DIGITAL LIBRARIES IN THE MAKING

By

Dr. Amjad Ali

Deputy Librarian

Aligarh Muslim University, Aligarh

Ess Ess Publications

4837/24, Ansari Road, Darya Ganj,
New Delhi-110002
✆ : 23260807
Fax : 23274173
E-mail: info@essessreference.com
url:http://www.essessreference.com

First Published 2005

ISBN : 81-7000-428-4

Price : Rs.875/-

Published by :

Ess Ess Publications

4837/24, Ansari Road, Darya Ganj,
New Delhi - 110 002
Phone : 23260807
Fax : 23274173
E-mail: info@essessreference.com
url:http://www.essessreference.com

Laser Typesetting:

Mukesh Graphics

L-2/8, DDA Market,
Mangolpuri, New Delhi
Ph. : 27924405
E-mail:mukeshgraphics29@hotmail.com

Printed at :

Print Line

Contents

Dedicated to My
MOTHER

Preface

The human tendency of preserving the records of their achievements and utilizing them for further gains dates back to the beginning of the civilization. The ways and means for doing so changed with the availability of the different kind of materials and methods. In the past, such records were laid down on stone slabs, clay tablets, parchments, leather, pieces of wood, cloth and surface of celluloid.

The advancements in science and technology led to miraculous changes in the art of recording and reproduction of knowledge making it possible to preserve it with greater accuracy and durability at a cheaper cost. An unimaginably vast amount of information is stored and reproduced now with the help of electronic devices.

Recently, digital libraries came into being as a result of technological advancements in the field of electronics engineering as well as the changing requirements and expectations from the traditional libraries. They are also referred as the collections of information stored in digital format and accessible over a communication network. Digital libraries, in fact revolutionized the process of collection, storage, management, accessibility and transmission of information without involving any constraints of space and time.

Digital libraries are the future avatars of the present day libraries. Most of them are in the process of making and are generally being developed in isolation by a number of organizations specially the educational institutions all over the world like the Universal digital Library, an Indo-US venture. Once developed and connected, the digital libraries will supercede all the traditional libraries of today reducing them to merely the museum of books. It is going to be happened within a short span of time since their vast capacity of accommodating resources, speed of information retrieval and accuracy in operations they offer is unparallel to the existing type of libraries.

This book covers the historical development of the various kinds of information media specially the digital technology of recording and reproduction of information, which led to the formation of the present day digital libraries. A reference has been made to the major projects of digitizing the library and information resources at the national as well as the international level. It has been found that India being strong enough technically is playing a major role in developing the digital libraries both domestically as well as internationally. The book also discusses about some of the major information networks and the digital sources of information available at present.

I am indebted to a number of individuals and organizations who contributed their information resources to the World Wide Web on the subject of digital libraries which I referred to bring out this volume. My special thanks are due to Prof. Raj Reddy, founder Director of the Universal Digital Library Project and Incharge of the Super Computer Educational Division at the Indian Institute of Science, Bangalore who through e-mail guided me to locate information resources on this topic. M/S Ess Ess Publications, New Delhi also deserve my thanks for giving the idea of writing this book being the need of the day.

It is hoped that the book will be useful for the students and faculty of library and information science, working librarians and information professionals, educationists and all those persons who are interested in recording, retrieval and utilization of information through the modern means.

Dr. Amjad Ali

Email: amjad_alig@yahoo.co.in

1
Paper to Paperless Media

Looking at the various stages of evolution of man, .it is found that A major breakthrough in the history was the transformation of man from *Homo Sapien to Homo febra*– a man who thinks. The records of thinking were preserved by one generation for the other and thus passed on to posterity. What we have today is, undoubtedly, the result of thousands of years of thinking, experimentation and rethinking. The quantum of know-how increased in geometrical proportions. There were darker times too as many civilizations got devastated prematurely. But despite all the setbacks, the human race continued to grow and multiply the available knowledge.

Different kind of materials; stones, clay tablets, leaves, cloth; parchment; vellum, etc. were used for the purpose of preserving the acquired knowledge depending upon the availability of the materials and man's capability to use them. The rate of shifting from one material to the other has been very slow and in consonance with the transition in the society as a whole. The invention of paper from papyrus in Egypt around two thousand years ago was perhaps the biggest gift to mankind. For centuries, paper made all forms of learning and research possible.

Paper has been used for the longest time as the basic material parchment for written communication and the dissemination of information comparing with stones, clay tablet, tree leave, cloth, and. It is one of the most widely used media, which dominated the scene of learning for the last many centuries. Paper coupled with the moveable types invented in the 15th century accelerated the rate of growth of the recorded knowledge. It was a cheaper and easily available medium and even mass production was not difficult. From this invention onwards, the quantum of publication was so high that whatever number of books the whole of Europe could have brought out till the 15th century was produced within a year of this invention. Paper became an indispensable reality in every civilized society ever since.

The word paper is derived from the name of the reedy plant papyrus, which grows abundantly along the Nile River in Egypt. In ancient times, the fibrous layers within the stem of this plant were removed, placed side by side, and crossed at right angles with another set of layers similarly arranged. The sheet so formed was dampened and pressed. Upon drying, the glue like sap of the plant, acting as an adhesive, cemented the layers together. Complete defibering, an indispensable element in modern papermaking, did not occur in the preparation of papyrus sheets. Papyrus was the most widely used writing material in ancient times, and many papyrus records still survive.

The Story of Paper

The history of papermaking can be traced to about AD 105, when Ts'ai Lun, an official attached to the Imperial court of China, created a sheet of paper using mulberry and other bast fibers along with fishnets, old rags, and hemp waste. In its slow travel westward, the art of papermaking reached Samarkand, in Central Asia, in 751; and in 793 the first paper was made in Baghdad during the time of Harun ar-Rashid, with the golden age of Islamic culture that brought papermaking to the frontiers of Europe.

The Arabs got papermaking 600 years later as one of the spoils of war. The Central Asian city of Samarkand was fighting the Chinese and captured a number of prisoners, two of whom were papermakers who were released in exchange for teaching the Arabs how to make paper. The Arabs wasted no time in improving papermaking techniques - they were probably the first to make paper from linen - and they spread the techniques throughout the Middle East and into Spain.

By the 14th century a number of paper mills existed in Europe, particularly in Spain, Italy, France, and Germany. The invention of printing in the 1450s brought a vastly increased demand for paper. Through the 18th century the papermaking process remained essentially unchanged, with linen and cotton rags furnishing the basic raw materials. Paper mills were increasingly plagued by shortages; in the 18th century they even advertised and solicited publicly for rags. It was evident that a process for utilizing a more abundant material was needed.

At the time when Gutenberg produced his first Bible around 1456, Europe was still predominantly using parchment and vellum for printing, rather than paper. Parchment is the skin of a sheep or goat prepared for writing; vellum is a fine parchment made from the skins of calves, lambs or kids. Gutenberg printed several copies of his Bible on parchment; to print just one, he had to use the skins of 300 sheep. Now with that kind of resource demand, obviously there were not enough goats and sheep and calves in Europe to allow the mass production of books. So there came this grand new technology - the printing press - and no way to realize its potential, until entrepreneurs saved the day by improving and expanding the technology of making paper from linen rags. At first, paper was called "cloth parchment."

Book production increased as a result of the easy availability of paper and newspapers started appearing in the late 1600s and early 1700s. Newspapers, and the increased communication they offered, began to affect the conduct of government and commerce. Newspapers played an important role in spreading political information in the pre-Revolutionary and Revolutionary period, not to mention during the formative period of nation's institutional and industrial history.

Booksellers in the Middle Ages seldom had many ready-made books in his shop. They were copied down by hand which took a lot of time and resources that everybody was not able to afford. It was done by simply borrow the first few pages of the book and take them home for copying. These pages were usually returned before borrowing the next few pages. There's a story, perhaps apocryphal, about Gutenberg's financial partner - when he offered 20 identical copies of the Bible to a bookseller in Paris, he was quickly forced to flee for his life. People were certain that the only explanation for this bizarre occurrence was that he was in league with the Devil.

The moveable types allowed lower cost of printing books on paper. Their subsequent availability, stimulated the foundation of new schools and universities. Because books were now more numerous, educational opportunities that were once restricted to the nobility and upper classes were now becoming somewhat more available to other classes in society, with dramatic increases in levels of education and literacy.

When changing from an oral culture, where everything is communicated in stories and the spoken word, to a literate culture, where people get their information by reading, one changes even such fundamentals as the process of thinking. Suddenly people don't have to carry all their knowledge in their heads. They don't have to develop elaborate ways of memorizing. They start to think in a more linear fashion because now they can work out on paper the complicated thought progressions that they hadn't been able to do in their heads.

The art world was also transformed by improvements in papermaking. Previously, artists had to practice their techniques and develop their drawing abilities on canvasses that they painted over and over again, so most paintings were actually lost - hidden under layers and layers of new paint. When paper became available as a cheap type of "canvas," artists could go wild practicing their sketching, and now these sketches could be saved. For the first time, drawing became an important art form in itself.

The breakthrough in papermaking technology fueled a huge expansion in business that eventually led to the development of the modern corporation, which was unable to function without tremendous supplies of paper. The paper industry in the 1850s crated changes so far-reaching that it was one of the transformation factors in the developing the nations. Not the least revolutionary change was the astounding drop in newsprint prices that advances in papermaking technology allowed.

Throughout the eighteenth century, there was an intense search in Europe and the U.S. for a new fiber source of paper. Contests were held, universities offered prizes, and inventors and laboratories worked feverishly to come up with a new source for paper. Inventors would often print a book on their newly-invented paper that described how the paper was made. And it ended up with books printed on paper made from asbestos, straw, swamp grass, marsh mallow, and esparto dune grass from certain beaches in Spain. The first patent for a paper using deinked waste paper as pat of its fiber source was issued in 1800 in London. It was not until the 1840s that the initial development of the papermaking machine in England and experiments in groundwood pulping in Germany and Nova Scotia enabled the commercial production of paper.

In 1800 a book was published that launched development of practical methods for manufacturing paper from wood pulp and other vegetable pulps. Several major pulping processes were gradually developed that relieved the paper industry of dependency upon cotton and linen rags and made modern large-scale production possible. These developments followed two distinct pathways. In one, fibers and fibre fragments were separated from the wood structure by mechanical means; and in the other, the wood was exposed to chemical solutions that dissolved and removed lignin and other wood components, leaving cellulose fiber behind.

Prior to the invention of the paper machine, paper was made one sheet at a time by dipping a frame or mold with a screened bottom into a vat of stock. Lifting the mold allowed the water to drain, leaving the sheet on the screen. The sheet was then pressed and dried. The size of a single sheet was limited to the size of frame and mold that a man could lift from a vat of stock.

Now, the production is done on mass level with the help of machines. Rags are received at the paper mill and once cooked, the rags are washed, then mechanically beaten. The beating shortens the fiber, increases the swelling action of water to produce a softened and plastic fibre, and fibrillates or frays the fiber to increase its surface area. All of these actions contribute to better formation of the paper sheet, closer contact between fibers, and the formation of interfiber bonding that gives the paper strength and coherence.

Since cellulose fiber is a major constituent of the stems of plants, a vast number of plants represent potential sources of paper; many of these have been pulped experimentally. A rather substantial number of plant sources have been used commercially, at least on a small scale and at various times and places. Indeed, the use of cereal straws for paper predates the use of wood pulp and is widely practiced today throughout the world, although on a relatively small scale of production. Because many parts of the world are deficient in forests, the development of the paper industry in these areas appears to depend to a considerable degree upon the use of annual plants and agricultural fibers.

There is abundance of bamboo in Southeast Asia, where increased production of paper is greatly needed, Much interest has been displayed in bamboo pulp development. The growing cycle of bamboo is favorable, for the culms can be harvested without destroying the root system. Under ideal conditions of soil fertility and moisture, an established stand of bamboo probably would produce more fiber per hectare (or acre) per year than any other plant. Wild bamboo, however, is difficult to harvest and transport economically; so far, the interest in it has not been translated into any large-scale production. Pulp mills make use of bamboo in India, Thailand, and the Philippines. Considerable quantities of bamboo pulp are said to be made in China, but details are lacking

In the ancient time, the media of communication had durability but lacked portability. This was achieved with the invention of paper. Later, the celluloid medium contributed in reduction of size of documents and made mass transfer of information possible through microfilms, microfiches and ultra fiches. This new medium also presented a different kind of material for understanding of reality and that was in the form of motion pictures. But the route to theses developments goes to the printing technology.

The Printing Technology

The current information revolution is actually the fourth information revolution in human history. The first one was the invention of writing 5,000 to 6,000 years ago in Mesopotamia; then—independently but several thousand years later—in China; and some 1,500 years later still, by the Maya in Central America. The second information revolution was brought on by the invention of the written book, first in China, perhaps as early as 1300 B.C., and then, independently 800 years later, in Greece, when Peisistratos, the tyrant of Athens, had Homer's epics—only recited until then—copied into books. The third information revolution was set off by Gutenberg's invention of the printing press and of movable type between 1450 and 1455, and by the contemporaneous invention of engraving. We have almost no documents on the first two of these revolutions, though we know that the impact of the written book was enormous in Greece and Rome as well as in China. In fact, China's entire civilization and system of government still rest on it. But on the third information revolution, printing and engraving, we have abundant material.

Everybody today believes that the present information revolution is unprecedented in reducing the cost of, and in the spreading of, informaticn whether measured by the cost of a "byte" or by computer ownership and in the speed and sweep of its impact. These beliefs are simply nonsense. At the time Gutenberg invented the press, there was a substantial information industry in Europe. It was probably Europe's biggest employer. It consisted largely of thousands of monasteries, many of which housed hundreds of highly skilled monks. Each monk labored from dawn to dusk, six days a week, copying books by hand. An industrious, well-trained monk could do 4 pages a day, or 25 pages during a six-day week, for an annual output of 1,200 to 1,300 handwritten pages.

Fifty years later, by 1500, the monks had become unemployed. These monks (some estimates go well above 10,000 for all of Europe) had been replaced by a very small number of lay craftsmen, the newly minted class of "printers," totaling perhaps 1,000, but spread over all of Europe produce a printed book required coordinated teamwork by up to 20 such craftsmen, beginning with one highly skilled cutter of type, to a much larger number, maybe 10 or more, of much less skilled bookbinders. Such a team produced each year about 25 titles, with an average of 200 pages per title, or 5,000 pages ready to be printed. By 1505, print runs of 500 copies were becoming increasingly common. This meant that a printing team could produce annually 25 *million* printed pages, bound into 125,000 books ready to be sold—or *2.5 million* pages per team member as against the 1,200 or 1,300 the individual monk had produced only 50 years earlier.

As a result of Gutenberg's invention prices of books felt dramatically. Before it books were such a luxury that only the wealthy and educated could afford them. But when Martin Luther's German Bible came out in 1522 (a book of well over 1,000 pages), its price was so low that even the poorest peasant family could buy one. The cost and price reductions of the third information revolution were at least as great as those of the present, the fourth information revolution. And so were the speed and the extent of its spread. Cotton was by far the most desirable of all textile fibers. It is easily washable and can be worked up into an infinite variety of different cloths. It was a time- and labor-expensive process. For it took 12 to 14 man-*days* to produce a pound of cotton yarn by hand, as against 1 to 2 man-days for wool, 2 to 5 for linen, and 6 for silk.

Between 1764, when machine tools to work cotton were first introduced—triggering the Industrial Revolution—and 1784, the time needed to produce a pound of cotton yarn fell to a few hours. The price dropped by 70% and production rose 25-fold.

Just as important as the reduction in costs and the distribution speed of the new printing technology was its impact on what information meant. The first printed books, beginning with Gutenberg's Bible, were in Latin and still had the same topics as the books that the monks had earlier written out by hand: religious and philosophical treatises and whatever texts had survived from Latin antiquity. But only 20 years after Gutenberg's invention, books by contemporary authors began to emerge, though they still appeared in Latin. Another 10 years and books were being printed not only in Greek and Hebrew but also, increasingly, in the vernacular (first in English, then in the other European tongues). And in 1476, only 30 years after Gutenberg, the English printer William Caxton (1422Ð1491) published a book on so worldly a subject as chess. By 1500, popular literature no longer meant verse—epics, especially—which lent themselves to oral transmission, but prose, i.e., the printed book.

In no time at all, the printing revolution also changed institutions, including the educational system. In the decades that followed, university after university was founded throughout Europe. but unlike the earlier ones, they weren't designed for the clergy or for the study of theology. They were built around disciplines such as law, medicine, mathematics, natural philosophy (science).

Printing's greatest impact, however, was on the core of pre-Gutenberg Europe: the church. Printing made the Protestant Reformation possible. Its predecessors, the reformation of John Wycliffe in England (1330-1384) and of John Huss in Bohemia (1372-1415), had met with an equally enthusiastic popular response. But those revolts could not travel farther or faster than the spoken word and could thus be localized and suppressed. This was not the case when Luther in 1517, nailed his 95 theses to a church door in an obscure German town. He had intended only to initiate a traditional theological debate within the church. But without Luther's consent (and probably without his knowledge), the theses were immediately printed and distributed gratis all over Germany, and then all over Europe. These printed leaflets ignited the religious firestorm that turned into the Reformation.

Printing publicized every single advance the Portuguese seafarers made along the west coast of Africa in their search for a sea route to the India. Printing provided Columbus with the first (though totally wrong) maps of the fabled lands beyond the western horizon, such as Marco Polo's China and the legendary Japan. Printing made it possible to record the results of every single voyage immediately and create new, more reliable maps. Noneconomic changes cannot be quantified. But surely the impact on society, education, culture—let alone on religion—of the printing revolution was easily as great and surely as fast, if not faster, as the impact of the present information revolution.

The most important lesson of the earlier information revolution may, however, be found in the fates and fortunes of its technologists. The printing revolution immediately created a new and unprecedented class of information technologists, just as the most recent information revolution has created any number of information businesses, MIS and IT specialists, software designers, and chief information officers. The IT people of the printing revolution were the early printers. Nonexistent—and indeed not even imaginable—in 1455, they flourished throughout Europe 25 years later and had become great stars. Unlike earlier craftsmen, they were great gentlemen. These virtuosi of the printing press were known and revered all over Europe, just as the names of the leading computer and software firms are recognized and admired worldwide today. Printers were courted by kings, princes, the pope, and rich merchant cities and were showered with money and honors.

The first of these printing tycoons was the famous Venetian printer Aldus Manutius (1449-1515). He realized that the new printing press could make a large number of impressions from the same plate—1,000 by the year 1515. Thus he created the first low-cost, mass-produced book. Aldus Manutius created the printing industry: He was the first to extend printing to languages other than Latin and also the first to do books by contemporary authors. Altogether his press turned out well over 1,000 titles.

The last of these great printing technologists, and also the last of the printing princes, was Christophe Plantin (1520-1589) of Antwerp. Starting as a humble apprentice binder, he built Europe's biggest and most famous printing firm. By marrying the two new technologies, printing and engraving, he created the modern illustrated book. He became Antwerp's leading patrician (Antwerp was then one of the richest cities in Europe, if not the world), and he became so wealthy that he was able to build himself a magnificent palace, still preserved today as a printing museum. But Plantin and his printing house began to decline well before his death and soon faded into insignificance.

By 1580 or so, the printers, with their focus on technology, had become ordinary craftsmen, respectable tradesmen but definitely not of the upper class. Their place was soon taken by what we now call publishers (though the term was not coined until much later), people and firms whose focus was no longer on the "T" in IT but on the "I." This shift got under way the moment the new technology began to have an impact on the

MEANING of information, and with it, on the meaning and function of the 15th century's key institutions such as the church and the universities. It thus began at the same juncture at which we now find ourselves in the present information revolution as we undergo the shift in business information and, with it, the redefinition of the function and purpose of business.

The Era of Writers

The genius of 17th century Britain lay with its writers rather than its printers. Shakespeare, Bunyan and Dryden led the way and it is testament to them that their work still inspires today. For the printer this meant greater variety and new markets. Reading was still not widespread in the sense that we know it now and the majority of printed works remained biblical and theological. But giant strides were made.

The romance novel was already established by the turn of the century and continued to go from strength to strength. Playwrights flourished as did their stage counterparts. Farming books began to appear such as Worlidge's Systema Agriculturae (1669) which reflected the importance of farming as an industry and, with the introduction of the horsedrawn carriage, travel books also became popular.

The lion's share of the trade remained in books and pamphlets. So few technological changes were made between Gutenberg's time and the invention of lithography in the late 18th century, that printed matter remained an expensive acquisition enjoyed by relatively few. The jobbing printer was basically unknown, and understandably so, as the vast majority of the population remained illiterate. And the printing process continued to be both slow and tedious.

The compositor would sit or stand (depending upon the generosity of his employer) beside an angled frame upon which he would set type. There were usually two cases of type in use at a given time - one upper and one lower case - and the frame could often store up to eight other pairs below. One pair would be laid on the frame in such a way that the most commonly used letters were closest to hand.

Words were compiled using an iron composing stick which was just over eight inches long and two inches broad. This was held in one hand while the other was free to select the required type, piece by piece. The compositor could work on six or so words at a time and would often have to rearrange at the end of a line to justify. Each line was then carefully set into a metal frame which resembled a picture frame and each page would have to be proof read before the next could be started. Mistakes were commonplace and rectification was time consuming.

There were other serious difficulties which the 17th Century printer and his staff had to deal with, but over which they had no control: principal among these was censorship.

In the previous century, illuminators and calligraphers had opposed printing as they felt their trades were threatened. In fact they were misguided as printing brought them new markets. But in the 17th Century the realization of the power of the printed word brought opposition from both Parliament and the Church.

In 1637 an Act was passed to limit the number of printers in England by decree and in 1644 a Licensing Act followed, which required all publications to go before an official censor for approval. By the end of the century there were just 20 master printers in England and 18 of these were in London.

These moves reflected the mood of the country as a whole, and the determination of those in power to protect their status. For this was the century which witnessed the English Civil War, Great Plague, Great Fire of London and one economic depression after another. As the power brokers sought security for their authority, printing became a dangerous occupation with the penalties for breaches of the Licensing Act including fines, imprisonment, confiscation of equipment and even death.

But things eased in the 1690s and the way was set for a mini-financial revolution which eventually led to the industry's progress to the late 18th Century. In 1694 the Licensing Act expired and was not renewed, largely because of Parliament's Declaration of Rights in 1689.

Also in 1694 the Bank of England, then a joint stock company, was born. Shortly before this, stockbrokers and jobbers had been recognised by an Act of Parliament and the foundations for the present day financial structure were laid.

The 18th Century was one of vastly changing fortunes for the people of Britain. In the early years the man in the street enjoyed a level of wealth such as none previously encountered. much of this resulting from improved overseas trade due to colonisation. However, from 1750 onwards things began to change as the American War of Independence, the Napoleonic Wars and the Industrial Revolution took their toll. Severe new taxes were introduced to bolster the war ridden economy and unemployment reached serious levels as a result of mechanisation leading to unorganised strikes and rioting.

Changes were also made to the printer's end product and from 1740 most books were sold in paper covered boards. The principle behind this was that it would allow the buyer to arranging binding to his own taste. A side effect of the move was undoubtedly that it brought the basic price of a book within the financial means of a wider reading public.

During the latter years of the century, another new practice was introduced whereby books were sold in subscription copies. These were advertised before publication (allowing the printer to assess demand) and the names of subscribers were often included in the printed copy.

Censorship remained prevalent throughout the 1700s and writing about the government was forbidden, especially in newspapers. The campaign to allow reports on government business was led by John Wilkes, a Member of Parliament, and in 1762 he founded the North Briton. But the establishment was determined to resist the actions of this activist and he was expelled from Parliament and imprisoned for a short time. He became a cult figure both in England and America, whose independence he supported.

Two other important political changes were the passing of the first Copyright Act by Parliament in 1709 and the introduction of Stamp Duty on newspapers in 1712. The Copyright Act recognised the rights of authors and illustrators and provided protection for a period of two years after their deaths. The introduction of Stamp Duty was less favourable. It amounted initially to a halfpenny or one penny on the price of a newspaper, depending upon the size. In subsequent years, this amount was to be increased and the duty was not abolished until as late as 1855.

Working conditions made little progress generally and printing on wooden presses remained laborious. The process of inking and manually operating the press had not changed substantially since Gutenberg's invention hundreds of years earlier. A competent printer could expect to produce perhaps 100 printed sheets in an hour. One 100 copies of a 300 page book might therefore take a number of weeks just to print the loose pages p; even working a 16 hour day, which was not uncommon at that time. But in the latter years of this period, the Industrial Revolution stamped its mark on printing.

As the iron industry grew and mechanisation began to take shape, the life of the wooden press drew to a close. In 1772, William Haas of Basel built a new press where all parts which were the subject of stress were made from iron, including both the bed and the platen. His work was superseded in 1798 when Earl Stanhope built a press made entirely from iron.

Printing as Industry

By the turn of the 19th century, the Industrial Revolution had taken hold and, when Queen Victoria came to the throne in 1837, the printing industry had been transformed. As had been the case in the second half of the 18th century, the country was gripped by social, political and industrial unrest. Numerous Combination Acts were passed by Parliament up to 1824, designed to prevent workers from combining to organise industrial action, and to prevent their employers from joining together to fix prices.

The larger towns and cities grew with their industries, but were ill equipped to cater for the influx of workers from rural districts. Widespread poverty and unhealthy epidemics prevailed as workers and their families lodged in overcrowded damp cellars.

Water supplies were contaminated and taxes remained high, even after the Napoleonic Wars, and there were attempts in the 1830s to form organised unions. Although these foundered, they were a foretaste of things to come for an industrialized Britain. Yet under such difficult circumstances, the transformation was made.

Aloys Senefelder's work with lithography continued. He began as a playwright but was unsuccessful in getting his work printed so he experimented with different printing processes, ultimately hoping to produce his own work. His earliest experiments involved etching onto pieces of calcareous stone in relief, but he soon discovered that pure limestone - which is absorbent of grease and water - would overcome the need to work in relief. He etched the limestone with a weak solution of nitric acid and gum Arabic, dampened the surface and then passed an inked roller over it. The undrawn parts of the stone refused the ink and the first principle of lithography was established: grease and water do not mix.

The Power Press

At around the same time Friedrich Koenig of Suhl was working on a power press but his first attempt, called the Suhler press, was eventually aborted as was a second. But by 1812 he had built a steam operated twin cylinder machine and within two years this was adopted by The Times newspaper in London.

At that time the paper was published by John Walter II,

having taken over from his near bankrupt father in 1803 but by 1837 distribution of The Times was approaching the 30,000 mark. This had been made possible by the invention of Koenig's power press. The output of the new machine was 1,100 sheets an hour, more than four times higher than that of the manually operated press previously used by the newspaper.

The invention of lithography and the power press combined to make printing an altogether more affordable medium. Book production, business and personal stationery benefited from the revolution in the sense that these ceased to be almost exclusively enjoyed by large companies and the landed gentry. Printing developed an altogether wider marketplace. But the progress and changes in the industry were not limited solely to the press.

In 1804 Henry and Sealy Fourdrinier bought the patents for a papermaking machine invented five years earlier in France. Bryan Donkin, the Fourdriniers' engineer, made significant changes to the earlier design and the adapted machine formed the basis for modern papermaking. By 1838, over 100 of the Fourdrinier machines were in operation throughout the UK.

By 1837 the industry was almost unrecognizable from its form 90 years earlier. The Industrial Revolution was all but over, Victoria came to the throne, and a period of consolidation was to follow.

The first 50 years of the 20th century were dogged by international unrest and two world wars, the like of which had never been seen before. For the industry, it represented a period of consolidation and moderate progress, with several signs of what was to come in the modern age. The nascent 19th century technological advances started to deliver on their promises. For example, web printing using removable letterpress shells became the norm and the use of etching baths allowed the rapid development of photography.

The use of steam to drive printing presses did not really

catch on in spite of the competition going on between advocates of the two modes of electricity, AC or DC. The introduction of transformers based on selenium meant that press manufacturers were not bound to one method at the expense of the other.

With great numbers of young men serving in France and economic priorities often laying elsewhere meant that the quality of print during the First World War and for a time afterwards was extremely variable. A hunger for illustrations of the war resulted however in methods of image capture and reproduction being developed at a phenomenal rate.

Great numbers of weekly periodicals were produced and even today these magazines are immensely popular and can be seen. It speaks volumes for the methods of reproduction that these periodicals catch the mood of the time without appearing overly dated. The demand for copper engravers, woodblock carvers and the like held strong till well after the Second World War.

Skills were becoming much more specialized, with fewer printers being all- rounders. During the Great Depression in the 1930s, demarcation disputes first started to appear, particularly as the various education acts meant that the workforce was now well educated, articulate and more organised.

Broadcasting never really became a threat. In fact it was a blessing, for the ability to transmit pictures and text increased the relevance of newspapers rather than diminishing its role in informing the population. It was here too that specialist typefaces started to appear, in effect branding producers of publications and print; Eric Gill for the London Underground - Times; Roman; the list of new typefaces generated throughout the period could go on forever.

Perhaps the 20th century is most marked by the arrival of offset printing, particularly for colour. In 1904, a New York lithographer by the name of Ira Rubel was the first to develop the process of lithographic offset printing onto paper. This was achieved largely because of the widespread introduction of metal plates, as previously the process had only been suitable for printing from stone to tin.

It was two years before the first British offset lithographic press was built by George Mann and although the invention was ostensibly American, most improvements in the following years (notably the 1920s) were made by European printers.

Print also influenced society as a whole. The growth of print, particularly spurred on by periodicals inspired by the British Empire's expansion, meant the need for a new Copyright Act. This was introduced in 1911, repealing the 21 previous Acts and for the first time it afforded protection to writers for the duration of their lives and 50 years beyond. At the time, book printers might well have felt the new Act would have a shrinking effect on their market but it rather went the other way by opening more doors to new authors.

Educational print was a remarkable driver of book production, but also of related industries, such as mechanical section sewing machines and in time the use of perfect binding in publications was completed by Allan Lane and his Penguin Books. The industry is now so large and complex that a history could be written on each of the individual sectors that make up the whole of the printing trade p; an industry so large that it is now the UK's sixth largest manufacturing industry.

The Advent of Audiovisuals

It is often said that a picture is worth a thousand words as it may communicate a huge mass of ideas, which may mean differently to different people. Photography emerged as an appropriate medium for such presentation, which coupled with the technology of sound proved to be the greatest and the most significant form for presentation of ideas.

The present day photography is the result of the early observations by alchemists and chemists based on the action of light on the photosensitive materials. The technique developed towards the end of the 18th century when the demand for the pictures grew. A major advancement in photography took place with substitution of glass for paper as a carrier for the light sensitive material. In 1851, once the manufacture of photographic materials was established as a commercial industry, the photographic techniques followed steady growth. In 1912 Kodak Company introduced flat film in place of glass plates for making negatives. The technique was advantageous for manufacturers. A few years later, the development in new sensitizing dyes made it possible for preparing panchromatic materials of improved quality.

Radio emerged as one of the most potent media of mass communication since it made possible the transmission and reception of signals by means of electronic wave and without the use of connecting wires. Within a century of its invention radio has grown enormously going out of Marconi's workshop to a permanent fixture in almost all the homes the world over.

CBS was the largest radio network at the time with 90 member stations. Runner-up NBC had 85 stations. By 1937, that balance had shifted. NBC's 111 affiliates topped CBS's 97, and the fledgling Mutual Broadcasting System claimed 39. By 1938, the three webs were commanding a total annual income of approximately $69.2 million.

Many forms of presentations emerged and met extinction within a short life span of radio spreading over the last fifty years. By 1975, the once-popular nostalgia format was fading, drama radio had been dead for more than a decade, and the disco format was "being studied based on the records played in the growing number of discotheques throughout. Since its development in 1895, the radio has long since been revolutionizing the world. It has become so common that it is very improbable that one could ever pass a day without coming into contact with radio in some shape or fashion. In the beginning, radios were the only form of entertainment other than family outings and live shows such as those seen on Broadway. However, it seems like radio has outlived its passion for the programs and evening news and now concentrates almost completely on music.

The radio not only revolutionized the world but also created a new form of entertainment and education that will more than likely carry on for many centuries to come. Perhaps this invention will soon be able to travel through space, collect tremendous amounts of data from the universe, and spell out for us the reality of new frontiers waiting to be explored. Truly the radio will live on forever.

Photography coupled with sound heralded a new era in field of communication of ideas. It followed the invention and application of a variety of technologies for recording and presentation of information. It began with the art of sight and sound which later transformed into tape slide shows. But with further improvements in synchronization of sound with the moving images, the present day cinematography took its birth.

The development in photography and cinematography brought significant changes in the world of learning. Now more sense organs were involved in the perception process. The human nature is so that the maximum of ones total knowledge is perceived through the senses of sight and sound and the new media of communication available as a result of these advancements exploited this potential of man to its fall, facilitating learning at a higher speed and with a greater ease. The trend was on for about thirty years in India from the mid of the last century. The celluloid medium was primarily adopted for entertainment but soon it became equally popular in the academic circles. Film became the medium of instruction within fifty years of its existence.

Cinematographic film consists of a transparent flexible support or base on which is laid a photosensitive adhesive emulsion. They are now available in different widths ranging from 8 mm to 70 mm. The more the width the higher is the cost of the film. They are used for varied purposes depending upon the cost and the quality of the film. The super 8 mm is used very rarely as the infrastructure for production on this format is not generally available. But this is certainly the cheapest cinematographic medium available so far. The 16 mm film is used by most of the institutions for education and development. This has advantage over 8 mm because of comparatively higher resolution being suitable to be magnified on slightly larger screen.

Both the 8 mm and' 16 mm films are used depending upon the size of the audience as well as the cost of the production involved. The 35 mm and 70 mm films are normally used for entertainment and commercial purposes. 'They are suitable for larger gatherings like the audience of feature films in cinema halls. The advertisement agencies produce ads on these formats. The advantage of their having larger width is that the picture contain: very high resolution and does not blow up while magnified on larger screens. Sound for cinematographic films can be recorded magnetically or optically depending upon the circumstances.

Video is basically a picture and sound recording medium. It is also cheaper in comparison to the cinematographic film. The great advantage of this medium is its instant playback facility. Video Productions are generally available on video tapes and video cassettes. Their width vary from super 8 mm to 2". VHS is the most suited format for home viewing and a small gathering. 'The formats of video are changing very fast. In India, within a decade the production studios have witnessed reel to reel videotapes, 1" BCN, 3/4" U Matic in low and high band and currently the Betacam in 1/2". There is also a possibility of shifting the medium to digital in the coming times since this format has certain advantages over the existing ones.

The audiovisual medium was used basically for entertainment purposes but its potential was soon recognized in the academic circles. Film became the medium of instruction. In India many institutions such as the Central Institute of Educational Technology (CIET), State Institutes of Educational Technology (SIETs) came into being apart from the Films Division and the National Films Development Corporation. The teaching and learning institutions too were attracted by the power of this medium. As a result, open universities with the multimedia approach to instruction were established. The University Grants Commission took special interest in popularizing education through the audio-visual media. Within a span of 9 years of inception of the UGC/INSAT/TV Project at the Mass Communication Research Centre in Jamia Millia Islamia, New Delhi, the number of media production centres, popularly known as the Educational Media Research Centres/Audio Visual Research Centres rose to 17 from only one in 1984.

Motion pictures are now available on cinematographic film as well as on video. Their basic and common characteristic is the movement of picture on the screen. The movement is achieved by running a film or video through a projector or player at a speed of 24 frames per second. The stills are recorded in a situation where all of them are comparatively similar and differ only at the point where movement has to be visualized. Motion pictures include silent and sound films as well. Nowadays, nearly all of them are being recorded in color.

Motion pictures are being accepted increasingly by the academic circles as a learning aid as well as the medium for preservation of information. We always need good instructional and enrichment films available in the international market. But there are hurdles in their import Even for the academic and research purposes. This requires urgent attention of all concerned so that motion picture can also be imported like books for the purpose of education and research. Moreover, just as there are renowned authors so are there well known filmmakers who have a series of worthwhile films to their credit and which could be an intrinsic part of every library.

Looking at the newer electronic media of audiovisuals, we find the difference quite visible. The audiovisual programs are being produced mainly on cassettes now which arc becoming cheaper despite the fact that the human factor is involved in their production and that the human labor is becoming costlier everywhere in the world. Computers, modems, discs, antennas, TV sets, VCRs/VCPs, nearly all the equipment and accessories used in the information storage and retrieval and based on the electronic devices are becoming cheaper. The main reason is the availability of improved technology based on Very Large Scale Integration (VLSI) and the mass production of electronic goods. The cost of audiovisual programs too has gone down about 10 times with the adoption of video in place of celluloid. On celluloid, the shooting of sequences involved much pain and the result was known only after developing the prints whereas video offers instant playback facility. Thus, the wastage of efforts or resources is minimum in the electronic media.

2
Making of the Digital World

We are living in a digital world. The evidence is everywhere. In advanced countries, keyboards outnumber office workers. Everybody has a web page. Nobody carries cash. There seems to be a growing concern in libraries and archives that if we are not going digital, being digital, or dreaming digital, then we are relegating ourselves to the great museum of paper. But it may be that our biggest challenge may not be embracing digital technology but rather building a common language to describe the transformations that are having such a phenomenal impact on our everyday lives. A shared vocabulary is the key element in the development of a community of practice and a shared vision of the future among those of us who have responsibility to shepherd the nation's cultural resources

Digital technologies are in fact an extension of the long history of the way we communicate with each other. The desire to communicate provides the motive and the ultimate rationale for the development of technologies of all sorts. Today's digital world is concerned with creating, sharing, and using information in digital form. Digital information is data that are structured and manipulated, stored and networked, subsidized and sold. Information takes many forms. One way to think about these forms is to distinguish between symbolic information and coded information.

The period from the time Gutenberg invented in the middle of the fifteenth century through the year 1500 is referred to generally as the period of incunabula. During this time printers and book designers went to great lengths to make their products—type faces, format, and layout—look and function much like the manuscript books of the preceding centuries. Only when a theory of the alphabet and a theory of the book emerged around the time of Geoffrey Tory's classic text on the structure of the roman alphabet were book designers able to begin taking full advantage of Gutenberg's technological innovation.

The world defined by strings of 1's and 0's has existed for a long time. The idea of the digital computer originated over 300 years ago in the fertile mind of a German mathematician, Gottfried Wilhelm von Leibnitz. In 1679, Leibnitz imagined a device in which binary numbers were represented by spherical pellets, circulating within a kind of pinball machine controlled by a rudimentary form of punched cards. He described a comprehensive numerical system in which all calculation can be expressed in combinations of 1 and 0—the identical approach that all digital technologies use today.

At present, the digital system uses numbers to represent a concrete object or an abstract idea. Digitization is the process of transforming the object or idea into a numerical code. The baseline of digital technology is a coding system with only two numbers—1 and 0—hence the term binary. Each numerical place in the system is a bit. In the digital world bits are things; they take up space; they take time to move from one place to another. A collection of bits can be described and counted, much like anything.

A bit-mapped image is a digital picture made up of row after row of bits in a grid. In a digital image, a bit is commonly referred to as a pixel, short for "picture element." As objects, digital images are described in terms of three characteristics: resolution, dynamic range, and pixel size.

The information revolution is still well under way. But it is not happening where information scientists, information executives, and the information industry in general are looking for it. It is not a revolution in technology, machinery, techniques, software, or speed. It is a revolution in concept.

So far, for 50 years, the information revolution has

centered on data; their collection, storage, transmission, analysis, and presentation. It has centered on the "T" in IT. The next information revolution will surely engulf all major institutions of modern society. But it has started, and has gone farthest, in business enterprise, where it has already had profound impacts. It is forcing us to redefine what business enterprise actually is and should be. This largely underlies the new definition of the function of business enterprise as the "creation of value and wealth," which in turn has triggered the present debate about the "governance of the corporation," that is, for whom the business enterprise creates value and wealth. Yet, despite its importance and impact, the next information revolution has so far been largely ignored by the information establishment.

A half century ago, around 1950, prevailing opinion overwhelmingly held that the market for that new "miracle," the computer, would be in the military and in scientific calculations, e.g., astronomy. A few persons argued even then that the computer would find major applications in business and would have an impact on it. These few also foresaw—again very much at odds with the prevailing opinion that in business the computer would be more than a very fast adding machine doing clerical chores such as payroll or telephone bills. On specifics, we dissenters disagreed, of course. But all of us nonconformists agreed on one thing: The computer would, in short order, revolutionize the work of top management. It would have its greatest and earliest impacts on business policy, business strategy, and business decisions.

The improved technology for storage and dissemination of information has made available a wide range of products that accommodate a fairly larger body of information. Reduction in size of documents by photographic process was one of the first measures in reducing the space required for housing information. All these discoveries were based on optics and chemical processes. The documents required utmost care in handling and preservation and in the normal circumstances it was almost impossible to preserve them beyond a few decades.

Computers

Computer is regarded as the greatest invention of all the times. It facilitates the storage, processing and distribution of information much easier with its vast memory speed and accuracy. The advancements in calculator, which was invented to carry out mathematical calculations led to the invention of computer.

A more visible change took place when calculators acquired the capability of processing textual data proceeded by the capacity to process information available in varied formats. Further improvements in computer design during the 1960s enabled the integration of text and graphics, a move that encouraged the development of computer based training programs. Such use was however limited, as programming was costly, slow and cumbersome, and the computing relied on a mainframe, or central computer to do all the work. The release of the first microcomputers during the late 1970s saw computing become more portable and affordable. Ease of use took a quantum leap with the introduction of the Apple Macintosh computer in 1984. Operation of the computer and its programs became more intuitive, largely as a result of research in the area of human-computer interaction.

The adoption of computers in the area of vocational training also increased, with some industries recognizing that the technology offered benefits that were largely cantered on efficiency gains. This was particularly the case in industries such as finance and insurance, manufacturing, health care, and the armed forces where training was a critical but costly component of operation. These types of organizations, with large staff numbers requiring training to an industry standard, or with staff located across national and international borders, found cost savings could be achieved by using technology to distribute training programs to the workplace, rather than bring staff to a central training centre. Computer programs could deliver training at a time and place convenient to all parties, provide flexibility in terms of progression and pace, generate and score tests, record all interaction between the learner and the system and produce detailed reports of this interaction. These attributes were welcomed in organizations where staff development programs were valued as a means of motivating staff and maintaining the standard of service. These programs are commonly based on competency standards that clearly define objectives, and set standards of performance that may be observed and measured against defined criteria.

The notion of providing training when it was needed to where it was needed was extended through the development of performance support systems. These systems allowed an employee to use a computer as both a tool and a tutor - the tutor would provide step by step assistance in the performance of specific computer related tasks, in much the same way as help "wizards" incorporated within many Microsoft products try to anticipate users needs in designing a new spreadsheet or database. Computer based training has also been a logical choice where there was substantial risk in allowing a novice to train in an operational environment. It is safer and more cost effective to allow the operator of a steel rolling mill to practice the procedure using a computer simulation, or a pilot to manage an engine failure without leaving the ground. Computers can be an asset in education, but the knowledge of appropriate applications, limitations and advantage needs to be clearly understood.

CD ROMs

The electronic media has the capability to store, manipulate and transfer information in the form of text as well as audiovisuals. It is also possible to combine both of them. Multimedia is and hypermedia can be cited as examples. The electronic media is useful in learning both in a classroom situation or individually. It includes information networks and

CD ROMs. The information is recorded electronically, hence greater speed, accuracy and memory is available to the users. It is presumed that within the coming decade, the electronic media will supersede all the available media for storage, management and dissemination of information. This will particularly affect the educational institutions as it is more effective and economic both in terms of money and time spent in learning. It will also affect the nature of classroom instruction. A new learning culture is in the offing, which can be seen in the open system of education where attendance in class is not a prerequisite to earn a degree.

The advances in electronics and telecommunications brought newer technology capable of accommodating very large quantities of information in a very little space. Magnetic tapes, CD-ROMs, multimedia and hypermedia are a few examples. One CD-ROM can accommodate 3,00,000 pages of A4 size text that is equal to 10 full sets of the Encyclopedia Britannica spreading over 300 volumes containing approximately 1,000 pages each. The space required for storing one Compact Disc is negligible. One floor of a library stack normally accommodating around 30 volumes of books can easily hold 300 discs. Thus a double-faced library stack with 28 shelves is capable of storing materials equal to 25,20,00,000 pages or nearly 25,20,000 volumes of books. Further, the storage capacity may be doubled if the stacks are partitioned according to the size of the disc and not the size of books which require more space. CD ROMs have the capacity to record and display large amount of information through computer system. The information contained in them can be manipulated and produced in varied sequences. They are easy to consult and make the searches convenient. The Microsoft Corporation has come out with a set of two CD ROMs that contains information equal to about twenty encyclopedia and the information it holds can be searched through various options.

CD ROMs have an edge on print as well as online

resources. On the one hand they save a lot of physical space required for their print counterpart while on the other hand they allow to work on huge resources independent of online connectivity that is far expensive. The ever-increasing cost of Internet connectivity also suggests that CD ROM technology is more suited to education and research. Document in an ever-increasing number are being directly published on CD ROMs without involving prints. Now experts believe that the shift from page to screen once a fantasy is approaching reality now. Students in many university use textbook that exist online. Similarly there are CD ROMs, which hold valuable academic information and are the only sources of information in certain areas of study like medicine and technology.

In the electronic media, search time has been reduced miraculously. Bulky reference tools like the *Chemical Abstracts, Dissertation Index, Index to Higher Theses*, encyclopedias and dictionaries, etc. can be searched within a fraction of a second by just pushing the keys of a computer. Further, the search is very easy as most of the databases are user friendly. Any of the related words can be taken as 'Search Term' and fed into the system for retrieval of information. This is followed by appearance of a detailed list of documents available on the same topic from which one can select the most relevant and pinpointed information and even download it in the memory of the computer or on auxiliary memory for future use. There are some restrictions. Words, which can create hindrance, are debarred from the retrieval process. They are called stop words. This is achieved by maintaining a separate file for them.

Another advantage of electronic media is the updating of the reference tools. Unlike the printed medium, which requires repeating the whole mechanical process for improvement or updating, the information is updated instantly in the electronic media. This is achieved with the push of a button. In fact, the agencies dealing in the electronic sources of information enter into an agreement with the consumers. The same discs can be sent to the agencies and returned updated. Now, with the Electronic Mail facility, updating can be carried out instantly on line. 'This practically involves no time and saves expenditure as well. In the print as well as the celluloid, mass copying leads to deterioration of prints by way of generation loss. But in the electronic media, the same text can be generated again and again without any loss or deterioration in the quality of the original or its copy.

In a tropical country like India the fluctuation in temperature and humidity leads to deterioration in the quality of print as well as celluloid by way of chemical reactions. This process of degeneration goes on with the passage of time. It is very difficult to maintain quality of print beyond a century and of celluloid beyond a decade. The solution lies to some extent in erection of specialized dehumidified chambers and providing air conditioners but this too is not practicable for many other reasons such as frequent breakdowns in supply of electricity and the huge expenditure involved.

eBooks

The invention of printing press by Johannes Gutenberg about 550 years ago transformed society for centuries to come. The moveable types provided an efficient way to produce large volumes of written information. As a result, knowledge spread quickly, sparking the Renaissance and the worldwide exchange of ideas that exists today. Similarly, we are now on the brink of an invention that promises to radically change society.

Now information is available anywhere, anytime and the books will never go out of print like the past tragedies. The change that this is going to bring about in society is as fundamental as the change brought out by the printing press.

Like the printed book, the electronic book or "eBook" will be a special device that is easy to read, has a vertical layout and allows users to flip from page to page. It will be just as comfortable to read as a printed book, yet it will offer more opportunities. The readers will be able to store a whole library of books on a single device of the size of a paperback book.

They will be able to search for specific information or look up words while they read. They will also be able to download any book they want from the Internet and any time they want. The electronic book can do a lot of things that a printed book cannot do, and will never be able to do. It's going to change every area of life one can think about where reading goes on.

At present it does not look advantageous to read books available electronically as it is easier in case of a book available on paper but once the technology is popularized and people get them easily available the electronic books will also be advantageous and easy to read. When reading electronically becomes easier, people will want to do it, and the advantages will become obvious.

One advantage is that consumers and businesses will be able to greatly reduce the amount of storage space they reserve for books since they will be able to store hundreds of books on a device the size of a paperback novel. Another is that they will no longer have to weigh themselves down with books while traveling.

Another benefit is that eBooks will offer people with disabilities the same access to books as the rest of the population. For example, people who are blind will be able to download any book and play software that reads the books aloud. Moreover, people with visual impairments won't be limited to the few books currently available in large print. It means that every book is available in large print sizes automatically because it just comes with the system.

Yet another benefit is that eBooks will reduce the world's consumption of paper. A lot of paper is used in the world's businesses in a year? There's a huge infrastructure in place to deal with that—to grow trees, cut them down, transport them, pulp them, print on them, store that print, transport the printed material and send the unsold books back to the pulp plant to get pulped again and turned into other books. Think of what happens if we eliminate that infrastructure. There's obviously going to be a certain amount of trauma associated with that change. But it's inevitable, and in a world with a finite amount of resources.

Ultimately, the price of books will become cheaper because the infrastructure required to produce them electronically will be far less labor-intensive. Picture what this does to education in third world countries. Countries like China, India and Africa where people are unable to afford books or don't have access to the books they need. As the cost of the hardware drops, these countries will come in the position to set up a local public library anywhere, with instant access to as much content as the Library of Congress, for a fraction of what a library costs today. It will have the same level of access for any village school.

Digital Communication

In the early times, it was smoke that communicated meanings to the responders at the other end. Then it took the form. Now information is transferred to other places in a number of ways. The telecommunication has brought a revolution in the ways of sending messages at distant places virtually without involving any considerable amount of time.

Wire remained the main career of messages for the last two centuries and improvement in wire-based technology increased efficiency of transmitting messages across the geographical boundaries of the nations. Different materials were used to manufacture them ranging from copper, aluminum, steel etc. Recently fiber optics has taken a lead over all the existing wire-based communication devices.

Fiber optics communicates data in digital form and is a very reliable channel for communication of huge quantity of data. A single glass fiber is thinner than the size of a human hair and it can transmit all the characters in dozens of books of the same size across the country in a single second. Such a quantity of information will normally take about 21 hours to send over a copper telephone line. Fiber Optic technology is a cutting edge method of transmitting information over great distances (150 km without using a repeater) using pulses of light.

Fiber optic technology sends data without electricity through a conductor. Instead of electrical signals, modulated light is used to quickly transmit data over great distances through an insulated glass Fiber-type material.

Fiber optics is currently the best long distance communications method because it provides much faster data transfer speeds when compared to traditional interconnection media such as copper wire. The signal cannot be disrupted by outside sources like electricity, rain, humidity, or other things that tend to damage conventional copper wire signals. Fiber Optic Cables are ideal for volatile environments because there is no fear of damage should they break like there is with traditional copper wiring.

Optical Fiber is lightweight compared to copper cabling because it is a thin glass strand and has huge bandwidth because information travels along the Fiber at the speed of light. Thousands of fibers can be fit in the same amount of space as required for one cable. The developments in fiber optics suggest that the future cost of broadband transmission capability will be within the reach of small organizations and individuals.

Significant developments were made in wireless communication during the twentieth century and many forms. But the most significant mode of communication that revolutionized the process of information exchange in the satellite.

Satellite Communication has turned the entire world into a global village. Satellites relay or transmit information such as TV, phone, weather, military intelligence, and data. Communications satellites provide a worldwide link. In 1960, Echo 1 was launched becoming the first communications satellite. The primitive Echo 1 was an inflatable metallic sphere with instruments that bounced radio signals back to earth. Two years later, Telstar 1 became the first active communications satellite. These satellites orbit the earth at a relatively low altitude. This made them difficult to track and not very suitable for communication. Active satellites receive, amplify, and retransmit signals to different locations. Telstar 1 was responsible for the relay of the first live television broadcast across the Atlantic Ocean.

Perhaps the first person to carefully evaluate the various technical options in satellite communications *and* evaluate the financial prospects was John R. Pierce of AT&T's Bell Telephone Laboratories who, in a 1954 speech and 1955 article, elaborated the utility of a communications "mirror" in space, a medium-orbit "repeater" and a 24-hour-orbit "repeater." In comparing the communications capacity of a satellite, which he estimated at 1,000 simultaneous telephone calls, and the communications capacity of the first trans-atlantic telephone cable (TAT-1), which could carry 36 simultaneous telephone calls at a cost of 30-50 million dollars, Pierce wondered if a satellite would be worth a billion dollars.

After the 1957 launch of Sputnik I, many considered the benefits, profits, and prestige associated with satellite communications. Because of Congressional fears of "duplication," Federal Communications Commission (FCC) for permission to launch an experimental communications satellite with a view to rapidly implementing an operational system. In 1965, Intelsat 1, nicknamed "early bird", became the first commercial geosynchronous satellite. It was launched by COMSAT. A network of 19 Intelsat satellites provide instantaneous communications throughout the world. The current generation Intelsat 8, can handle 22,500 two-way phone calls and three color television broadcasts simultaneously. Recent advances in electronic equipment could increase the number of telephone circuitry to 112,500. There are also communication satellites launched by individual countries, organizations, and businesses in orbit.

Within the last ten years the first direct broadcast satellites were launched.

Weather forecasting has undergone a revolution because of the availability of pictures from geostationary meteorological satellites—pictures we see every day on television. All of these are important aspects of the space age, but satellite communications has probably had more effect than any of the rest on the average person. Satellite communications is also the only truly commercial space technology.

The basic communications component of the satellite was the traveling-wave-tube (TWT). These had been invented in England by Rudoph Kompfner, but they had been perfected at Bell Labs by Kompfner and J. R. Pierce. All three early satellites used TWTs built by a Bell Labs alumnus.

In 1965, when EARLY BIRD was launched, the satellite provided almost 10 times the capacity of the submarine telephone cables for almost 1/10th the price. Satellites are still competitive with cable for point-to-point communications, but the future advantage may lie with fiber-optic cable. Satellites still maintain two advantages over cable: they are more reliable and they can be used point-to-multi-point (broadcasting). Cellular telephone systems have risen as challenges to all other types of telephony. It is possible to place a cellular system in a developing country at a very reasonable price. Long-distance calls require some other technology, but this can be either satellites or fiber-optic cable. Cellular telephony has brought us a new technological system, the personal communications system (PCS). In the fully developed PCS, the individual would carry his telephone with him. This telephone could be used for voice or data and would be usable anywhere. Several companies have committed themselves to providing a version of this system using satellites in low earth orbits (LEO).

The inherent "broadcast" nature of satellite communications has made direct-broadcast a recurrent theme—yet one never brought to fruition. Each year many communications satellites are launched making the process of communication of information more easy and effective day by day.

The confluence of satellite and multimedia resulted in making the communication technology available at an unimaginably lower cost to the betterment of the common man although it originated in labs for scientific researchers. Now, Internet services are primarily based on these technologies.

Multimedia represents the convergence between computers, digital video, digital audio and sound synthesis. It has initially culminated the re-evaluation of the ways in which we communicate information combining still and moving images, sound, text and audio. Day to day applications of multimedia can be visualized considering information activities around us. Multimedia is being increasingly adopted for education and training, reference, business, entertainment etc.

Multimedia

Multimedia is widely acknowledged as an environment with great potentiality for education. It is able to assist both the people and teachers in new ways since for teacher it provides a means of putting across information and ideal and for students it can represent a one-to-one teaching environment which moves at the required pace.

Distribution of multimedia lessons, lectures and courseware on CD ROM or CD-1 discs adds another dimension to multimedia in education providing a vehicle of information to the students to take home. Its potential is enormous for the rural communities and isolated geographical regions where schools are inaccessible. The Open University teaching will certainly depend more upon the means and methods presented by advances in multimedia in the time to come.

As projected in the past we have now libraries without

space. An information specialist sitting comfortably at his place of work just connecting his computer can establish contact with the desired number of foreign databases and an interaction can follow for the desired information. These services are being offered now on commercial basis too. The information thus selected can be downloaded on computer for further use.

Pupils traveled long distances in the past in search of information. Now information is knocking at their doors. The electronic devices have made it possible to transfer information at the speed of light. Pictures and sounds too are being transmitted from one place to the other. What is important today, is the selection of information and its dissemination for application. The quantum of information available is so much that everybody can have enough to learn individually. This is because of the coordination of efforts at the global level and presentation of this vast amount of information in a way that makes it convenient for the users to determine what is relevant to their needs.

Many academic institutions in the West have made database search an integral part of their educational process. Now thanks to the power of CD-ROM technology, information on nearly all the disciplines of education is available within reach of virtually every academic institution, its teachers, students and researchers. One can search as broadly, as deeply and as long as he or she wishes. The Indian National Scientific Documentation Centre is providing professional expertise in this regard to the academic and research institutions in India. Some other agencies like the Videsh Sanchar Nigam, the National Informatics Centre and the Faxon Informatics, Bangalore also coordinate in subscribing to these services. The data available from these agencies reveals steady growth in demand of the On-Line Information Services by the academic institutions in India.

The electronic media allows portability as well as durability. Information recorded digitally can last for centuries virtually with no effect of humidity, dust or temperature. The quality of recording is not affected because the information i , not recorded on the surface but within the medium itself. The electronic media seems to be ideal for preservation of manuscripts and other valuable records. There are two ways of recording from paper on to the digital media-one is the transfer of text page wise and the other is that the contents of rare manuscripts may be entered word by word. Thus, not only the life of the documents increases but also they can be retrieved rapidly and made available to the researchers.

The present situation has become an ideal one for adoption of Internet as in the words of Bill Gates "For the first time, all kinds of information-numbers, text sound video-can be put into a digital form that any computer can now store, process and forward. For the first time, standard hardware combined with a standard software platform has created economies of scale that make powerful computing solutions available extensively to all kinds of companies" (Business @ the speed of thought: Penguin Books: London (1999).

The Internet

Internet has emerged as the most powerful medium for storage and retrieval of information. It works round the clock and connects every nook and corner of the globe. With an unprecedented growth in the quantum of knowledge worldwide and the easy accessibility, Internet has become an unavoidable necessity for every institution of higher learning and research. Internet is continuously growing internationally. Within a short span of ten years, its services have been spread among all the nations of the world. In 1991 it was within reach of 73 countries but within four years of its existence Internet reached 148 countries. The number of Internet users is also increasing tremendously as they are almost doubled after every two years. In the meanwhile Internet widened its scope. Now it is used for storage, manipulation and dissemination of textual data as well as the multimedia.

Internet became more popular by its feature of the World Wide Web in 1991, Tim Berners-Lee, a young scientist working in European Particle Physics Laboratory (CERN) produced Internet's first browser. According to him, "the dream behind the Web is of a common information space in which we communicate by sharing information. "By its application, someone could scan every document or photo or video on the net. It gave an opportunity to share the resources by individuals and organizations on the basis of mutual understanding.

So much is the impact of Internet that even the textbook industry is going to witness a fundamental shift leave alone the periodical publications and the other forms of print media. Once a sizeable number of traders agree for sharing ideas electronically along with a higher percentage of students having access to personal computers, the situation will be quite different. Having textbooks available electronically at lower cost will enable cash strapped institutions to redirect money spent on printed textbooks for other needs. The faster the growth of technology the shorter is the time to apply it for proper gains.

With the increasing dependant on micro literature for research in the universities and the availability of improved technology for information handling, the traditional library practices of classification and cataloguing are proving to be less relevant. As the information needs of users even in the academic institutions are satisfied with some alternate means. The growing use of Internet by medical and engineering institutions is a clear indication of what is in store for the libraries of the future? PUBMED, a service of the National Library of Medicine provides access to over 11 millions of citations back to the mid 1960s and additional life science journals. It includes links to many similar websites providing full text articles and other related resources. The service is available free of cost. Journals are the most pertinent sources of information for research in the universities. They are available in plenty on Internet. Moreover a large number of them is free of cost and if priced they cost less compared to their print counterpart. After the print media, journals could not figure in any other format except the digital media. The audiovisuals remained short lived and barring a few political ones no worth mentioning journal could surface in the audiovisual media.

Internet has also democratized the process of higher education in the true sense librating it from the clutches of the few knowledgeable and powerful without whom research was a distant dream for the students. It has affected almost every sphere of human activities. In the field of education, the work of traditional gurus has been taken over by Internet now, which provides information on the latest advancements and researches taking place in the various disciplines of study. It also supports further activities of collecting data, analyzing and synthesizing it. Moreover it presents the events in international perspective hence the research work is supposed to be unique whereas the chances for repetition were higher in the past when things were perceived in the limited geographical limits.

Internet has not only facilitated resources sharing across the boundaries of the countries but also it has freed libraries from many complicated and inconvenient practices such as the inter library lending where the documents were required to be dispatched physically. It involved risk of loss. Only the trusted institutions could render the service on the basis of mutual understanding. The idea was always good but it could never work satisfactorily.

Internet services are easily available and affordable as the cost of connectivity and computer hardware, software has come down considerably during the last few years. Moreover, there has been standardization in the ever-changing configuration of systems. The software has been made more user friendly for computer as well as netsurfing. Now, the services are also being offered through cable TV and in case this facility widens there will be no need to purchase the computer hardware and software at all.

Growth of the Internet

A mere fifteen years ago, hardly any one knew that the Internet existed. Since then, its growth has been astonishing in various aspects. Now, it is hard to decide what to include in estimating its size and measure the growth of the Internet as it is a loose collection of networks. However, because no single entity is in control, nobody knows everything about the Internet. Measuring it is especially hard because some parts choose to limit access to themselves to various degrees.

In the given circumstances however, we have various methods of surveying and estimating the size of the Internet. There are widely differing estimates for the growth rate of the Internet. Over the years, the growth rate of the Internet has not been stable with more rapid growth surfacing in some years compared to others, but a decline has never taken place. A surprising statistic is that a large majority of the Internet growth is due to men. Approximately 70% of the users of the internet are men and 30% women world wide. This is partially due to the dominance of men in the workforce, and the fact that half of Internet users are professional and technically related. The two most popular ways to measure Internet growth is by the number of hosts and by the number of Internet users/ traffic.

Growth Measured By Hosts

The most popular way to measure the growth of the Internet is by the number of hosts (the number of machine addressed on the net as reported by the nameservers). Their growth in chronological order is being illustrated Below:

Date	Hosts
August 1981	213
May 1982	235
August 1983	562
October 1984	1,024
October 1985	1,961

November 1986	5,089
December 1987	28,174
October 1988	56,000
October 1989	159,000
October 1990	313,000
October 1991	617,000
October 1992	1,136,000
October 1993	2,056,000
October 1994	3,864,000
January 1996	9,472,000
January 1997	16,146,000
January 1998	29,670,000
January 1999	43,230,000
January 2000	72,398,000
January 2001	109,574,429
January 2002	147,344,723

As the table above shows, in 1981 there were only 213 hosts and the increase through 1982 was very minimal. Beginning in 1983, the number of hosts started to double and in many years they came close to tripling. The latest results from the Internet's most basic and longest continuing measurement of its size were just released by the Internet Software Consortium from data collected by Network Wizards. The survey attempts to locate every host of the Internet by using the Domain Name System. These results were gathered around late January 2001. ISC's measurements show that the Internet currently has 109,574,429 connected computers (hosts) that reside in 230 countries and territories. Thirteen additional countries and territories were listed in the Domain Name System, but no hosts were discovered under those domains. As of March 2002, the 109 million Internet host mark has already increased to 170,849,000, which is a 59% increase from January 2001.

The result of 170 million hosts represents a significant new benchmark for the number of Internet hosts. The current annual growth rate now stands at 51 percent. It's right in the range of the 46-67% we have experienced over the past two years. The 109 million mark shows a strong growth, with the 100 million host barrier being broke in the fourth quarter of 2000. If the same growth rate is sustained, the Internet would cross the 1 billion host mark in mid 2005. The largest domain is COM, which has increased by 7.8 million (32% annual growth rate) hosts since January to a new high of 36.3 million hosts. The countries with the largest number of host are: 1)United States of America, 2)Japan, 3)Canada, 4)Germany, 5)UK, 6)Italy, 7)Australia, 8)Netherlands, 9)Taiwan, and 10)France. The Internet is now expanding at a rate of 63 new hosts and 11 new domains per minute worldwide.

Growth Measured By Internet Usage/Traffic

Most recent studies, as of, 2002, show that there are now almost half a billion people around the world with internet access. According to Nielsen NetRatings, 498 million people had home Internet access by the end of 2001, which is up by 5.1 percent. The number of online users surpassed the half-billion point in 2001. The main reasons for 2001's surpassing of the half-billion mark was the continuing e-commerce growth and online business became more mainstream. As of 1995, it was estimated that 10 percent of the population of the United States used (home or elsewhere) the Internet on a regular basis. The increase in Internet usage in the United States has been on a steady pace and is currently estimated to be at 61 percent. If future projections are correct, by the year 2005 an unbelievable 75 percent of American will use the Internet. How many people are online around the world: world total 544.2 million, Africa 4.15 million, Asia/Pacific 157.49 million, Europe 171.35 million, Middle East 4.65 million, Canada & USA 181.23 million, and Latin America 25.33 million. Forty percent of home users were in North America, 27 percent were in Europe (almost half of UK homes have online access), the Middle East and Africa, and 22 percent were in Asia.

The continent with the fastest growing home Internet population is Asia. The number of people with online access grew 5.6 percent in the fourth quarter of last year, compared to a 4.9 percent increase in Europe, 2.5 percent in the United States 3.3 percent in Latin America. Lower income groups are not prevalent on the Web due to limited resources and education. Surveys show that mid range income families at about $60 thousand a year had the largest amount of users on the Internet. The percentages decreased rapidly on either side of the median. Current trends show that the majority of new Internet users are not English speaking. More Asian and non-english speaking European countries are starting to use the net.

Traffic and the capacity of the public Internet grew at rates of about 100% per year in the early 1990's. A brief period of explosive growth was experienced in 1995 and 1996 with traffic growing at a rate of 1,000% per year, but starting in 1997, traffic slowed back down to the 100% per year rate. If the number of people using the Internet were to keep doubling every year, then by mid year 2005, 100 percent (6,005,829,368) of the world's population would be using the Internet. The number of unique indexable Web pages has grown from 1 billion in January 2000 to more than 2 billion in June 2000. The number of people who use the Internet on a regular basis has dramatically increased from fewer than 90,000 in 1993 to more than 304 million in 2000. Overall, the online access market showed a sluggish growth of barely one percent, growing from about 68.6 million users at the start of 2001 to 69.3 million by the close of the year according to TR's Online Census report. When compared to a 52 percent growth rate for 2000, the growth was very stale.

Recent studies show that home Internet users account for almost one eighth of the world's population and there is still significant growth potential for Internet access. Analyst estimate that 24 million people used the Internet for the first time in the fourth quarter of 2001, which is an increase from the 15 million who went online in the third quarter. The fastest Internet growing countries are: 1)India, 2)Indonesia, 3)Mexico, 4)Portugal, 5)Slovakia, 6)Romania, 7)Ukraine, 8)Brazil, 9)Estonia, and 10)Soviet. The fastest growing Internet countries are mainly the countries that are just getting the Internet established and realizing its benefits. Countries like the United States where the Internet is already widespread has a smaller growth potential. If traffic on the Internet continues to double each year, data should exceed voice on U.S. long distance networks around the end of 2002.

There seems to be no reason to expect a slowdown in the next decade, and there could even be periods of more rapid growth. Internet application is increasing in the education section like the other human activities. People depend more and more on information delivery through in escalating proportions. A survey of the University of Waterloo is given here to illustrate this point.

Growth in traffic between the University of Waterloo (Canada) and the Internet backbones.

For each school term, the table displays the volume of data transmitted during the month of highest traffic.

Month	MB/day in	MB/day out
March 1993	453	227
July 1993	541	271
October 1993	648	324
April 1994	977	543
August 1994	1,377	915
November 1994	2,098	1,426
April 1995	2,285	1,730
July 1995	3,229	2,588
November 1995	6,000	3,450
March 1996	7,229	4,275

July 1996	7,823	4,572
November 1996	10,962	5,984
March 1997	11,463	6,235
July 1997	12,087	7,223
November 1997	24,621	10,572
March 1998	24,676	9,502

The 100% annual growth rates for the Internet were a result of increase in number of users as well as increased traffic from existing users. While there will surely continue to be growth in users of the Internet, it will not be by a factor of 100 or even close to it over the next decade, since that would require more people than live on the Earth. However, rapid growth has been observed even from small communities. The University of Waterloo also appears to have experienced roughly a doubling of traffic to and from the Internet each year for the last five years.

The Library of Congress statistics (Table below) also show more than a doubling each year. Thus it appears that organizations find IP sufficiently attractive that they double their traffic each year, although the sources of demand may change.

Growth in data traffic at the Library of Congress.

For each year, total traffic in gigabytes given during February of that year

year	GB/month	increase from previous year
1995	14.0	
1996	31.2	123%
1997	109.4	251%
1998	282.0	158%

There is room for further expansion in this area. About half the households in the U. S. have PCs, and of these only half have residential Internet service. Further, 45 minutes per day is a small fraction of the time that American families watch television. As more people join the network, they create more content, and make it more attractive for others to create content for the Internet, which draws in more users, and so on, as predicted by Metcalfe's Law.

Once broadband technologies such as cable modems, various DSL technologies, or wireless data links are deployed, residential customers will be able to substantially increase their traffic per house-hold. In the very near future, though, rapid growth is most likely to come from institutions such as corporations, which have the broadband communication infrastructure to increase increased traffic. Costs of providing local access at high speeds from corporate WANs are dropping rapidly with the deployment of HDSL (although that is not reflected in prices yet), and fiber will be increasingly feasible for higher speeds. Even without novel applications, such as packet telephony and videoconferencing, ordinary Intranet and Extranet applications could lead to continued growth at historic rates. We could also see spurts of growth even faster than 100% per year if some of the novel applications start growing. The public Internet could also grow at high rates if more of the growth in internal private line networks shifts to it.

3
Dawn of the Digital Libraries

Digital technologies are transforming scholarly communication. These technologies provide an unprecedented opportunity to rethink how a social organization creates, uses, publishes, accesses, and manages the information resources. The greatest impact of these technologies can be seen in the creation of new knowledge and how scholars, researchers, and students are increasingly finding new means of providing education services and collaborating via the networked environment. Digital libraries have emerged as a suitable substitute to the traditional libraries with more positive features to serve the society. In digital libraries a significant proportion of the resources are available in machine-readable format, rather than in print or on microform.

Digital libraries are emerging as substitute to the traditional libraries with more and more facilities at a lower cost. It may be said that the infrastructure does not exist suitably to be benefited equally but a precedent may be taken of the expansion of computer in the same conditions.

Digital technology can make the works of man permanently accessible to the billions of people all over the world. J.N. Tata and other great philanthropists, and visionary information scientist like Dr S. R. Ranganathan, in past centuries have recognized the great potential of public libraries to improve the quality of life and provide opportunity the citizenry. Now a language independent digital library, widely available through free access on the Internet, will improve the global society in ways beyond measurement. The technological advances today make it possible to think in terms of storing all the knowledge of the human race in digital form by the year 2008.

In libraries, the process of digitization began with the catalog, moved to periodical indexes and abstracting services, then to periodicals and large reference works, and finally book publishing. A digital library is an assemblage of digital computing, storage, and communications machinery together with the content and software needed to reproduce, emulate, and extend the services provided by conventional libraries based on paper and other material means of collecting, cataloging, finding, and disseminating information. A full service digital library must accomplish all essential services of traditional libraries and also exploit the well-known advantages of digital storage, searching, and communication.

Digital libraries are emerging to satisfy the information needs of organizations at the national and international level and also in different environments of the working of libraries. In advanced countries, they are more visible and active compared with the developing and the under-developing countries. It is therefore necessary to study some of the leading digital libraries of the world.

The concept "library" has been refined over several centuries. It would be injudicious to depart from what people expect merely because a digital service is replacing a material one. The Digital Library is the collection of services and the collection of information objects that support users in dealing with information objects and the organization and presentation of those objects available directly or indirectly via electronic/digital means.

Different people define digital libraries in different ways. According to William Arms, a digital library is " a managed collection of information, with associated services, where the information is stored in digital formats and accessible over a network". The Digital Library Federation of United States of

America defines digital libraries as " organizations that provide the resources including the specialized staff, to select. Structure, offer intellectual access to, interpret, distribute, preserve the integrity of, and ensure the persistent overtime of connections of digital works so they are readily available for use by a defined community or set of communities".

Digital libraries are like traditional libraries in that they involve large collections of diverse information and there are common issues concerning organization, retrieval, access, storage, archiving and preservation of information. However, digital libraries are different in that the properties of physical location and storage of local copies for individual use no longer need apply. This decoupling of storage, organization and access along with the ease of authoring, annotation and support for collaborative work groups of a significant advantages.

Digital libraries differ from the electronic libraries because all of the information that they contain exists only in a digital electronic format. The information itself may reside on different storage media such as electronic memory or magnetic and optical disk, but users will not necessarily perceive any differences between. Because of the way in which information in stored, digital libraries do not, therefore contain conventional books. The major types of publications contain in this type of libraries will be various types of electronic document.

A digital Library is an assemblage of digital computing, storage, and communications machinery together with the content and software needed to reproduce, emulate, and extend the services provided by conventional libraries based on paper and other material means of collecting, cataloging, finding, and disseminating information. A full service digital library must accomplish all essential services of traditional libraries and also exploit the well-known advantages of digital storage, searching, and communication.

Digital library is a concept that has different meanings in different communities. To the engineering and computer science community, digital library is a metaphor for the new kinds of distributed data base services that manage unstructured multimedia data. To the political and business communities, the term represents a new marketplace for the world's information resources and services.

Digital libraries are a set of electronic resources and associated technical capabilities for creating, searching, and using information. In this sense they are an extension and enhancement of information storage and retrieval systems that manipulate digital data in any medium (text, images, sounds; static or dynamic images) and exist in distributed networks. The content of digital libraries includes data, metadata that describe various aspects of the data (e.g., representation, creator, owner, reproduction rights), and metadata that consist of links or relationships to other data or metadata, whether internal or external to the digital library.

Many potential advantages of a digital library over a paper library are similar to those of any digital database over its paper counterpart:

- faster addition to the collection with better quality control
- improved search functionality and faster access to information found, and
- more freedom and reduced bureaucracy for individual users.

Achieving these advantage depends not only on efforts traditionally undertaken by computer scientists, but also on the highest quality engineers.

Characteristics of digital Libraries

Following are the characteristics of digital libraries:

- users are usually elsewhere than the information they want, and often wish to correlate things from several sources;

- whoever wants to use a library must show permission to do so;
- different patrons are permitted different actions and to see different parts of each collection;
- to find specific information, each user must understand the catalog structure;
- the catalog may describe items not actually held as part of the collection at hand;
- the catalog and the collected items are used differently and not necessarily housed in the same place;
- documents are cataloged with text descriptors and also with conventional properties, such as author names;
- documents contain cross references to other documents;
- document identifiers are different from document names; a document may have several names, one for each context, e.g., "Tales of Hoffmann" in English, "Les contes d'Hoffmann" in French, and "Hoffmanns Erzaehlungen" in German;
- translations of a document may express essentially the same information, e.g., versions of classic literature in different languages;
- each stored item is valuable, often with part of its residual value owned by its authors or authors' assignees;
- part of the value provided by a library is the provenance information it holds for each item;
- items are put into libraries because, while each is thought valuable for future reference, the specific individuals who will read it and the times when this will occur are not known.

Any organization like school, business, department, family, individual can create and manage its own library, and most individuals can access to many libraries. All libraries should do certain things similarly adhere to certain standards

— so people do not need to learn new methods for each library and so information can be exchanged.

At the general level found in requests for proposals, in the trade literature, and in business publications, there is broad consensus on what services the digital library should have in 5-10 years. For a few of the generic components, such as storage subsystems and document markup languages and interpretation, detailed requirements analyses exist; typically they include hundreds of well-justified requirements. For most of the other generic components suggested earlier, similarly comprehensive requirements analyses are not available in the generally accessible literature.

To prioritize the requirements for academic and cultural Digital Library services we must consider a range of objectives which will differ among different institutions. For some the premier objective will be improved accessibility to rare and valuable materials for scholars. For others, as in the TULIP project mounted by Elsevier in partnership with computer science groups at several universities, it will be easier information search by electronic publication of professional journals

The radically new possibility for Digital libraries is storage and dissemination of collected items. In contrast, digital catalogs have been in practical use for some time, and there is a considerable body of experience, both good and bad, or at least questionable, and some standards in this area.

The preparation of a catalog may seem a light task, to the inexperienced, ant to those who are unacquainted with the requirements of the learned world, respecting such works. In truth, however, there is no species of literary labor so arduous and perplexing. The peculiarities of titles are, like the idiosyncrasies of authors, innumerable.

An analysis done by IBM Research identified several hundred specific requirements — too many to tabulate here. However, several broadly applicable elements emerged, and are summarized below because they typify what needs to be worked out for each library:

- accessibility from all workstation
- application independence;
- catalog service from all kinds of operating system platforms;
- joining libraries to other databases;
- automatic capture and indexing;
- document managers;
- large and small items;
- low entry point, with growth to giant collections, maintaining performance;
- low installation and administration overhead;
- open subsystem
- standard interfaces and protocols;
- customer-defined data formats;
- support for all kinds of item storage;
- tools for "amateur" application programmers.

Development of Digital Libraries

It is not clear when the first digital library came into being, but the concept did not appear until late 1980s. The emergence and development of digital libraries at this stage were driven by two main forces. First, digital technological development, especially in multimedia and networking, offered more efficient and sometimes new ways in information processing and management. Second, people wanted to better share important information like library materials, scientific databases in education and research. So digital library systems came into being

Most early "digital libraries" were various types of digital collections and information systems. Personal information resources, workgroup and organizational information collections and collaboration environments are some of the examples. Edward Fox in his Digital Libraries Overview offered a detailed account of some early projects in the field. According to his timeline, Electronic Theses started as early as 1987. Libraries were also working towards this direction. Many libraries started to replace their card catalogs with OPAC systems, and were beginning to store abstracts and periodicals on CD-ROMs.

In 1989, the World Wide Web project was first proposed and since mid 1993, it quickly grew at an exponential rate. Users could browse and set up a node on the network to put information on it. It was called by some people the beginning of a true digital library. But the Web is a library without a card catalog, and many search tools or services were crude at the early stage.

High levels of attention and funding were first given to digital libraries in the early and mid 1990s, which led to a booming era with large number of visions and projects. Scholars in the field wanted to find ways to apply or create technologies in order to better use and share information on the network systems, which themselves are developing at an amazing speed. The shared vision is best illustrated in the mission statement of Digital Library Initiative: "the Initiative's focus is to dramatically advance the means to collect, store, and organize information in digital forms, and make it available for searching, retrieval, and processing via communication networks. Digital Library Initiative (DLI) is the biggest, and the most important digital library research project among all.

Starting from 1994, DLI is a four-year multiagency research initiative sponsored by the National Science Foundation, Advanced Research Projects Agency, and the National Aeronautics and Space Administration. It demonstrates the US government's effect in building the National Information Infrastructure. Six large-scale research projects, each funded with about $1 million per year, are involved. They are:

1. The University of Michigan Digital Library Research Project

The core of the Digital Library at the University of Michigan has been the "agent architecture that supports the teaming of agents to provide complex services by combining limited individual capabilities". The content focus is on earth and space sciences.

2. The University of Illinois at Urbana-Champaign Digital Library Research Project

The research is concentrated on building an experimental testbed with tens of thousands of full-text journal articles from physics, engineering, and computer science.

3. The University of California at Berkeley Digital Library Research Project

The project's goal is to develop the technologies for intelligent access to massive, distributed collections of photographs, satellite images, maps, full text documents, and "multivalent" documents on environmental information.

4. Carnegie Mellon University Digital Library Research Project

The Informedia Digital Video Library at Carnegie Mellon University studies how multimedia digital libraries with digital video, audio, images, and text information can be established and used.

5. The Stanford University Digital Libraries Project

The Stanford Digital Libraries project focuses on interoperability. It aims to develop a single, integrated "virtual" library that will provide uniform access to a variety of services and information sources.

6. The Alexandria Project at The University of California at Santa Barbara

The Alexandria Digital Library focuses on geographically-referenced information. It aims to provide easy access to collections of maps, images, pictorial materials and other spatially referenced information.

(The above information is from NSF/DARPA/NASA Digital Libraries Initiative Projects page and each university's digital library project homepage.).

There is no clear-cut between the above era and this period. In many cases, they co-exist. The rapid expansion of the Internet and Web triggered, in some way, the sudden advances in the research and development in digital libraries, and at the same time proposes many questions to researchers.

Since 1995, various kinds of conferences, workshops and forums on digital libraries were held, and articles flooded discussing all kinds of questions from various perspectives on digital libraries. Digital libraries and digital library researches in Asia and Europe are also playing an active role. Recently, Digital Libraries Initiative Phase Two is proposed which "seeks to provide leadership in research fundamental to the development of the next generation of digital libraries, to advance the use and usability of globally distributed, networked information resources, and to encourage existing and new communications to focus on innovative applications areas. We believe digital libraries will continue developing with all these efforts.

Resources and Projects

The developments taking place all over the world suggest that the digital libraries are gaining popularity in about all the nations. They are more visible in the developed countries. But as per the established trends the developing countries follow the suit and try to bring them at par with the developed nations. Following are some factors which suggest steady growth of the digital libraries in the time to come.

Conferences

The origin and development of ideas take place in the form of symposia, seminars and conferences. The number of conferences held on the themes of digital libraries is quite large which shows a steady acceptance of digital library in the society. The following are the conferences which were held during the last eight years.

International Summer School on the Digital Library

Course 1: Leaders' Visions on the Library of the Future

Tilburg University, Tilburg, The Netherlands, 10 - 12 August 2003

URL: http://www.ticer.nl/summer03/course1/

Course 2: Change: Making it Happen in your Library

Tilburg University, Tilburg, The Netherlands, 12 - 15 August 2003

URL: http://www.ticer.nl/summer03/course2/

Course 3: Libraries, Electronic Resources, and Electronic Publishing

Tilburg University, Tilburg, The Netherlands, 24 - 27 August 2003

URL: http://www.ticer.nl/summer03/course3/

ACM SAC 2002: Special Track on Database and Digital Library Technologies

March 10 - 14, 2002: Madrid, Spain

URL: http://notesmail.cs.odu.edu/faculty/zubair/workshop.nsf/sacdl02?OpenPage

The Sixth International Summer School on Digital Libraries

- Course 1: The Management of Change (Tilburg University, the Netherlands, 30 July - 3 August 2001)
- Course 2: Ditial Libraries and the Changing World of Education (Tilburg University, the Netherlands, 5 - 10 August 2001)
- Course 3: Electronic Publishing (European University Institute, Italy, 7 - 12 October 2001)

URL: http://www.ticer.nl/summer01/

(The 2001 Summer School was discussed in a D-Lib

article

http://www.dlib.org/dlib/november01/prinsen/11prinsen.html)

The Fifth International Summer School on the Digital Library

July31 - 11 August, 2000: Tilburg University, Netherlands

URL: http://www.ticer.nl/summer00/

Digital Libraries '99: Fourth ACM Conference on Digital Libraries.

August 11-14, 1999: University of California, Berkeley.

URL: http://fox.cs.vt.edu/DL99/

ADL '99: Advances in Digital Libraries Conference.

May 19-21, 1999: Baltimore, MD.

URL: http://cimic.rutgers.edu/adl99/

Ninth DELOS Workshop: Digital Libraries for Distance Learning.

April 15-17, 1999: Brno, Czech Republic.

URL: http://www.ercim.org/publication/ws-proceedings/DELOS9/index.html

Eighth DELOS Workshop: User Interface in Digital Libraries.

October 21-23, 1998: Stockholm, Sweden.

URL: http://www.ercim.org/publication/ws-proceedings/DELOS8/index.html

Second European Conference on Research and Advanced Technology for Digital Libraries.

September 19-23 1998: Heraklion, Crete, Greece.

URL: http://www.ics.forth.gr/2EuroDL/

Digital Libraries '98: Third ACM Conference on Digital Libraries.

June 24-27, 1998: Pittsburgh, PA.

URL: http://www.acm.org/pubs/contents/proceedings/dl/276675/

Sixth DELOS Workshop: Preservation of Digital Information.

June 17-19, 1998: Tomar, Portugal.

URL: http://www.ercim.org/publication/ws-proceedings/DELOS6/index.html

Digital Libraries Asia 98 Conference & Exhibition: The Digital Era: Implications, Challenges & Issues.

March 17-20, 1998: Singapore.

URL: http://dla98.digilib.org.sg/

ISDL '97. The International Symposium on Research, Development & Practice in Digital Libraries.

November 18 - 21, 1997: Tsukuba Science City, Japan.

URL: http://www.DL.ulis.ac.jp/ISDL97/

Fifth DELOS Workshop: Filtering and Collaborative Filtering.

November 10-12, 1997:Budapest, Hungary.

URL: http://www.ercim.org/publication/ws-proceedings/DELOS5/index.html

First European Conference on Research and Advanced Technology for Digital Libraries.

September 1-3, 1997: Pisa, Italy.

URL: http://www.ercim.org/publication/Ercim_News/enw31/peters.html

ELVIRA 4 (Electronic Library and Visual Information) Conference on Digital Library Research.

May 6-8, 1997: Milton Keynes, UK.

URL: http://www.iielr.dmu.ac.uk/ELVIRA/ELVIRA4/

ELVIRA'96 3rd International Conference on Electronic Library and Visual Information Research

The UK Digital Libraries Conference. 30 April - 2 May 1996.

URL: http://educate.lib.chalmers.se/IATUL/montfort.html

First DELOS Workshop: An Overview on Projects and Research Activities in Digital Library Related Fields.

March 4-6, 1996: INRIA - Sophia Antipolis.

URL: http://www.ercim.org/publication/ws-proceedings/DELOS1/index.html

Social Aspects of Digital Libraries

February 16-17, 1996: Workshop held at the UCLA Department of Library and Information Science.

URL: http://dlis.gseis.ucla.edu/DL/

Final Report PDF: http://www.ifla.org/documents/libraries/net/ucladl01.pdf

Proceedings of the First IEEE Metadata Conference

April 16-18, 1996: Silver Spring, Maryland.

URL: http://www.computer.org/conferences/meta96/meta_home.html

ACM Digital Libraries '96.

First ACM International Conference on Research and Development in Digital Libraries (announcement).

URL: http://fox.cs.vt.edu/DL96/

ISDL'95: International Symposium on Digital Libraries 1995.

August 22 - 25, 1995: University of Library and Information Science, Tsukuba Science City, Ibaraki, Japan.

URL: http://www.DL.ulis.ac.jp/ISDL95/

Digital Libraries '95.

Proceedings of the Second International Conference on the Theory and Practice of Digital Libraries. June 11-13, 1995: Austin, Texas.

URL: http://csdl.cs.tamu.edu/DL95/

1995 Workshop on Digital Libraries.

IITA - Interoperability, Scaling, and the Digital Libraries Research Agenda. May 18-19, 1995: Reston, Virginia.

URL: http://www-diglib.stanford.edu/diglib/pub/reports/iita-dlw/main.html

ADL '95: Forum on Research and Technology Advances in Digital Libraries, May 15-17, 1995.

May 15-17, 1995: McLean, VA.

URL: http://sdcd.gsfc.nasa.gov/DIV-NEWS/adl.html

AAAI Spring Symposium on Information Gathering from Heterogeneous, Distributed Environments.

March 27-29, 1995, Stanford University. This was an Artificial Intelligence Symposium that looked at machine-assisted retrieval of networked information.

URL: http://www.ai.mit.edu/people/las/aaai/sss-95/sss-95-cfp.html

Digital Libraries '94.

Proceedings of the First Annual Conference on the Theory and Practice of Digital Libraries. College Station, Texas, USA. June 19-21, 1994.

URL: http://csdl.tamu.edu/DL94/

W3 Consortium. Collaboration, Knowledge Representation and Automatability.

URL: http://www.w3.org/Collaboration/Overview.html

Workshop on WWW and Collaboration, September 11-12, 1995.

URL: http://www.w3.org/Collaboration/Workshop/

Workshop on Wide-Area Collaboration and Cooperative Computing, at Second International WWW Conference, October 19th, 1994.

URL: http://www.ai.mit.edu/projects/iiip/colab/workshop.html

GENERIC CONFERENCE RESOURCES

International World Wide Web Conferences.

URL: http://www.w3.org/Conferences/Overview-WWW.html

YAHOO! WWW Conferences List.

URL: http://dir.yahoo.com/Computers_and_Internet/Internet/World_Wide_Web/Conferences/Organizations

A large number of organizations have come into existence which moot the creation and development of digital resources and libraries. The trend of their coming into being is more visible in the advanced nations. The following are the organizations which are more visible.

IEEE. Digital Library Task Force.

URL: http://cimic.rutgers.edu/ieee_dltf.html

International Institute for Electronic Library Research.

URL: http://www.iielr.dmu.ac.uk/

[Australia] Management of Material in Electronic Format Working Party. Towards Federation 2001 - Linking Australians and their Heritage.

"A national consultative conference, hosted by the National Library of Australia, on access to Australia' recorded documentary heritage was held in Canberra, Australia on 23-26 March 1992. The conference has 86 resolutions as its outcome and since that time the National Library of Australia has engaged in a thorough assessment of each resolution, its progress or lack thereof, and possible changes in the objective or action mechanism which might lead to faster and better progress in the future."

URL: http://www.nla.gov.au/pub/tf2001.html

[Australia] Preserving Access to Digital Information (PADI).

URL: http://www.nla.gov.au/padi/

[Australia] Photographic Libraries

URL: http://www.photographiclibraries.com/

[European Union] European Commission. Telematics for Libraries Programme.

Research and Development in the libraries sector of the

Telematics Programme aims to facilitate access to the wealth of knowledge held in libraries throughout the European Union, while reducing disparities between national systems and practice. This is a comprehensive and important entry point for information about European digital library projects.

URL: http://www.echo.lu/libraries/en/libraries.html

[Europe] DLM-FORUM Electronic Record.

URL: http://www.echo.lu/dlm/en/home.html

[Europe] European Preservation Information Centre (EPIC).

URL: http://www.knaw.nl/ecpa/

[International] International Council of Archives. Committee on Electronic Records.

URL: http://www.ica.org/

[International] Digital Library Colaboratory Working Groups.

URL: http://www.si.umich.edu/UMDL/EU_Grant/home.htm

[International] International Standards Organisation (ISO). Open Archival Information (OAIS) Standard.

URL: http://ssdoo.gsfc.nasa.gov/nost/isoas/overview.html

[Japan] University of Library and Information Science. Digital Library Network (DLnet).

Tsukuba Science City, Japan. August 31, 1994

URL: http://www.dl.ulis.ac.jp/DLW_E/

[South Asia] Digital South Asia Library (DSAL)

The Digital South Asia Library is a global collaborative effort to make important and rare resources available to the international community. DSAL includes resources from many disciplines as well as a variety of data types. The component parts of the project include maps, statistics, bibliographies, union lists, indexes, photographs, books and journals, as well as a reference collection that is strong in pedagogical tools for South Asian language learning.

URL: http://wwwcrl.uchicago.edu/dsal/

[United Kingdom] International Institute for Electronic Library Research.

URL: http://www.iielr.dmu.ac.uk/

[United Kingdom] Public Record Office. International Institute for Electronic Library Research.

The PRO has established two digital preservation programmes, EROS (Electronic Records from Office Systems) for the records created in the office networks being introduced by government bodies, and NDAD (UK National Digital Archive of Datasets at <http://ndad.ulcc.ac.uk>) for structured datasets, such as survey files and databases, in government departments.

URL: http://www.pro.gov.uk/

[UNESCO] Memory of the World.

"The twofold purpose of the UNESCO's "Memory of the World" programme is to safeguard and promote the endangered world documentary heritage."

URL: http://www.unesco.org/webworld/memory/mempage.htm

[US] Association of Research Libraries (ARL).

URL: http://arl.cni.org/

[US] National Archives and Records Administration. Records Center Program.

URL: http://www.archives.gov/records_center_program/index.html

[US] Center for the Study of Digital Libraries.

Texas A&M University.

URL: http://www.csdl.tamu.edu/

[US] Center for Networked Information Discovery and Retrieval (CNIDR).

URL: http://www.cnidr.org/

[US] Coalition for Networked Information.

URL: http://www.cni.org/

[US] Commission on Preservation and Access.

URL: http://www.clir.org/pubs/cpanews/cpanews.html

[US] Consortium for the Computer Interchange of Museum Information (CIMI).

URL: http://www.cimi.org/

[US] Inter-university Consortium for Political and Social Research (ICPSR).

A strategic undertaking of the ICPSR is the acquisition and long-term preservation of social science data.

URL: http://www.icpsr.umich.edu/ICPSR/

[US] Massachusetts Historical Society.

URL: http://www.masshist.org/

[US] Museum Computer Network.

URL: http://www.mcn.edu/

[US] National Archives and Records Administration. Center for Electronic Records.

URL: http://www.nara.gov/nara/electronic/homensx.html

[US] National Digital Library Federation (NDLF).

URL: http://lcweb.loc.gov/loc/ndlf/

[US] National Science Foundation (NSF).

Digital Libraries Initiative.

URL: http://www.dli2.nsf.gov/

[US] OCLC: Online Computer Library Center

URL: http://www.oclc.org/

[US] Research Libraries Group.

URL: http://www.rlg.org/

[US] Digital Library SunSITE.

University of California, Berkeley

URL: http://sunsite.berkeley.edu/

[US] Universal Preservation Format.

This site disseminates information about the proposed universal preservation format and related initiatives.

URL: http://info.wgbh.org/upf/

Digital Library General Projects

Adams Family Papers: An Electronic Archive

URL: http://www.masshist.org/digitaladams/

Digitisation Forum Online.

URL: http://www.acn.net.au/projects/digit.htm

Thomas Jefferson Papers: An Electronic Archive

URL: http://www.thomasjeffersonpapers.org/

Library Produced WWW Services and Guides

The Argus Clearinghouse.

URL: http://www.clearinghouse.net

Berkeley Public Library Home Page.

URL: http://www.infopeople.org/bpl/

BYU Libraries Information Network .

URL: http://www.lib.byu.edu/

Connecticut Library Home Page.

URL: http://www.ctstateu.edu/libraries.html

INFOMINE.

A collaborative project which includes participants from all 9 University of California campuses and Stanford University. One of the first academic virtual libraries.

URL: http://infomine.ucr.edu/Main.html

Larry Schankman's Best of the Best.

URL: http://www.clark.net/pub/lschank/web/subject.html

Directories. Indices, Databases and Guides for Information Access and Orgainzation

Association of Research Libraries Digital Initiatives Database.

URL: http://www.arl.org/did/

EFF's (Extended) Guide to the Internet.

URL: http://www.eff.org/papers/eegtti/

EINet Galaxy.

URL: http://www.einet.net/galaxy.html

The HCI Bibliography Project.

A free-access online extended bibliography on Human-Computer Interaction

URL: http://www.hcibib.org/

The Internet Services list.

Based on Yanoff's Internet List

URL: http://www.cs.indiana.edu/internet/internet.html

Joel's Hierarchical Subject Index.

URL: http://www.teco.uni-karlsruhe.de/~michael/joels.html

NCSA's Internet Resources Meta-Index.

URL: http://www.ncsa.uiuc.edu/SDG/Software/Mosaic/MetaIndex.html

WWW Virtual Library.

URL: http://www.vlib.org/

Yanoff's Special Internet Connections.

URL: http://www.spectracom.com/islist/

Projects in America

Abacci Books Free literary resources on the net

At Abacci Books they combined two literary resources of the net: Project Gutenberg and Amazon, to produce a new view of the world's best free literature.

URL: http://www.abacci.com/books/default.asp

Carnegie-Mellon. Digital Video Library.

"The Informedia (tm) Digital Video Library project will establish a large, on-line digital video library by developing intelligent, automatic mechanisms to populate the library and allow for full-content and knowledge-based search and retrieval via desktop computer and metropolitan area networks. Initially, the library will be populated with 1000 hours of raw and edited video drawn from video assets of WQED/ Pittsburgh, Fairfax County (VA) Public Schools, and the Open University (U.K.). We will deploy the library at Carnegie Mellon University and local area K-12 Schools."

URL: http://www.informedia.cs.cmu.edu/

Columbia University. Oversized Colour Images Digitization Project.

"This URL contains the results of a project, under contract to the Commission on Preservation and Access, to identify the most acceptable preservation and access techniques available for oversize, color images associated with text. Five maps from brittle volumes have been scanned, as have single-frame color microfiche of the maps (produced during an earlier Commission-sponsored project) and 4 x 5" color transparencies. Paper printouts have been made from each digital version."

URL: http://www.columbia.edu/dlc/nysmb/

Columbia University. Project Bartleby: The Public Library of the Internet.

"Bartleby's 3,000 pages of text on-line may not seem monumental at first, but consider that Whitman's Leaves of Grass released in March 1994 was one of the first on-line books of classic literature that was "native" to hypertext on the WorldWide Web; that Project Bartleby is currently one of the largest public collections of on-line literature; and that it's considered the finest example of public electronic publishing—maintaining strict editorial and quality-control procedures."

URL: http://www.bartleby.com/

Cornell University. CUPID - Consortium for University Printing and Information Distribution.

"'CUPID' is an acronym for the Consortium for University Printing and Information Distribution, an informal and open collection of colleges and universities interested in the distributed printing over the Internet of finished, high-quality, production documents. CUPID was created four years ago by the Xerox University Advisory Panel and now exists as a project under CNI (the Coalition for Networked Information), receiving financial support from Kodak, Sun, and Xerox."

URL: http://www.cni.org/projects/CUPID/

Elsevier Science, et. al. TULIP - The University Licensing Project.

"TULIP is an initiative of Elsevier Science Publishers to explore the issues involved in electronic distribution of scholarly journals. The TULIP project involves nine universities and about forty Materials Science journal titles."

URL: http://www.elsevier.nl:80/homepage/about/resproj/tulip.htm

Emory University. Digital Library Project.

"In today's environment access to networked information is rapidly transforming libraries and reducing reliance on vast, locally-owned print collections. With support from the Luce Foundation in New York City, Emory University has undertaken a three year project to develop a blueprint for a prototype digital library. [...] Emory will explore the many governance, organizational, economic, educational, and technological issues to be faced in developing and implementing this prototype."

URL: http://www.library.emory.edu/VL/vlhome.html

IBM. Digital Library.

Includes work with the Vatican Library, Institute for Scientific Information, and the Los Angeles Public Library.

URL: http://www-4.ibm.com/software/is/dig-lib/

Library of Congress. Digital Library Collections.

URL: http://lcweb.loc.gov/

American Memory.

URL: http://lcweb2.loc.gov/amhome.html

American Memory Background Papers and Technical Information.

URL: http://lcweb2.loc.gov/ammem/ftpfiles.html

American Special Collections.

URL: http://lcweb.loc.gov/spcoll/spclhome.html

Country Studies/Area Handbook Program.

URL: http://lcweb2.loc.gov/frd/cs/cshome.html

Electronic Exhibits.

URL: http://lcweb.loc.gov/exhibits/

THOMAS: Legislative Information on the Internet.

URL: http://thomas.loc.gov/

National Aeronautics and Space Administration (NASA). Digital Library Technology Project - Core Technologies for the National Information Infrastructure.

"The Digital Library Technology (DLT) project and the Public Use of Remote Sensing Data (RSD) project, are two related elements of the Information Infrastructure Technology and Applications component of NASA's High Performance Computing and Communications Program. The DLT Project supports the development of new technologies to facilitate public access to NASA data via computer networks. Of highest priority are those technologies that develop tools, applications, and software and hardware systems that are able to scale upward to accomodate evolving user requirements and order-of-magnitude increases in user access. Although most of the technology is envisioned to be developed in the private sector, an inhouse skill base must be acquired and maintained in key areas of developing technology such as the integration of multimedia data, wide-area networking, resource discovery, and intelligent information retrieval."

URL: http://learn.arc.nasa.gov/education/topics/digital.shtml

National Aeronautics and Space Administration (NASA). Public Use of Remote Sensing Data - Core Technologies for the National Information Infrastructure.

The RSD Program is part of the Information Infrastructure Technology and Applications (IITA) component of the High Performance Computing and Communications (HPCC) initiative.

URL: http://rsd.gsfc.nasa.gov/rsd/

National Library of Canada. Electronic Collection.

"The NLC electronic collection incorporates formally published Canadian online books and journals. These publications are being acquired, catalogued, and permanently stored at the NLC. Public access is provided on the Internet through the World Wide Web. Catalogue records for Electronic Collection titles, including the Uniform Resource Locators (URLs), are available on NLC's AMICUS system and on resAnet."

URL: http://collection.nlc-bnc.ca/e-coll-e/index-e.htm

National Library of Canada. Inventory of Canadian Digital Initiatives.

"The Canadian Inventory of Digital Initiatives provides descriptions of Canadian information resources created for the Web, including general digital collections, resources centred around a particular theme, and reference sources and databases."

URL: http://www.nlc-bnc.ca/initiatives/erella.htm

Research Libraries Group. Electronic Publications Pilot Project.

"RLG and its members will use their experience and collaborative infrastructure in digital collection projects —

coordinating selection and digitization; resolving intellectual control and access issues; establishing digital archives and protocols for their lasting operation — and bridging the gap between bibliographic citations and digitized information objects. "

URL: http://www.rlg.org/toc.html

Arches — Archival Server and Test Bed.

URL: http://www.rlg.org/strat/projarch.html

Digital Collections Project — "Studies in Scarlet".

URL: http://www.rlg.org/strat/projdcp.html

New Access to Archival Collections — The FAST Track.

URL: http://www.rlg.org/strat/projfast.html

Stanford University. Digital Libraries Project.

"The goal of the Stanford Digital Library project is to develop the enabling technologies for a single, integrated and "universal" library, composed from the large numbers of emerging individual heterogeneous repositories. Our definition of a constituent repository includes everything from personal information collections to the collections in conventional libraries and large data collections shared by scientists. Our technology will provide the "glue" that will make this worldwide collection usable as a unified entity, in a scaleable and economically feasible fashion."

URL: http://www-diglib.stanford.edu/diglib/index.html/

University of California, Berkeley. Digital Library Project.

"This project will produce a prototype digital library with a focus on environmental information. The library will collect diverse information about the environment to be used for the preparation and evaluation of environmental data, impact reports and related materials. The research prototype is intended for eventual full-scale deployment in the State of California's CERES production systems. To create the prototype, researchers will need to produce technologies which allow untrained users to contribute to and find relevant information in other world-wide digital library systems. Research areas include automated indexing, intelligent retrieval and search processes; database technology to support digital library applications;new approaches to document analysis; and, data compression and communication tools for remote browsing."

URL: http://elib.cs.berkeley.edu

University of California: Santa Barbara. Alexandria Digital Library.

"Project Alexandria will develop a digital library providing easy access to large and diverse collections of maps, images and pictorial materials as well as a full range of new electronic library services. The project is centered at the University of California, Santa Barbara, with its major collections of maps and images and its strong research focus in the area of spatially-indexed information. It also involves the State University of New York at Buffalo (SUNY-Buffalo), the University of Maine and several industrial partners."

URL: http://alexandria.sdc.ucsb.edu/

University of Illinois. Building the Interspace: Digital Library Infrastructure for a University Engineering Community.

"The NSF/DARPA/NASA Digital Libraries Initiative (DLI) project at the University of Illinois at Urbana-Champaign (UIUC), 1994-1998, had the goal of developing widely usable Web technology to effectively search technical documents on the Internet. Our efforts were concentrated on building an experimental testbed with tens of thousands of full-text journal articles from physics, engineering, and computer science, and making these articles available over the World Wide Web, often before they were available in print. The DLI Testbed focused on using the document structure to provide federated search across publisher collections."

URL: http://dli.grainger.uiuc.edu/

University of Michigan. Internet Public Library.

"The Internet Public Library Project seeks to challenge and redefine the roles and significance of libraries in an increasingly distributed and digital world. Libraries have always been places of learning and excitement, opening new worlds of information, enlightenment and entertainment to all who enter. Libraries and the people who work in them are committed to democracy and equality of access, the dignity of their patrons, and the freedom to express and investigate all points of view."

URL: http://www.ipl.org/

University of Michigan, et. al. JSTOR - Journal Storage Project.

JSTOR is a project of The Andrew W. Mellon Foundation for development of a digital library in support of the arts and sciences. It will initially consist of about ten journal titles in the areas of economics and history and will initially contain approximately 750,000 journal page images.

URL: http://www.jstor.org/

University of Michigan. Digital Library Production Service (DLPS).

"The Digital Library Production Service grew out of the Digital Library Program at the University of Michigan. The service was formed in response to a felt need for production level (twenty four hour a day, seven days a week) support for digital library resources. DLPS exists to provide ongoing development and support of digital library content and to provide a clearly articulated framework for production support and future project activity. The DLPS is responsible for the operation and maintenance of existing and new collections, including SGML text collections, journal images, museum images, and numeric/spatial data collections."

URL: http://www.umdl.umich.edu/

University of Pittsburgh. Digital Resesrch Project.

"The Digital Research Library supports the teaching and research mission of the University of Pittsburgh and serves users of the University Library System through creation and maintenance of digital research collections.

URL: http://digital.library.pitt.edu/

VE Multimedios. Biblioteca Electrónica Cristiana.

Spanish-language Catholic library

URL: http://www.multimedios.org/

XEROX. Digital Library related work at Xerox.

We at Xerox are searching for ways to enhance the productivity of document intensive activites in the context of group work and within a variety of enterprises. Our method is to bring together our core competence in the areas of new document types, interface research, collaborative systems, information access to build practical systems that can be tested in actual use. e library represents a social activity in each of our core areas, and exposes a set of document issues that other organizations have only begun to recognize. The research initiative on Digital Libraries represents a unique opportunity to apply some of the technologies we have developed in conjunction with university partners in a function that will dominate work-practice in the NII-enabled work-force. This package contains overviews, bibliographies, and a prospectus of digital-library related research that we might engage in at PARC in conjunction with one or more partners in this initiative.

URL: http://www.parc.xerox.com/parc-go.html

Yale University. Project Open Book.

"Yale University Library Project Open Book is a research and development program that is exploring the feasibility and costs of large-scale conversion of preserved material from microfilm to digital imagery."

URL: http://www.library.yale.edu/preservation/pobweb.htm

Projects in Europe

British Library. CATaloguing and Retrieval of Information Over Networks Applications (CATRIONA).

"CATRIONA is a 6 month feasibility study funded by the British Library Research And Development Division. The purpose behind the CATRIONA project is to investigate the technical, organisational and financial requirements for the development of applications programs and procedures to enable the cataloguing, classification, and retrieval of documents and other resources over networks, and to explore the feasibility of a library system supplier led collaborative project to develop such applications and procedures and integrate them with one or more existing library housekeeping systems and associated OPAC interfaces."

URL: http://bubl.ac.uk/org/catriona/cat1rep.htm

European Union. I3 - intelligent - information - interfaces.

ESPRIT programme initiative on future interfaces to information.

URL: http://www.cordis.lu/esprit/src/iii.htm

Joint Information Systems Committee. Follett Implementation Group on Information Technology (FIGIT). (United Kingdom). Electronic Libraries Programme (eLib).

The Higher Education Funding Bodies in the UK have invited proposals for projects which would "transform the use and storage of knowledge in higher education institutions". £315 million was allocated to the "Electronic Libraries Programme", m[illegible]y the Joint Information Systems Committee on be[illegible]ding bodies. Currently, about 60 projects are bei[illegible]gh this number changes as some projects are co[illegible] new ones are funded.

URL: http://ww[illegible]c.uk/services/elib/

Lancaster University. ARIADNE Collaborative Database Browsing Project.

URL: http://www.comp.lancs.ac.uk/computing/research/aai-aied/information/ariadne/

ARIADNE Links Index: locally used hotlist of digital libraries related resources.

URL: http://www.comp.lancs.ac.uk/computing/research/aai-aied/information/ariadne/links.html

Oxford University. Scoping the Future of Oxford's Digital Collections.

This report, funded by the Andrew W. Mellon Foundation, makes concrete recommendations which can be implemented rapidly to satisfy the known and increasing needs of readers for digital materials, and proposes the establishment of a new body: the Oxford Digital Library Services (ODLS). This body would provide a co-ordinated set of services, building on Oxford's expertise in this area, to help in the creation, management, and delivery of digital surrogates. The core component would be an on-demand digitization service, which would provide both a reactive (on-demand) service in response to user requests, and a proactive service that would target specific collections for digitization. The remit and components of the ODLS are outlined in the report.

URL: http://www.bodley.ox.ac.uk/scoping/

From the above factors, it is clear that the digital libraries are in the making and once the required infrastructure is available for them they will become as popular in the society as their print media counterparts. With the growth factors it is very much expected that the current century will be dominated by the digital devices i field of human activities and libraries will b en every ion.

4
Universal Digital Library

Universal Digital Library is a project proposal under the Indo-US Science and Technology Collaboration initiatives. It is intended to develop a digital library containing on million books and to make the same available for the mankind on the World Wide Web.

The aim of the project is to digitize around a million books in the next three years. This joint initiative is planned to synergetically capitalize on the availability of the state-of-the-art of hardware and software in the US for digitizing, storing and accessing of information and the quality manpower available in India. This would act as a forerunner for many such initiatives with other countries, particularly in China and Korea and would culminate in the grandiose vision of digitizing all the formal knowledge and make available in a location and time independent way for the benefit of the mankind.

Today's scanning technology offers the possibility of digitizing an entire book in two hours. In order to take million books to the web, it is estimated that around 1000 man years would be needed. If the project is carried out in a developed country like the United States of America, it would cost at least around 40M $ besides the cost of the hardware, space and energy. It is economically feasible to try this out in developing nations like India.

As part of this project, it is planned to create 10 centres across India that would be commissioned to run three shifts with a work force of 40 in each centre. This would be adequate to meet the manpower demand of 1000 man years in 3 years. Each centre would then require around 15 scanning stations (Total 150 Scanning Stations). The cost of each scanning station including its maintenance over the three years period would be approximately US $ 30,000. Thus with a hardware and software cost of 5M $, over the three years period, it looks plausible to think in terms of the Universal Digital Library that will hold at least a million books.

It is proposed that the hardware and software costs are met from the US side while the manpower needs are met by the Indian side.

Copyright Laws

Currently, the copyright laws do not permit books published in the last 50 years in India and 100 years in the US to be digitized and distributed free. These laws are based on the earlier era wherein the life cycle of Information products was large. Currently, obsolescence is the common thing in science and technology and in many areas the obsolescence rate is so rapid that the life cycle of Information products such as books is reduced to a few years. There is a world wide awareness of this and WIPO is seriously directing its efforts towards this issue. Indo-US team could generate critical inputs to shape the copyright laws world over in general and in India and the USA in particular, that would be in tune with the aspirations of the Digital Economy. This would also ensure that the copyright laws protect the interest of the creator and consumer of information and still make economic sense.

Further, it is proposed that most of the books, in the 'million books to the web' project would come from the United States. After scanning, modality could be worked out by which the books may be retained in the respective retained Centres. The latter may be justified by the fact that the cost of the transportation back to the US after digitizing may be high.

Research and Development

Several attendant technologies are to be developed besides the hardware and software and the identification of books for scanning in order to ensure that the books of Indian Origin are included dominantly in the digitization. First is the research and development needed to ensure that an error free character recognizer in Indian Languages is made available to the centres. Further, an appropriate software to identify various fonts and the title, heading etc and to create meta files that can be used for accessing the information has to be perfected. Most of the Indian knowledge particularly in Sanskrit etc may not be available in printed form at all and even if unavailable, the quality of the paper and the background may not be suitable for feeder based scanner and character recognizer. In such cases, appropriate speech technologies to convert speech to text in Indian Languages and / or photographic scanner technologies may have to be developed.

The technology development described above would also form the focus of the R&D efforts proposed under the Indo-US collaboration. On the Indian side, the Indian Institute of Science, Bangalore would act as a nodal agency to coordinate amongst various academic institutions and governmental agencies from the Indian side. The Carnegie Mellon University would play the same role from the US side.

Vision

For the first time in history, all the significant literary, artistic, and scientific works of mankind can be digitally preserved and made freely available, in every corner of the world, for our education, study, and appreciation and that of all our future generations.

Up until now, the transmission of our cultural heritage has depended on limited numbers of copies in fragile media. The fires of Alexandria irrevocably severed our access to any of the works of the ancients. In a thousand years, only a few of the paper documents we have today will survive the ravages of deterioration, loss, and outright destruction. With no more than 10 million unique book and document editions before the year 1900, and perhaps 100 million since the beginning of recorded history, the task of preservation is much larger. With new digital technology, though, this task is within the reach of a single concerted effort for the public good, and this effort can be distributed to libraries, museums, and other groups in all countries.

Existing archives of paper have many shortcomings. Many other works still in existence today are rare, and only accessible to a small population of scholars and collectors at specific geographic locations. A single wanton act of destruction can destroy an entire line of heritage. Furthermore, contrary to the popular beliefs, the libraries, museums, and publishers do not routinely maintain broadly comprehensive archives of the considered works of man. No one can afford to do this, unless the archive is digital.

Digital technology can make the works of man permanently accessible to the billions of people all over the world. Andrew Carnegie and other great philanthropists in past centuries have recognized the great potential of public libraries to improve the quality of life and provide opportunity the citizenry. A universal digital library, widely available through free access on the Internet, will improve the global society in ways beyond measurement. The Internet can house a Universal Library that is free to the people.

Mission

The mission is to create a Universal Library which will foster creativity and free access to all human knowledge. As a first step in realizing this mission, it is proposed to create the Universal Library with a free-to-read, searchable collection of one million books, primarily in the English language, available to everyone over the Internet. Within 10 years, it is expected that the collection will grow to 10 Million books. The result will be a unique resource accessible to anyone in the world 24x7, without regard to nationality or socioeconomic background.

The first major project of Universal Library is the Million Book Digital Library project. Typical large high-school libraries house fewer than 30,000 volumes. Most libraries in the world have less than a million volumes. The total number of different titles indexed in OCLC's WorldCat is about 48 million. One million books, therefore, is more than the holdings of most high-schools, and is equivalent to the libraries at many universities and represents a useful fraction of all available books.

One of the goals of the Universal Library is to provide support for full text indexing and searching based on OCR (optical character recognition) technologies where available. The availability of online search allows users to locate relevant information quickly and reliably thus enhancing student's success in their research endeavors. This 24x7 resource would also provide an excellent testbed for language processing research in areas such as machine translation, summarization, intelligent indexing, and information retrieval.

The Universal Library will be mirrored at several locations worldwide so as to protect the integrity and availability of the data. Several models for sustainability are being explored. Usability studies would also be conducted to ensure that the materials are easy to locate, navigate, and use. Appropriate metadata for navigation and management would also be created.

The primary long-term objective is to capture all books in digital format. It is believed that such a task is impossible and could take hundreds of years, and never be completed. Thus, as a first step it is planned to demonstrate the feasibility by undertaking to digitize 1 million books (less than 1% of all books in all languages ever published) by 2005. Such a project has the potential to change how education is conducted in much of the world.

A secondary objective of this project will be to provide a test bed that will support other researchers who are working on improved scanning techniques, improved optical character recognition, and improved indexing. The corpus this project creates will be one to three orders of magnitude larger than any existing free resource.

Technical Details

1. Database creation

Creating a scalable database to support the Universal Library is one of the desired objectives. The resulting globally distributed database will appear to be a virtual central database from any place around the world. Mirroring the database in several countries will also ensure security and availability. The database will house both an image file and a text file at about 50-60 megabytes per book. A 100 terabytes of online storage currently costs around $150,000 and is expected to be under $5000 by year 2005 and thus making it possible to mirror the site in many countries.

2. Scanning

Earlier in the project, the scanner of choice was an inexpensive duplex scanner that required the books to be disbound so that the pages could be fed through in batches. While the economy and speed of this technique were most attractive, several technical problems occurred. The pages had to be cut on all four edges for smooth feeding. The project required the purchase of a $10,000 guillotine to accomplish this. The guillotine was somewhat dangerous, required in-depth training in use and safety, slowed the process, and nullified the economy of the inexpensive scanner.

Dust, an inevitable accompaniment to older books, proved to be a formidable opponent. Dust caused frequent jamming and subsequent cleaning of the scanner. Paper fixatives were employed to counteract the dust. Spraying on the fixative slowed the project and was not entirely satisfactory.

Currently, the Universal Library project uses a Minolta PS7000 overhead scanner, which is potentially able to scan 10000 pages operating on a 3-shift basis. Although this scanner was 5 times more expensive than the conventional roll-fed double sided scanner we used earlier, it proved to be more reliable. Books did not have to be disbound. The image processing software for curvature correction, deskewing, despeckling and cropping allows for thick books to be scanned either flat or in an angled cradle that reduces wear on the spine. Careful training is required to operate the scanner, and several different employees were successfully trained in our pilot experiment.

In summary, the advantages of the Minolta scanner were:

* Disbinding via a guillotine is not necessary.
* Books can be reused in their original form.
* Dust, thick paper, and long books can be easily accommodated.
* Training requirements are reasonable.
* Equipment is reliable

3. Data Production

The current approach for document scanning is to digitize the documents at the archival quality of 600 dots per inch (dpi) as a binary image (1 bit per pixel). The resulting images are stored as TIFF (Tagged Image File Format) files. (TIFF version 5.0 is acceptable. Subject to testing, version 6.0 (or later) may also be acceptable). The resolution of the images is high enough so as to permit reading of the the original pages directly on a computer screen.

4. Optical Character Recognition (OCR)

We do not plan to correct the OCR output as part of this project. The primary function of OCR is to allow searching inside the text. Unlike in other efforts, the output of the OCR text will not be used for direct viewing by the public. It will only be used for creating a searchable index (where errors tend to have limited impact).

Because words are often repeated, the 98% success rate will allow students and scholars to find relevant passage. In the pilot projects, the OCR program Abby Fine Reader was run after the scanning was completed.

Chinese and Japanese OCR programs are also available

and will be used whenever needed. This project has also stimulated efforts towards the development of OCRs in Indian Languages. Providing a testbed that will allow for the creation of even better OCR programs is one of the goals of this project. Scholars will be able to run newer OCR programs over the scans and possibly correct the output manually.

5. Metadata

Digital Library Federation standards and metadata best practices will be used throughout this project. Bibliographic metadata for the pilot project will be derived from existing library catalog records. Carnegie Mellon libraries developed software that uses the standard Z39.50 protocol to search and retrieve relevant metadata from catalog records fields. Thus, author, title, and publication data do not have to be rekeyed.

Entering metadata information manually is time-consuming. One of the current research projects is the creation of software for "automatic discovery of document structure". This will permit users to create hyperlinks which are not present in the original printed version of the book and navigate through the chapters.

Administrative metadata supports the maintenance and archiving of the paper or digital objects and ensures their long-term availability by providing information about how the files were created and stored. Administrative metadata will be maintained internally as file descriptions in the project databases and externally as part of the copyright permission database.

The Digital Library Federation, a supporter of this project, has several initiatives underway that will allow commercial browsers to harvest metadata more aggressively. The results of DLF's metadata harvesting project will be explored for possible application to the resources produced in this project (www.diglib.org).

6. Quality control

The standards established for quality control are those

currently endorsed by the Digital Library Federation, whose missions include the establishment of best practices and the development of standards. The project must maintain a 98% accuracy rate for the quality of images and the inclusion of all pages.

The process of scanning a book involves finding a library that owns the book, pulling the book, transporting the book to the scanning site, scan the pages, and returning the book to the original library. This process will be expensive. Maintaining high quality the first time the book is scanned will be essential. A demonstration of high quality, reliable work done on materials currently in China and India will give U.S. libraries confidence that their collections should be shared.

Benefits

The principal benefit of the Universal Library will be to supplement the formal education system by making knowledge available to anyone who can read and has access. Libraries have played a vital role in the advancement of human society. Societal advance depends on young people having access to books via libraries and other means. Making this unique web resource available free to everyone around the world will enhance the learning process.

Libraries are unevenly distributed around the world and within each country. In the U.S., the NCES Survey noted that in 1996, 3,408 of 3,792 institutions of higher education had libraries holding 806.7 million volumes. The 112 largest university libraries in the United States and Canada each have at least 1.8 million books. They are members of the Association for Research Libraries. Massachusetts has about 25 million volumes; New York has about 31 million volumes, and California has about 40 million volumes in their ARL Libraries (Association for Research Libraries, 1999/2000). Other states, such as North and South Dakota, have no large libraries. A few large public libraries have several million volumes. However, most junior colleges, high schools, and public libraries have much smaller collections. Making this large knowledge repository can revolutionize research at all levels of education and give a much-needed boost at minimal cost to our national educational infrastructure. This impact will be further enhanced given the convenience of online access, and the benefit of full text searching at word and phrase levels.

A secondary benefit of online search is to make locating the relevant information inside of books far more reliable and much easier. Student success in finding exactly what they seek will increase and increased success will enhance student willingness to perform research using this large resource. NCES reports that 84 percent of libraries around the country are open between 60 and 80 hours a week. This digital library would be open all the 168 hours the week on a 24x7x365 basis. More than one individual will be able to use the same book at the same time. Thus, popular works will not be checked out and thus unavailable to others.

This million-book project will produce an extensive and rich testbed for use in further textual language processing research. It is hoped that at least 10,000 books among the million will be available in more than one language, providing a unique resource for example based machine translation.

Many believe that information is now doubling every two years. Machine summarization, intelligent indexing, and information mining are tools that will be needed for individuals to keep up in their discipline work, in their businesses, and in their personal interests. This large digitization project will enable extensive research in these areas.

Philosophy of Content Selection

The Million Book Project envisages to develop a collection of one million digital books by adopting a staged approach as described below. The Million Book project will adhere to the U.S. copyright law.

U.S. collections will primarily include the following types of materials:

1. Coordination of Selection

Creating one digital copy and mirroring it in different locations will suffice, and will support the multiple uses at any time. Preliminary discussions with OCLC as a host for a registry of scanned items are underway. Certain key projects, such as the Making of America project, are already represented in the OCLC database as digital books. Other large digitization projects may require some data entry of their content in order to avoid duplication.

2. Non-copyrighted materials

Materials published before 1920 are in the public domain and may be scanned for this project. Several large academic libraries are considering shipping materials from their repositories of little used books to India or China. These books will be scanned there and then returned to where they came from. To reduce the costs of selection, the project will probably develop a strategy of selecting key topics and then removing large runs of books and journals from a selected repository. Having a reasonable turn-around time will be essential to the success of the project. A strategy has been devised to understand the logistics of shipping the materials and the impact of their absence from the home library.

The 1909 copyright law granted copyright for 28 years. Rights holders could then renew the copyright for another 28 years; many publishers and authors did not exercise that renewal option. Thus, some books published after 1922 (56 years prior to the 1978 effective date of the 1976 act) may be out of copyright. In order to provide for the efficient checking of status of these books, the copyright renewal records for books for these years have been scanned and made available online at www.ulib.org. Similar records for other formats, such as serials and audiovisual material, will also be made available as a part of this resource.

Government documents are also in the public domain and may be included in this project. Many participating libraries are repositories for full runs of government documents and could supply them to the project, as could the Library of Congress. The inclusion of these documents will allow for more recent material to enter the project legally and to become available to a broader audience and in a more accessible manner. Many government documents are currently available in digital form. The creation of these back files would enhance those resources.

The Chinese delegation is most eager to have technical reports and science and technology dissertations as a part of this project. Scholars and universities producing these scientific material have copyright interests in them. Gaining university permission might be fairly straightforward. A good-faith attempt would also have to be made to obtain the permission of the scholars. That could be a part of an externally funded copyright clearance project, but no pilot-study has been made to allow for an estimate of contact rate and subsequent success. If some arrangement could be made with University Microfilms to scan dissertations of selected universities from microfilm, which would be cheaper and easier to transport, such an initiative might satisfy a strong desire among all participants to increase science content.

3. Copyrighted materials

The 1998 Copyright law grants copyright to authors for their lifetimes plus 70 years or for 95 years. Patent law, by contrast, gives 20 years. A.W. Mellon's JSTOR project developed the concept of a moving wall that allowed the inclusion of materials over five years old. Journal publishers generally agreed that the economic value of that material was greatly reduced and granted permission for its inclusion in this most successful project. A similar broad publisher agreement about the point at which economic value of a print book declines is greatly needed. Books often go out of print in two or three years but remain in copyright and thus be unavailable for over 90 years.

Dr. Raj Reddy and Dr. Peter Shane, Director of the Institute for the Study of Information, Technology and Society recently had a conversation with a major book publishers to explore the possibility of taking a broad publisher approach to receiving copyright permissions. Certain publishers, including the National Academy Press, have had the experience that when they digitized their books, sales increased because attention was focused on the material and the users were not yet ready to read the books online. Authors' guilds will also be contacted to see if they would be interested in granting permissions.

Three conditions seem to be necessary to attract publishers to the scanning of their out of print but in copyright titles:

* Publisher should receive a tax deduction for contributing the title to this project. The tax deduction might reflect revenues previously generated by the title.
* When a print on demand feature becomes a part of this project, publishers should collect royalties on books printed.
* If a book were to return to general popularity, as the effect of the movie Titanic had on the sales of out of print titles, the publisher should be able to withdraw the permission for a fee. The publisher might be expected to reimburse the project for the costs of digitizing the title and maintaining it online.

Dr. Michael Shamos, a Director of Carnegie Mellon's Universal Library project and an intellectual property attorney, recommends the following approach to copyright clearance: The million book project will make a good faith effort to clear copyright on appropriate materials by sending the publisher of record a letter asking for permission. Replies will be recorded in the administrative metadata. If the publisher has returned the rights to the author, the author will be contacted. Subsequent copyright holders will be contacted as needed.

4. Best books approach

The project will seek publisher permission to scan books from Books for College Libraries (BCL), one source for core academic books in English. A previous study done at Carnegie Mellon University Libraries indicates that 22% of publishers granted permission for scanning and mounting on the web. The materials in the study were a random sample of Carnegie Mellon Libraries' books and included a broad range of dates, publishers, and in and out of print status.. Numerous difficulties from out of business publishers, lack of publisher records, return of copyright to authors, and other circumstances were identified. Subsequently, Carol Hughes, the collections development officer for Questia, corroborated Carnegie Mellon's experience.

OCLC owns a database of books from the latest edition of Books for College Libraries. BCL contains about 50,000 titles. A 22% success rate in clearing copyright would result in 10,000 of the best books for college students being included in the project. Clearing copyright is labor intensive and expensive. Bradd Burningham's recent article estimated those costs ("Copyright Permissions" in Journal of Interlibrary Loan, Document Delivery, and Information Supply, 11:2 (2000), 95-111). The BCL database, however, will allow for sorting by publisher so that permission requests can contain the names of several books. A quick sample indicates that as many as 25,000 publishers may be represented there. Despite the expense, this commitment to quality should be attempted. Carnegie Mellon University Libraries will seek private foundation funding to undertake this project.

Publishers increasingly see that digital presentation of their works can attract buyers. They are interested in exploring ways in which their out of print titles may be returned to profitability. Continued work with publishers through the course of this project may attract many of them to it. That would be most beneficial in enriching the content to be made available.

Current Status

Now we will describe activities used to establish protocols, to select standards to be used, and to address issues of indexing and retrieval. Workflow and training programs to support the larger project are being developed. Both the content and the mechanisms for using it will be made available in open source code.

One of the key activities has been to work with libraries within United States who will participate in providing content for scanning for the Universal Library. Members of the U.S. Digital Library Federation met on November 15 and 16, 2001 to work out the logistics of selecting and transporting materials from U.S. collections. Participants included the executive director of DLF, representatives of the NSF, OCLC, the Center for Research Libraries, collection development officers, and other librarians from the Library of Congress, the University of Washington, the University of California Berkeley, Stanford University, University of Illinois, University of Chicago, Penn State University, and the University of Pittsburgh.

The collection development librarians discussed:

* Collection focus to achieve a consensus on how to select the million books to be digitized.
* Involvement of outside scholars in selection issues to consider how non-librarian scholars might participate in selection.
* Copyright considerations to consider seeking permission for a set of in copyright "best books", such as those in Books for College Libraries.
* Standards for the work to review the current Digital Library Federation standards with a view to rapid adoption.
* Registry issues to move forward with OCLC in establishing a registry for books selected.
* Methods of transport to consider alternative means of transport and return.

* Timing to weigh the advantages of air containers and sea containers.
* Level of participation to determine minimum levels for contributors to the project.
* Incentives for participation to establish means of recognition for contributions through screen display and copies of the archives.

The outcome of this meeting was a plan for the selection and transmission of almost a million books to China and India over a multi-year period and a plan for assessing the success of the project annually.

The National Science Foundation's 2000 ITR grant cycle provided $500,000 for equipment to begin a Million Book pilot project. That grant will allow the purchase of 18 Minolta scanners to be located in India and China. These scanners have already been deployed to begin the scanning process. Additional scanners from other donors have permitted increase in the number of scanners deployed in India and China.

Participation of China

In August of 2001, the Chinese University Presidents, a Ministry of Education officials, and Chinese Academy of Sciences leaders visited the U.S. to reach agreements and to form a steering committee. Dr. Michael Lesk and Dr. Stephen Griffin from NSF attended this meeting and also hosted the Chinese delegation at the National Science Foundation. Professor Pan Yunhe, President of Zhejiang University; Dr. Gao Wen, Deputy President of the Graduate School, Chinese Academy of Science; Professor Chi Huisheng, Vice President of Beijing University; Professor Hu Dongcheng, Vice President of Tsinghua University; Professor Xu Zhong, Vice President of Fudan University; Professor, Zhang Yibin, Assistant to the President, Nanjing University; Mr. Guo Xinli, Vice General Director, Ministry of Education of China; Mr. Chen Jianping, Vice Director, State Planning Commission of China; and Dr. Ching-Chih Chen of Simmons College attended.

Indian Contribution

A delegation from India visited US in May of 2002. This includes officials from from the Central and State Governments in India, Presidents of Universities and leading academicians. The Indian team included Prof MGK Menon, Chairman, Council of IIIT-A and IIT-B, Mr Yashwant Bhave, Jt Secretary, Ministry of Communication and Information Technology, Dr. IV Subbarao, Secretary Education, Government of Andhra Pradesh, Dr P. Krishniah, Executive Officer of TTD, and Mr Ajay Sawhney, Special Secretary for IT, Government of Andhra Pradesh, Dr Om Vikas, Senior Director, and Dr Chaturvedi, Director, of the Ministry of Communication and Information Technlogy, Government of India, Mr Surendra Bagde, Joint CEO MIDC, Mumbai. Dr. N. Balakrishnan, Chairman of the Division of Information Sciences, Indian Institute of Science, Prof Ashok Kolaskar, Vice Chancellor, Pune University, Dr MD Tiwary, Director, IIITA, Dr. Thangraj, Principal, AKCE, Mr Shreedhar, Secretary, AKCE, Dr Vaidhyasubramanian, Dean, SASTRA, representing the academia.

The meeting at CMU reviewed the current status of the work in India and created plans for the Million Book project in India, including technological challenges, legal and copy right issues, selection of books, meta data standards, search engines and server management. It was concluded that one of the Central Government agencies will take ownership of the Million Book Initiative in India, and will form a consortium that will give large impetus to the Indian efforts in a coordinated way.

Logistic Challenges

Accessing, scanning and webhosting of a million books is a major logistical challenge. A million books can be expected to be about 300 to 500 million pages. Throughput of each Minolta PS7000 scanner is about 6,000 to 10,000 pages per day based on three-shift operation. Using a 100 scanners, and about a 1000 person workforce, we can expect to complete the task of scanning a million books in 500 working days, or roughly two years of three shift operation. Given the uncertainities of quality of workers, equipment failures and power failures, we anticipate the scanning to be completed in less than four year time frame. This website will provide a graphic visualization of the progress after full speed of operation.

Movement of books from U.S. to India and China

India and China have large academic libraries and will contain much of the material to be included as part of the Million Book project. Over 700 of these libraries are OCLC members whose holdings can be easily ascertained. Because the scanning centers can be established anywhere, It is planned to establish them close to the libraries so that the books can be transported with minimal difficulty. It may be feasible to locate some of the scanning centers within the academic libraries, space permitting.

The task of shipping materials from the U.S. to China and India has been examined. The current plan is to primarily use air containers rather than shipping containers so as to reduce the damage to books and time of absence of the books from their owning libraries.

The books can be packed at originating libraries in small vendor boxes. It may be desirable to shrink wrap the books to ensure their intact arrival. The basic cost of shipping per book is expected to be about one to two dollars per book. Some libraries may select some materials that do not need to be returned because they are in the process of being discarded, but the default will be that materials will return to their originating libraries.

The Center for Research Libraries is willing to supply some of its own books to the project. It might also serve as a collection place towards the end of the project when the quantity of material to be shipped falls below the whole container level.

Future Sustainability

Sustainability is a long-term issue for this project; further research will be done on developing economic models to support this major contribution to education. Partial answers to this significant challenge are discussed below. Three establishments have potential for offering a sustainable model for this project—the Library of Congress and similar national libraries, OCLC, and other commercial concerns.

The million-book project will be a public good and as such must have a suitable repository that will continue to make it available to the public at no charge. That responsibility belongs most clearly to the national library in each country. Having a network of national libraries mirroring the resource around the world would be an appropriate and desired outcome.

Library of Congress

In the United States, the Library of Congress whould be the natural choice to act as the repository of all knowledge, because the national interest is so clearly served. However, the Library of Congress is not the national library of the United States, although many people assume that it is. In the LOC's own words in its mission statement: "THE FIRST PRIORITY of the Library of Congress is to make knowledge and creativity available to the United States Congress." It is only a lesser goal to make knowledge available to the public, and that is why the million-book project had to be undertaken outside of the scope of LOC. LOC is also the guardian of the copyright office and is apparently unwilling and/or unable to digitize anything to which there might be a copyright claim.

In 2001, Congress appropriated 100 million dollars for Digital Preservation, contingent on LOC's raising of $75 million in matching resources. The law allows the acceptance of gifts in kind as a part of the matching funding. The possibility of pledging the million-book project to LOC as matching funding for the Digital Preservation initiative is being explored. Even if the value of the project were only assessed on its inputs (equipment and labor), the Million Book project represents a significant investment.

OCLC

Another alternative might be for OCLC to maintain a free version of the resource. OCLC is a non-profit organization whose member libraries are committed to enhancing access to information. OCLC might cover its costs by charging member libraries a small fee when the million-book project is accessed through the 48 million-title database. For the millions of OCLC users, that convenience would be worth a small payment in an already existing fee relationship. OCLC's recent strategic planning initiatives identified the addition of more full text to the database, exploring archiving responsibilities, and becoming more international as important thrusts. OCLC would also be able to cover partial costs through some of the strategies listed below for publishers.

Commercial alternatives

The marketplace for electronic books is chaotic at this moment. Questia, designed to be an online source with at least 50,000 of the best books with sophisticated software to support searching and the creation of footnotes, marketed itself directly to students at a $20-30 monthly fee. Although the project was well capitalized and attracted a great deal of media attention, its operations have been significantly scaled back over the past year. Librarians have long observed that charging for resources in the academic environment reduces use. Students' desire for the convenience of online information sends them to the web and to the much-used electronic resources of their own libraries. That love of convenience apparently does not extend to purchasing Questia under current pricing models.

During the same period, the company netLibrary has announced that it will provide new full textbooks online. NetLibrary marketed itself to libraries through consortia. Use of materials, thus, was at no direct cost to students and faculty. While students appreciated the convenience of being able to use the resource online, they had many complaints about its functionality—in particular they resented the fact that books could only be printed one page at a time and that books were unavailable if another individual were using them. The economic models behind netLibrary charges also seemed to reflect an adherence to those of paper books rather than recognizing the economies of digital materials. The assets of netLibrary have since been sold to OCLC.

At this time, the marketplace responses suggest that turning the million book project into a private, revenue-generating source would not offer a sustainable model. JSTOR, Project Muse, and other digital journal projects that offer online materials with superior functionality and sustainability continue to flourish.

Publishers

Another commercial alternative might revolve around relationships with publishers. As publishers find that making the book available increases sales, they might be willing to support the project. The Universal Library website would support "buy" buttons, in return for a small share of the revenues from print-on-demand sales of out of print materials.

People CMU

* Dr. Raj Reddy, Founder and Director of the Universal Digital Library (UDL)
* Dr. Michael Shamos, Director of UDL, Intellectual Property
* Dr. Jaime Carbonell, Director of UDL, Language Technologies
* Dr. Robert Thibadeau, Director of UDL, Privacy and Security
* Dr. Gloriana St. Clair, Director of UDL, University Librarian, Content Selection

* Others: Eric Burns, Madhavi Ganapathiraju, Krishna Konduru, Kishore Madhav, Gabrielle V. Michalek

US Advisors

* Dr. Ching-chih Chen, Co-Principal Investigator, China-US Million Book Project
* Dr. Daniel Greenstein, Executive Director of the Digital Library Federation
* Dr. Brewster Kahle, President, Internet Archive
* Dr. Victor Zue, Professor, LCS, MIT
* Dr. Michael Lesk, National Science Foundation
* Dr. Stephen Griffin, National Science Foundation

China

* Dr. Pan Yunhe, President of Zhejiang University
* Dr. Gao Wen, Deputy President of the Graduate School, Chinese Academy of Science
* Mr. Guo Xinli, Vice General Director, Ministry of Education of China
* Mr. Chen Jianping, Vice Director, State Planning Commission of China
* Dr. Chi Huisheng, Vice President of Beijing University
* Dr. Hu Dongcheng, Vice President ofTsinghua University
* Dr. Xu Zhong, Vice President of Fudan University
* Dr. Zhang Yibin, Assistant to the President, Nanjing University
* Others

India

* Prof. M G K Menon, Chairman, Council of Indian Institute of Information Technology, Allahabad and Indian Insitute of Technology-Bombay (Mumbai)
* Dr. N. Balakrishnan, Chairman, Division ofInformation Sciences, Indian Institute of Science

* Mr. Yashwant Bhave, Joint Secretary, Ministry of Communication and Information Technology
* Mr. Surendra Bagde, Joint CEO, Mumbai Industrial Development Corporation
* Dr. Chaturvedi, Director, Ministry of Communication and Information Techlnlogy, Govt. of India
* Dr. Ashok Kolaskar, Vice Chancellor, Pune University
* Dr. P. Krishniah, Executive Officer of Tirumala Tirupati Devasthanams
* Mr. Ajay Sawhney, Special Secretary for IT, Government of Andhra Pradesh
* Mr. Sridharan, Secretary, Arulmigu Kalasalingam College Of Engineering
* Dr. IV Subbarao, Secretary Education, Government of Andhra Pradesh
* Dr. Thangaraj, Principal, Arulmigu Kalasalingam College Of Engineering
* Dr. M D Tiwari, Director, Indian Institute of Information Technology, Allahabad
* Dr. Vaidhyasubramanian, Dean, Shanmugha Arts, Science, Technology & Research Academy
* Dr. Om Vikas, Senior Director, Ministry of Communication and Information Technlogy, Govt. of India
* Others: Kiran Kumar, S. Srinivas

Partners

China

* Beijing University
* Chinese Academy of Science
* Fudan University
* Ministry of Education of China
* Nanjing University

* State Planning Commission of China
* Tsinghua University
* Zhejiang University

India

* Arulmigu Kalasalingam College Of Engineering
* Goa University
* Indian Institute of Information Technology - Allahabad
* Indian Institute of Science
* International Institute of Information Technology - Hyderabad
* Shanmugha Arts Science, Technology & Research Academy
* Tirumala Tirupati Devasthanams
* Maharashtra Industrial Development Corporation
* University of Pune

Funding Sources

Funding for the Million Book Project is coming from multiple sources. National Science Foundation is providing funding for equipment, India and China are providing manpower resources for scanning, indexing and hosting, and various companies and foundations are providing partial support.

National Science Foundation is providing funding for Scanners, Computers, Servers, and Software. These resources from NSF are augmented by China and India who are providing the manpower, about 2,000 man years of effort each, over a five year period, as their contribution to this project. This represents a twenty-to-one relative contribution by China and India to this project. They will assist in the selection of documents, software development and in digitizing of the books. English language materials already resident in those countries would be scanned first, before books are shipped from the United States. Chinese and Indian language based books would also be scanned where such material is available free of copyright restrictions. U.S. libraries, primarily members of the Digital Library Federation, would ship materials as needed, to be scanned and returned.

Donations

Activities such as selection and acquisition of books, packing and shipping costs, and quality assurance of the content are unfunded, and would greatly benefit from your support.

Tax Deductible donations may be made payable to "Million Book DL Project, CMU", and mailed to:

University Librarian,
Carnegie Mellon University,
Pittsburgh PA 15213 USA.

The Knowledge Conservancy

The Knowledge Conservancy is being created as a complement to the Universal Library Project.

Knowledge Conservancy is expected to help in the following ways:

* Accepting undirected and directed gifts to digitize and make freely accessible the works of man. This includes gifts that guarantee specified numbers of books or specified collections under the rule that access is free to the people.
* Funding the digitization of works and the ongoing upgrading of the digital works to the public. This funding can be directed to ongoing or new digitization projects. In addition, the funding will support one central master registry site that other sites will mirror.
* Promoting awareness of these digital works, and their importance, to the public at large.
* Selection and digitization of works may be at the discretion of the Conservancy, the projects it funds, or its donors.

* For example, a donor might contribute money specifically for digitizing works in a particular subject area. Selection of works might also be made from lists drawn up by scholars, requests over the Internet, and books donated to the Conservancy.
* Coordinating the efforts of digitization efforts. The Knowledge conservancy maintains a database to keep track of all book editions, music editions, art, and motion pictures that have been digitized and whether they have free access. This includes the capabilities to
* determine through its catalog whether access to a known document is already available,
* claim to be digitizing a document within a certain time period,
* reference a document with a hyperlink that does not 'go bad,'
* reference the content of a document based on accepted practice in document tagging, and
* allow machine interpretation of copyright restrictions and other restrictions on access and use.

Supporting Knowledge Conservancy

The Knowledge Conservancy seeks donations and support from people and organizations wishing to help make the cultural treasures of the world available to all.

Tax Deductible donations may be made payable to "Knowledge Conservancy, CMU", and mailed to:

University Librarian,

Carnegie Mellon University,

Pittsburgh PA 15213 USA.

Rationale for the creation of Knowledge Conservancy

The mission of the Knowledge Conservancy is the preservation of the world's cultural, historical, and scientific works, and their free access to the world over the Internet.

Many projects are already underway to put works on-line for general reading, including projects like American Memory, Project Gutenberg, and the Universal Library. While these projects are making some headway at preserving the world's cultural heritage, they still face major obstacles:

* Digitization efforts are widespread but relatively small and too often associated with restricted access. Collection owners are not motivated to provide free access often through ignorance about available techniques for recovering costs.
* Funding for the digitization of information — and for its ongoing preservation, maintenance, and delivery, once digitized — is less than needed to make a large-scale digital library of millions of items available to the global public.
* There is no global organizations seeking only to provide coordination of digitization efforts, sharing of limited resources, and global public awareness.
* A large portion of the world's cultural heritage is copyrighted. Thus far, projects have largely avoided using copyrighted material, because of the difficulty of acquiring rights. Many works risk being lost in obscurity long before the copyright expires. The result is that important bodies of work may be unavailable in widely accessible for for a long time, and possibly forever.

The Knowledge Conservancy promotes the widespread duplication of digital collections at many sites, to increase accessibility and minimize the risk of single-point failure.

Conservancy policy is that a digital copyright may be retained by the collection owner but the conservancy will have a perpetual right to provide free viewing access to the material through its universal library. Furthermore, free viewing access will be automatically and perpetually granted to any site that agrees to the conditions of copyright and agrees to solely bear the cost of the mirroring. The copyright owner will always have a right to a link defined on any of his pages viewed, as will the Knowledge Conservancy.

The Knowledge Conservancy will actively support and endorse, but will not fund, money making activities around the material that is free to read. Examples include ordering copies of a book or manuscript, paying to print, paying for high fidelity access, ordering CD or DVD ROMs, ebook editions, selling supplementary materials, searching tools, indexing tools, multilingual tools, and portals that provide new media presentations of the material.

The Knowledge Conservancy will fund (a) digitizing a work and (b) providing metadata about a work including cataloging metadata, metadata about the structure of the content inside the work (e.g., chapters, stanzas, link maps for images), metadata that controls copyrights, and full text (symbolic) conversion. It will not fund, but will strongly endorse and otherwise support, interpretative efforts.

The conservancy is not a standards making organization, but will provide online cross-disciplinary support and assistance in order to improve quality in digitization, free-to-read presentations, and long-term preservation and migration of digital works. The conservancy may charge fees for this support or provide referrals to organizations that charge fees for such support.

Copyright Disclaimer

All the books available at the Universal Library are either out of copyright or permission to scan has been granted. If this is incorrect the offending content will be removed on receiving information from the aggrieved party.

Some Clarifications

Information storage and management

The MBP when completed will produce approximately 250 million pages or 500 billion characters of information. The storage requirements for the image files will be approximately 50 petabytes ? an order of magnitude larger than any publicly available information base. Creating and managing such a vast information base poses many technological challenges and provides a fertile test bed for innovative research in many areas (described below). The MBP is a multi-agency, multi-national effort that will require the database to be globally distributed. For location independent access, this globally distributed database should appear to be a virtual central database from any place around the world. Mirroring the database in several countries will ensure security and availability. The network speeds at the various nodes would be different. Research in distributed caching and active networks would be needed to ensure that the look and feel of the database is the same from any location.

Search engines

The search engines of today work on the principle of keyword matching and perform searches in one language at a time. With a large corpus of multilingual data provided by the MBP, along with multilingual summarization and translation tools, a well-directed research effort would be needed to ensure concept- and content-based retrieval of knowledge from across multilingual data.

Image processing

The accuracy of Optical Character Recognition (OCR), even in some of the most developed languages, is hindered by the bad quality of the images. This is particularly true for older books and those that use ancient fonts for which the OCR is not tuned. Even the very best OCR accuracy of the order of 98% may not be acceptable in some cases. In order to obtain an improved accuracy close to 100%, advanced image processing research that will perform recognition beyond the character level will be needed. With the availability of large test data from the MBP and the exponentially increasing computing power of the microprocessors, well-directed image processing research would lead to near perfect optical recognizers.

Optical Character Recognition (OCR) in non-Romanic languages

The MBP will have considerable content in many Indian and Chinese languages. The development of OCR in many of the Indian Languages is far more complicated. For example, some of the problems in the development of OCR for Indian languages are:

* There are1500 spoken Indian languages and 17 scripts.
* Unlike English, where the number of characters to be recognized is less than 100, Indian scripts have several hundred characters to be recognized.
* Non-uniformity in the spacing of the characters within a word because of the presence of Consonant Conjuncts (vowel + consonant) makes OCR more difficult. Also, the presence of Consonant Conjuncts results in improper line segmentation. Programs will have to do further processing to segment the lines.
* Consonants take modified shapes when attached with the vowels. Vowel modifiers can appear to the right, on the top or at the bottom of the base consonant. Such consonant-vowel combinations are called modified characters. In addition, two, three or four characters can combine to generate a new complex shapes called compound characters. These characters are very difficult for a machine to recognize.
* In scripts like Bangla and Devnagari, all the characters in a word are connected by a unique line called shirorekha (also called head line). In these scripts, character segmentation is especially difficult.
* In south Indian scripts, vowels occur only at the beginning of a word as against the vowels in Oriya, where they occur anywhere within a word. So, the language

morphology for some groups of scripts is different from the others.

* There is no universally acceptable standard encoding scheme for Indian scripts. This necessitates a scheme where the output labels from the OCR system can be mapped to the labels used by the typesetter through a mapping table.

Because of the non-availability of quality-segmented data, the recognition rate of the Indian language OCR cannot be pushed beyond 90% using character level recognition. To obtain a higher recognition rate, word level information in the form of dictionary has to be used. A word corpus is essential, but such a word corpus for most of the Indian scripts is not available today. The MBP will be able to provide this important missing piece. Once such data is available, it will be possible to use advances in image recognition to develop the OCR in Indian and other non-Romanic languages.

Copyright laws and digital rights management

In the new digital economy, providing democratic access to information while suitably and reasonably rewarding the innovator is possible. The largest repertoire of free software available on the web in many cases has been the outcome of state supported research. This free availability of software has in fact contributed to more developments and hence an exponential growth of knowledge. Even in literary and scholarly publications, authors have experienced increase sales of their work whenever they are made freely available on the web. This is in tune with observations in the new economy that the companies that make more and more of their software freely available on the web, have their market capitalization enhanced. The MBP, with its proposed plans to make a large knowledge base freely available, will provide useful statistics for testing many economic and sociological models.

Language processing

The MBP will produce an extensive and rich test bed for use in further textual language processing research. It is hoped that at least 10,000 books among the million will be available in more than one language, providing a key testing area for problems in example based machine translation. In the last stage of the project, books in multiple languages will be reviewed to ensure that this test bed feature is accomplished.

Many believe that knowledge is now doubling at the rate of every two to three years. Machine summarization, intelligent indexing, and information mining are tools that will be needed for individuals to keep up in their discipline work, in their businesses, and in their personal interests. This large digitization project will support research in these areas. This will be of greater significance for the Indian languages where new tools for summarization, grammar and spell checking, thesaurus and translation dictionaries need to be developed.

The data provided by the MBP with the right research inputs will facilitate the development of language- and location-independent intelligence amplifiers for furthering information creation.

Permission to digitize titles

The MBP approach is to request permission for a range of years, for example, everything published prior to 1990. A publisher could specify the cut-off year or, alternatively, specify the list of titles for which they grant non-exclusive permission to digitize in the MBP.

Value-added services

The MBP is not developing a for-profit system. All of the content will be available free-to-read on the Internet. Participating publishers will get copies of the digitized books and metadata, and can themselves provide or enable others to provide value-added services to access the digital books. Permission granted to the MBP is NON-exclusive.

Reading the case study of the National Academy Press's experience putting their books online free-to-read could facilitate understanding and appreciation of the benefits of this approach. The case study is available at: http://www.press.umich.edu/jep/04-04/pope.html (Journal of Electronic Publishing, Vol. 4, Issue 4, May 1999)

Participation in the Program

The National Academy Press has given us permission to digitize all of their books published prior to 1995 and negotiations are on with MIT Press.

Accuracy in Scanning

Carnegie Mellon has established a workflow (based on pilot ?100 book? and ?1000 book? projects) that includes steps to insure capture of high resolution images and essential metadata, post-processing to correct skewing and crop dark borders surrounding the page images, and OCRing to create searchable ASCII text with 98% accuracy.

Sscanning a title

We expect/hope to return TIFF images to the publisher in about three months from the time permission is granted, but the time will depend on how long it takes us to locate copies of the books (after permission to digitize them is granted) and how many books are included in the group.

Print-On-Demand (POD) standards of Replica and Lightning Source

The MBP follows the standards and best practices supported in ?A Framework of Guidance for Building Good Digital Collections? developed by the Institute for Museum and Library Services in 2001 and endorsed by the Digital Library Federation in 2002. See:http://www.diglib.org/standards/imlsframe.htm, http://www.imls.gov/pubs/forumframework.htm

More specifically, our guidelines for data production

(excerpted from the MBP NSF proposal and based on pilot projects) are:

* Bitonal images with a pixel depth of 1 bit-per-pixel scanned at a resolution of 600 dots per inch (DPI). Images will be stored as ?Intel? TIFF (Tagged Image File Format) files with the header content specified. The compression algorithm used is ITU (Formerly CCITT) Group 4.
* TIFF version 5.0 is acceptable. Subject to testing, version 6.0 (or later) may also be acceptable.
* The initial-capture system includes dynamic thresholding or a similar feature to capture variability of darkness in the imprint and possibly darker (e.g., foxed) backgrounds from decay. Images should be as readable as the original pages.
* Typical expected data will be provided for most TIFF tags (normally, the data supplied by software default settings). A specification for the TIFF header will be produced to include scanner technical information, filename, and other data, but to be in no way a burden on the production service.
* Images will be written in sequential order, with corresponding 8.3 filenames, e.g., 00000001.tif as the first image in volume sequence and 00000341.tif as 341st image in volume sequence.
* Volumes provided to the MBP will be assigned unique identifiers that conform to 8.3 format. The images will be in directories named with the corresponding identifier (e.g., the volume identified as akf3435.001 will have a directory with the same name, and 00000001.tif through 0000000N.tif files within that directory).
* Images and directories (as specified above) will be written to gold CD-ROM according to agreed upon specifications and using ISO9660 format.
* Skew will be within a specified range of degrees allowed.

Administration of the MBP

Neither the consortium nor participating publishers will have an administrative role in the MBP. Administrative responsibility for the MBP belongs to officials at participating universities.

At Carnegie Mellon, the administrative officials are:

Dr. Raj Reddy, University Professor, School of Computer Science

Dr. Gloriana St. Clair, University Librarian

Dr. Mark Kamlet, Provost

The establishment of the Universal Digital Library id going tc set a landmark in the history of libraries and learning. If it goes well that is very much expected, the largest full text database of books will be made available that can be accessed from any corner of the world by an unlimited number of users simultaneously.

5
California Digital Library

The California Digital Library (CDL) was established in 1997. Within the last seven years it has become one of the largest digital libraries in the world. The Library supports the assembly and creative use of the world's scholarship and knowledge for the University of California libraries and the communities they serve. Presently it has more than 32 million items in their collective holdings, the University of California (UC) libraries make up the largest university research library in the world. The California Digital Library supports the assembly and creative use of the world's scholarship and knowledge for the University of California libraries and the communities they serve.

Overview & Mission

The California Digital Library is the University of California's 11th University library. It was established in 1997 by University of California President Emeritus Richard Atkinson to build the University's digital library, assist campus libraries with sharing their resources and holdings more effectively, and provide leadership in applying technology to the development of library collections and services. Organizationally housed under the UC Office of the President the CDL operates in close collaboration with all UC campuses and their libraries.

The mission of the library is to harness technology and innovation, and leveraging the intellectual and cultural resources of the UC. The CDL supports the assembly and creative use of the world's scholarship and knowledge for the UC libraries and the communities they serve.

To achieve its mission, the CDL utilizes strategic partnerships and technical innovation to:

* Focus on digital library collections by investing in the means of developing, acquiring access to, and persistently managing digital collections.
* Invest in applications that help campus libraries and others build meaningful, cost effective, and customized services for the use of the University's scholarly, cultural, and learning resources.
* Provide collaborative leadership in the development of new forms of scholarly communication.
* Leverage its investments to influence the marketplace for scholarly information in the interest of the University, its libraries, and the communities they serve.

Organization

The California Digital Library is housed under the University of California Office of the President, and is directed by Daniel Greenstein, the University Librarian and Executive Director. UC library groups, CDL advisory groups, CDL staff, and third-party partners all contribute to the workings of the CDL. Because the CDL is one of the UC libraries, it participates in systemwide library groups. CDL advisory and working groups provide guidance for specific CDL programs and initiatives.

The CDL staff support the CDL's mission and programs. Many staff members also serve on advisory committees and working groups focusing on the development of digital libraries. CDL departments include:

* Administration
* Built Content
* Business Development
* Communication
* Digital Library Services
* Digital Library Technologies

* Digital Preservation Programs
* Office of Scholarly Communication
* Shared Digital Content

The CDL also has valuable partnerships with organizations outside the UC system. Third-party partners include California libraries and museums, and national and international digital library organizations and researchers.

Planning the Library

The California Digital Library was founded as a collaboration of the University of California campuses and, by nature, creates and manages shared resources. Successful collaboration depends upon advisory and operations groups whose memberships include faculty, administrators, and staff from all UC campuses.

Systemwide Library Planning

The planning and advisory processes which guide the CDL are well integrated with Systemwide Library Planning (SLP), which is directed by the CDL University Librarian and Executive Director. The CDL often implements the plans created by the SLP. The SLP collectively works through representative groups for the UC libraries and their constituencies. CDL Advisory and Working Groups directly advise the CDL in specific domains. These working groups:

* **Joint Steering Committee on Shared Collections (JSC):** This group is responsible for identifying appropriate mechanisms for the systemwide development of digital collection frameworks and priorities. Its members come from the UC campus libraries.
* **Online Archive of California (OAC) Steering Committee:** The steering committee advises the OAC on broad issues of content, policy, sustainability, partnership, and scholarship. Members are drawn from the CDL and the UC campus libraries.

* **Online Archive of California Working Group (OACWG):** The OACWG advises the CDL and the OAC Steering Committee on issues concerning the administration, operation, and technical development of the OAC. Its members are nominated by the CDL.
* **Patron Initiated Request (PIR) Project Team:** Working on the Request service, this group identifies and makes recommendations to resolve policy issues, and coordinates implementation with campus library staff. Members include CDL staff.
* **Strategic Technology Architecture and Standards Working Group (STAS):** This group recommends and maintains architectural guidelines and standards for the UC shared digital collections. Its members are drawn from the UC campuses, the San Diego Supercomputer Center, and the CDL.
* **Text Encoding Interest Group:** This group focuses on topics related to the Text Encoding Initiative, an organization that helps standardize the way libraries, museums, publishers, and scholars encode text for online research and teaching. Members include CDL staff.
* **Tools and Services Working Group (TSWG):** The TSWG develops principles and guidelines for the identification, evaluation, selection, and implementation of online tools and services for sharing, manipulating, and integrating scholarly content in all forms. Its members come from the UC campus libraries.

CDL operations cover:

* **Users Council:** The Users Council is responsible for basic communication about public services and the use of the CDL. Its members include representatives from major user groups and catalog contributors, including those outside the UC system.
* **Resource Liaisons:** These liaisons are campus subject

experts who monitor and conduct ongoing evaluation of shared resources. Members include bibliographers and reference librarians.

* **eScholarship Liaisons:** Each campus library has an eScholarship liaison who provides information about eScholarship activities.
* **Evaluation Liaisons:** This group helps create and disseminate user evaluation information, and is made up of public service and instructional librarians.

In addition, most CDL programs and services have liaison groups that assist with systemwide communication and operations.

Programs

The California Digital Library supports the assembly and creative use of the world's scholarship and knowledge for the University of California libraries and the communities they serve. To accomplish these goals, the CDL partners with the UC libraries, publishers, and other institutions in broad-based programs and initiatives. Programs host specific digital collections and services.

The CDL's programs include:

Collections

The collection function includes acquiring scholarly content, hosting digitized materials from UC collections and non-UC library and museum partners, and enabling the publication of original scholarly materials.

The University of California's scholars and students conduct their research and learning while drawing from a significant portion of the world's knowledge held in the UC's library collections. Those collections grow and become more convenient to use through the California Digital Library's program to acquire and host scholarly materials in digital form.

The CDL leads a large collaborative effort to license electronic scholarly materials on behalf of the UC, in co-investment with the campus libraries. In addition, CDL hosts digital content created by the UC libraries and California partners, and makes these materials available for public use. The CDL:

* Provides the UC community with more digital material than is available at any other university, including more than 8,000 electronic journals, tens of thousands of electronic books, and more than 250 article and reference databases.
* Saves millions of dollars compared to what would be spent by the campuses acting independently.
* Allows campus libraries to focus on local research and curriculum by economizing on costs for commonly needed materials and acquisition processes.
* Provides a deep and broad collection of online cultural heritage materials from UC and California libraries, museums, and historical societies via the Online Archive of California (OAC).
* Enables the experimental publication of scholarly output in open-access repositories.
* Encourages interactive use of government and social science statistics and data via Counting California.
* Forges partnerships with university presses and societies to digitally publish scholarly works.

New activities and explorations are focusing on:

* Publishing scholarly monographs in XML.
* Hosting digital image collections managed by UC Visual Resource curators.
* Providing access to local history collections.
* Cultivating the interchange of California's botanical information resources.

More information:

* Collections & Services

* eScholarship Program
* UC Libraries

Services

The service functions cover enhancing services for discovering, sharing, manipulating, and integrating scholarly content. Services allow scholars and students to search for and use items in the University of California collections and elsewhere. Services are the necessary complement to collections and to the activities of acquiring, managing, and preserving scholarly materials.

The California Digital Library pursues technological innovations that provide solutions to the UC libraries for the discovery, integration, manipulation, and sharing of scholarly content in all forms. The CDL provides some direct online services and makes tools available to the UC libraries and others for the customization of local services.

The digital services program relies on systemwide collaboration to identify, build, and implement services and tools that benefit the UC libraries and other partners. Existing services, tools, and activities concentrate on:

* Discovering print and digital materials in the UC libraries and beyond, including the 32 million items in the UC libraries via the Melvyl® Catalog, and the large collections of cultural heritage materials from more than 70 California libraries and institutions in the Online Archive of California (OAC).
* Streamlining access to online and print materials by linking from article citations to the full online content or to the locations for printed materials via UC-eLinks.
* Manipulating content by providing tools to export citations to citation management software, or to create and export presentations using digital images.
* Creating and sharing scholarship by providing faculty with experimental publishing tools and infrastructure.

* Influencing commercial products by developing high-performance technical and functional requirements, and by working with UC subject specialist librarians, known as Resource Liaisons, who monitor and influence licensed products.
* Supporting UC librarians by communicating with the Users Council, sponsoring workshops, and providing a Help Desk and guides for troubleshooting.

New activities and explorations are focusing on:

* Digital image services, with tools designed for classroom instruction.
* Federated searching or portal tools for the discovery and integration of disparate collections.
* Instructional technologies that integrate digital materials into learning and course management systems.
* Delivery of digital books to classrooms, labs, libraries, and individual readers.

eScholarship

e Scholarship function includes fostering innovation and faculty experimentation in digital scholarly communication. Scholarly communication is the foundation of all academic activities. The traditional model of scholarly communication is based on journal publications, and in the current age, it has become expensive, restrictive, and increasingly limited in its ability to make information accessible. To address these concerns, the eScholarship program was initiated by the California Digital Library at the University of California.

The eScholarship program facilitates innovation and supports experimentation in the production and dissemination of scholarship. Through the use of innovative technology, the program seeks to develop a financially sustainable model and improve all areas of scholarly communication, including its creation, peer review, management, dissemination, and preservation. New modes of scholarly publication include:

* Repositories for research and scholarly output, including pre-publication materials and peer-reviewed content.
* Web-based publications of digitally reformatted content.
* Electronic editions of academic monographs of interest to both scholarly and general-interest readers.

In partnership with librarians, scholars, publishers, information technologists, and professionals in other memory organizations, the eScholarship program has developed several key collections and services:

* eScholarship Editions: Provides access to a growing collection of digital texts and monographs, including more than 1,400 UC Press titles. A significant number of the electronic books are available for free to the public.
* eScholarship Publications: Publications from the eScholarship program, including monographs from the UC International and Area Studies Digital Collection, journals and peer-reviewed series in the eScholarship Repository, experimental interactive publications like ECAI, and legacy content like the DOJ.
* eScholarship Repository: This free, open-access repository infrastructure supports the full range of scholarly output, from pre-publication materials to journals and peer-reviewed series, by offering UC departments direct control of publishing.

Digital Preservation

In partnership with the University of California libraries, the California Digital Library established the digital preservation program to focus on the persistent management of digital information. The program is supported by grants from the Institute of Museum and Library Services and The

Andrew W. Mellon Foundation, and partnerships with Stanford University and the San Diego Supercomputer Center. Activities focusing on digital preservation are:

* Identifying methods to preserve and persistently manage ejournals. The UC libraries have invested heavily in licensed content, but do not directly control the content. Because of this, the CDL is investigating methods to preserve and manage these materials. Currently, the CDL is participating in the beta test of experimental caching software that captures and locally manages licensed electronic journals and other content. The program, Lots of Copies Keeps Stuff Safe (LOCKSS), is an initiative based at the Stanford University library.
* Evaluating methods for gathering and persistently managing web-based materials under a grant from The Andrew W. Mellon Foundation. While the program deals with information produced or disseminated by U.S. state and federal governments, it provides the University libraries with an understanding of the preservation strategies for web archiving in general.
* Establishing a UC libraries digital preservation repository for the persistent management of digital assets created by the UC libraries. This project, conducted as a collaboration between the CDL and the UC Berkeley library, will create a preservation repository for digital materials conforming to the Open Archival Information System (OAIS) standards.
* Developing an implementation strategy for preservation. The CDL is investigating the implementation of persistent identifiers and standards for encoding descriptive, administrative, and structural metadata for objects in a digital library.

Education, Communication & Assessment

Furthering the understanding of digital library products and the digital library domain; discovering needs, testing usability, and evaluating the use and usefulness of digital collections and services. The California Digital Library has a variety of education, communication, and assessment activities that introduce the organization to others and help further the understanding of digital libraries. Through this program, the CDL collaborates with staff at each campus to foster successful use of digital collections and services and informs University of California and its partners about the wide range of digital library services and developments.

In addition, the CDL considers it critical to understand the information needs of the UC community and characteristics of the use of its digital collections and services. These assessment activities are fundamental to the CDL's own education and the informed pursuit of improving service.

The education, communication, and assessment program allows the CDL to:

* Foster independent and successful use of CDL collections, services, and tools: Activities include establishing usability tools for the selection and design of collections and services, and working with the Evaluation Liaisons, the Users Council, and other service staff on the campuses to develop outreach and instructional materials. User guides and help are included with all major collections and services.
* Develop an understanding of the needs of CDL patrons and their use of CDL resources: Projects include soliciting information from patrons, performing needs assessments for service design and enhancements, and coordinating the production of quantitative and qualitative use data.
* Articulate CDL directions, goals, and activities for a variety of audiences: Methods and venues include this web site and a variety of publications, press releases, and communiqués.
* CDL Technologies: Supporting the UC campus libraries

and others in the application of technology for the development of scholarly digital collections and services.

CDL Technologies

The CDL Technologies group is responsible for the technical design, implementation, and operations of the California Digital Library in support of the plans and policies formulated by the University Librarian.

CDL technologies provide enabling infrastructure for campus libraries and other information organizations by:

* Investing in technologies and applications that help campus libraries and others build cost effective, customized services that support the use of the University's scholarly, cultural, and learning resources.
* Continuously experimenting with innovative technologies in the provision of scholarly information and in the development of new forms of scholarly communication.
* Defining architecture guidelines and standards in cooperation with the University community.
* Implementing new systems within this framework.

Future Directions

Looking ahead, the CDL technologies group is working to develop the full range of infrastructures requisite to the ingest, preservation, and presentation of information to scholarly communities.

The CDL recognizes that new directions must be explored to leverage ingenuity in systems design for the delivery of content to users, and that these system's capabilities must be accessible, uniform, and well-characterized. The future lies in the services the CDL provides, not merely in the content the CDL preserves.

Partners & Research

Collaboration is a core value for the California Digital Library. The CDL's continuing success in delivering and sustaining digital collections and services for the University of California's teaching and research depends on its collaboration with the UC campuses as well as state, national, and international partners.

The CDL provides leadership to the digital library community through founding memberships in key organizations that are working to define and analyze library challenges and technological innovations. CDL staff members are active within many key standards development groups and initiatives.

In addition, the CDL has a very successful record of acquiring grants to explore strategic innovations in digital libraries. Granters have included the Andrew W. Mellon Foundation, the Library Services and Technology Act administered by the California State Library, the Institute of Museum and Library Services, and the Library of Congress.

Partners

The California Digital Library partners with the University of California's campus libraries and systemwide library planning to build and maintain a shared digital collection and a digital services infrastructure. In addition, the CDL partners with many other organizations based at UC, including museums, the UC Press, and the San Diego Supercomputer Center in order to expand the scope of its research and programs.

Outside of the UC, the CDL is deeply networked with national and international research, cultural, and education establishments. Through active memberships in several organizations, the CDL contributes to the development of digital libraries. Staff members participate in the definition of technical standards that support digital library activities, collections, and services.

Memberships and Standards Work

The CDL is a member of:

* Coalition for Networked Information
* Consortium for the Computer Interchange of Museum Information
* Council on Library and Information Resources (CLIR)
* Digital Library Federation (DLF)
* EDUCAUSE
* International Coalition of Library Consortia (ICOLC)
* National Information Standards Organization (NISO)
* Scholarly Publishing Academic Resources Coalition (SPARC)

CDL staff contribute to standards development efforts, including:

* **Metadata Encoding and Transmission Standard (METS):** CDL staff (Brian Tingle) serving on the editorial board.
* **Open Archives Initiative (OAI):** CDL staff (John Ober) serving on the steering committee.
* **OpenURL:** CDL staff serving on the National Information Standards Organization (NISO) Development Committee.
* **Preservation Metadata: Implementation Strategies (PREMIS):** CDL staff (John Kunze) serving on this working group sponsored by the Online Computer Library Center (OCLC) and the Research Libraries Group (RLG).
* **Shibboleth:** CDL and UC staff (Peter Brantley, David Walker, and David Wasley) serving on the Internet 2 development and implementation groups.
* **Z39.50:** CDL staff (Margery Tibbetts) serving on the Implementers Group Advisory Board.

Research

With its partners, the California Digital Library is actively engaged in applied research that contributes to the development of digital library content and services and the progress of scholarly communication.

At the CDL, applied research takes several forms. Results have directly shaped digital library collections and services at the University of California and throughout California, and have had national and international impacts.

Grant-funded initiatives: Impacts of externally funded projects include refined digitization and encoding standards for cultural materials, best practices for creating and sustaining digital collections, deeper understanding of digital preservation methods and collaboration, expanded alternatives for scholarly publishing, and insights on user behavior toward print and digital materials. Grants totaling more than $1 million per year have been awarded from the Andrew W. Mellon Foundation, the Library Services and Technology Act administered by the California State Library, the Institute of Museum and Library Services, and the Library of Congress, among others.

Co-development: The CDL is in a unique position to help surface the interests and skills of stakeholder organizations, and support applied research and co-developments among them. For example, support from the CDL has helped California museums and libraries to develop their digital collections, the University's herbaria to collaborate in the creation of online collections and services, and the Electronic Cultural Atlas Initiative to build new tools.

Standards development: The CDL lends its staff to the principle community efforts to understand digital library technology and infrastructure requirements, and to define, test, and establish related standards. Staff have participated in standards work for content encoding, digitization, systems interoperability, and security and authentication. See a list of

CDL memberships and standards work at the partners page.

Selective list of grant-funded activities:

* **Preservation of web-based government information:** Investigating of the technical alternatives for harvesting, organizing, and preserving web-based government information. $150,000 grant from the Andrew W. Mellon Foundation.
* **Management of mixed print and digital collections:** Systemwide Library Planning is exploring how scholars and libraries can best integrate and preserve collections of scholarly journals that are published in both print and digital forms. $670,000 grant from the Andrew W. Mellon Foundation.
* **Preservation of UC library materials:** Creating a pilot digital preservation repository for multi-institutional use, based on the Open Archive Information System (OAIS) model for digital preservation. $374,736 grant from the Institute of Museum and Library Services.
* **Contributions to the National Digital Library collection:** Supporting cooperation between the Online Archive of California (OAC) and the Library of Congress's National Digital Library Program. $600,000 grant from the Library of Congress.
* **Best practices for digitizing cultural heritage materials and finding aids:** Supporting the creation of and permanent access to standardized metadata and digital images through the OAC. $488,148 awarded in three grants from the California State Library's Library Services Technology Act (LSTA).
* **Alternative forms of scholarly communication:** Supporting experimentation in the dissemination of research findings. $167,836 grant from the Scholarly Publishing Academic Resources Coalition (SPARC).
* **Extension of library standards to museums:** Evaluating the capabilities of Encoded Archival Descriptions, a

digital finding aid technology, to integrate museum collection descriptions into the OAC collections. $828,533 awarded in two National Leadership grants from the Institute of Museum and Library Services.

* **Establishment of the Japanese American Relocation Digital Archive (JARDA):** Mining California's rich collections of Japanese American relocation materials to create JARDA. $358,724 grant from the Library Services and Technology Act, administered by the California State Library.
* **National Science Foundation's Digital Library Initiative–Phase 2:** The CDL is working with UC Berkeley, UC Santa Barbara, Stanford, and the San Diego Supercomputer Center on the "InterLib" suite of California projects in the NSF-funded Digital Library Initiative.

News & Publications

On a continuing basis, the California Digital Library acquires access to new online content, and develops services that help scholars publish, search for, and use information through the University of California campus libraries.

6
Digital Library of India

Up until now, the transmission of the cultural heritage has depended on limited numbers of copies in fragile media. The fires of Alexandria irrevocably severed our access to any of the works of the ancients. In a thousand years, only a few of the paper documents we have today will survive the ravages of deterioration, loss, and outright destruction. With no more than 10 million unique book and document editions before the year 1900, and perhaps 100 million since the beginning of recorded history, the task of preservation is much larger. With new digital technology, though, this task is within the reach of a single concerted effort for the public good, and this effort can be distributed to libraries, museums, and other groups in all countries.

Existing archives of paper have many shortcomings. Many other works still in existence today are rare, and only accessible to a small population of scholars and collectors at specific geographic locations. A single wanton act of destruction can destroy an entire line of heritage. Furthermore, contrary to the popular beliefs, the libraries, museums, and publishers do not routinely maintain broadly comprehensive archives of the considered works of man. No one can afford to do this, unless the archive is digital.

Digital technology can make the works of man permanently accessible to the billions of people all over the world. J. N. Tata and other great philanthropists, and visionary information scientist like Dr S. R. Ranganathan, in past centuries have recognized the great potential of public libraries to improve the quality of life and provide opportunity the citizenry. A language independent digital library, widely available through free access on the Internet, will improve the global society in ways beyond measurement.

The technological advances today make it possible to think in terms of storing all the knowledge of the human race in digital form by the year 2008.

Mission

The mission is to create a portal for the Digital Library of India which will foster creativity and free access to all human knowledge. As a first step in realizing this mission, it is proposed to create the Digital Library with a free-to-read, searchable collection of one million books, predominantly in Indian languages, available to everyone over the Internet. This portal will also become an aggregator of all the knowledge and digital contents created by other digital library initiatives in India. Very soon we expect that this portal would provide a gateway to Indian Digital Libraries in science, arts, culture, music, movies, traditional medicine, palm leaves and many more. The result will be a unique resource accessible to anyone in the world 24x7, without regard to socioeconomic background or nationality.

Typical large high-school libraries house fewer than 30,000 volumes. Most libraries in the world have less than a million volumes. The total number of different titles indexed in OCLC's WorldCat is about 48 million. One million books, therefore, is more than the holdings of most high-schools, and is equivalent to the libraries at many universities and represents a useful fraction of all available books.

One of the goals of the Digital Library of India is to provide support for full text indexing and searching based on OCR (optical character recognition) technologies where available. The availability of online search allows users to locate relevant information quickly and reliably thus enhancing student's success in their research endeavors. This 24x7 resource would also provide an excellent test bed for language processing research in areas such as machine translation, optical character recognition, summarization, speech and hand writing recognition, intelligent indexing, and information retrieval in Indian languages.

It is our expectation that the Digital Library of India will be mirrored at several locations worldwide so as to protect the integrity and availability of the data. The DLI will also partner with other country specific Digital Libraries initiatives as part of the Universal Library Project (www.ulib.org) spearheaded by Prof. Raj Reddy and Carnegie Mellon University.

Goals

The primary long-term objective is to capture all books in digital format. It is believed that such a task is impossible and could take hundreds of years, and never be completed. Thus, as a first step we are planning to demonstrate the feasibility by undertaking to digitize 1 million books (less than 1% of all books in all languages ever published) by 2005. We believe such a project has the potential to change how education is conducted in much of the world.

A secondary objective of this project will be to provide a test bed that will support other researchers who are working on improved scanning techniques, improved optical character recognition, and improved indexing. The corpus this project creates will be one to three orders of magnitude larger than any existing free resource.

Benefits

The principal benefit of the Digital Library will be to supplement the formal education system by making knowledge available to anyone who can read and has access. Libraries have played a vital role in the advancement of human society. Societal advance depends on young people having access to books via libraries and other means. We expect that making this unique web resource available free to everyone around the world will enhance the learning process.

Libraries are unevenly distributed around the world and

within each country. In the U.S., the NCES Survey noted that in 1996, 3,408 of 3,792 institutions of higher education had libraries holding 806.7 million volumes. The 112 largest university libraries in the United States and Canada each have at least 1.8 million books. They are members of the Association for Research Libraries. Massachusetts has about 25 million volumes; New York has about 31 million volumes, and California has about 40 million volumes in their ARL Libraries (Association for Research Libraries, 1999/2000). Other states, such as North and South Dakota, have no large libraries. A few large public libraries have several million volumes. However, most junior colleges, high schools, and public libraries have much smaller collections. Making this large knowledge repository can revolutionize research at all levels of education and give a much-needed boost at minimal cost to our national educational infrastructure. This impact will be further enhanced given the convenience of online access, and the benefit of full text searching at word and phrase levels.

A secondary benefit of online search is to make locating the relevant information inside of books far more reliable and much easier. Student success in finding exactly what they seek will increase and increased success will enhance student willingness to perform research using this large resource. NCES reports that 84 percent of libraries around the country are open between 60 and 80 hours a week. This digital library would be open all the 168 hours the week on a 24x7x365 basis. More than one individual will be able to use the same book at the same time. Thus, popular works will not be checked out and thus unavailable to others.

This million-book project will produce an extensive and rich testbed for use in further textual language processing research. It is hoped that at least 10,000 books among the million will be available in more than one language, providing a unique resource for example based machine translation.

Many believe that information is now doubling every two years. Machine summarization, intelligent indexing, and information mining are tools that will be needed for individuals to keep up in their discipline work, in their businesses, and in their personal interests. This large digitization project will enable extensive research in these areas.

Philosophy of Content Selection

The Million Book Project envisages to develop a collection of one million digital books by adopting a staged approach as described below. The Million Book project will adhere to the copyright law.

1. Coordination of Selection

Creating one digital copy and mirroring it in different locations will suffice, and will support the multiple uses at any time. Preliminary discussions with OCLC as a host for a registry of scanned items are underway. Certain key projects, such as the Making of America project, are already represented in the OCLC database as digital books. Other large digitization projects may require some data entry of their content in order to avoid duplication.

2. Non-copyrighted materials

Materials published before 1920 are in the public domain and may be scanned for this project. To reduce the costs of selection, the project will probably develop a strategy of selecting key topics and then removing large runs of books and journals from a selected repository. Having a reasonable turn-around time will be essential to the success of the project. A strategy has been devised to understand the logistics of shipping the materials and the impact of their absence from the home library.

4. Best books approach

The project will seek publisher permission to scan books from Books for College Libraries (BCL), one source for core academic books in English. A previous study done at Carnegie Mellon University Libraries indicates that 22% of publishers granted permission for scanning and mounting on the web.

The materials in the study were a random sample of Carnegie Mellon Llibraries' books and included a broad range of dates, publishers, and in and out of print status.. Numerous difficulties from out of business publishers, lack of publisher records, return of copyright to authors, and other circumstances were identified. Subsequently, Carol Hughes, the collections development officer for Questia, corroborated Carnegie Mellon's experience.

OCLC owns a database of books from the latest edition of Books for College Libraries. BCL contains about 50,000 titles. A 22% success rate in clearing copyright would result in 10,000 of the best books for college students being included in the project. Clearing copyright is labor intensive and expensive. Bradd Burningham's recent article estimated those costs ("Copyright Permissions" in Journal of Interlibrary Loan, Document Delivery, and Information Supply, 11:2 (2000), 95-111). The BCL database, however, will allow for sorting by publisher so that permission requests can contain the names of several books. A quick sample indicates that as many as 25,000 publishers may be represented there. Despite the expense, this commitment to quality should be attempted. Carnegie Mellon University Libraries will seek private foundation funding to undertake this project.

Publishers increasingly see that digital presentation of their works can attract buyers. They are interested in exploring ways in which their out of print titles may be returned to profitability. Continued work with publishers through the course of this project may attract many of them to it. That would be most beneficial in enriching the content to be made available.

People

The Principal Scientific Advisor to the Government of India.

Academia

* Dr. N. Balakrishnan, Chairman, Division of Information

Sciences, Indian Institute of Science

* Prof. M G K Menon, Chairman, Council of Indian Institute of Information Technology, Allahabad and Indian Institute of Technology-Bombay (Mumbai)
* Dr. Y.S.Rajan, Vice Chancellor, Punjab Technological University, Punjab
* Dr. Ashok Kolaskar, Vice Chancellor, Pune University, Maharashtra
* Dr. A.Vagiswari, Head Library, Indian Institute of Astrophysics, Bangalore
* Dr. M. D Tiwari, Director, Indian Institute of Information Technology, Allahabad
* Dr. P.V Konnur, Goa University, Goa
* Dr. Rajeev Sangal, Director, International Institute of Information Technology, Hyderabad
* Mr. S. Vaidhyasubramanian, Dean, Shanmugha Arts, Science, Technology & Research Academy, Tanjavur, Tamil Nadu
* Mr. V.R Gowri Shankar, Sringeri Mutt, Karnataka
* Dr. S Venkadesan, Indian Institute of Science, Bangalore
* Mr. Sridharan, Secretary, Arulmigu Kalasalingam College Of Engineering, Tamil Nadu
* Dr. Thangaraj, Principal, Arulmigu Kalasalingam College Of Engineering, Tamil Nadu
* Dr. Udaya Kumar, Anna University, Chennai
* Mr. Vasant Mehta, Sri Kanchi Kamakoti Peetham, Tamil Nadu

Government

* Mr. Kamal Kant Jaswal , Secretary, Ministry of Communication and Information Technology
* Mr. Yashwant Bhave, Joint Secretary, Ministry of Communication and Information Technology

* Dr. Ajeya Kallam, Executive Officer of Tirumala Tirupati Devasthanams
* Mr. Ajay Sawhney, Special Secretary for IT, Government of Andhra Pradesh
* Dr. G.V Subbarao, Director of Libraries, Government of Andhra Pradesh
* Dr. I.V Subbarao, Secretary Education, Government of Andhra Pradesh
* Dr. Om Vikas, Senior Director, Ministry of Communication and Information Technology, Govt. of India
* Dr. P. K. Chaturvedi, Director, Ministry of Communication and Information Technology, Govt. of India
* Dr. R.K. Arora, Ministry of Communication and Information Technology, Govt. of India
* Dr. Gulshan Rai, Executive Director, ERNET

CMU

* Dr. Raj Reddy, Founder and Director of the Universal Digital Library (UDL)
* Dr. Michael Shamos, Director of UDL, Intellectual Property
* Dr. Jaime Carbonell, Director of UDL, Language Technologies
* Dr. Robert Thibadeau, Director of UDL, Privacy and Security
* Dr. Gloriana St. Clair, Director of UDL, University Librarian, Content Selection

US Advisors

* Dr. Ching-chih Chen, Co-Principal Investigator, China-US Million Book Project
* Dr. Daniel Greenstein, Executive Director of the Digital Library Federation

* Dr. Brewster Kahle, President, Internet Archive
* Dr. Victor Zue, Professor, LCS, MIT
* Dr. Michael Lesk, National Science Foundation
* Dr. Stephen Griffin, National Science Foundation
* Gabrielle V. Michalek, Carnegie Mellon University

China

* Dr. Pan Yunhe, President of Zhejiang University
* Dr. Gao Wen, Deputy President of the Graduate School, Chinese Academy of Science
* Mr. Guo Xinli, Vice General Director, Ministry of Education of China
* Mr. Chen Jianping, Vice Director, State Planning Commission of China
* Dr. Chi Huisheng, Vice President of Beijing University
* Dr. Hu Dongcheng, Vice President of Tsinghua University
* Dr. Xu Zhong, Vice President of Fudan University
* Dr. Zhang Yibin, Assistant to the President, Nanjing University

The Team

* S.Srinivas, Indian Institute of Science, Bangalore
* Sheik Dawood, Indian Institute of Science, Bangalore
* J.Anandh, Indian Institute of Science, Bangalore
* Jiju Vargheese, Indian Institute of Science, Bangalore
* Vishwas Sharma, Indian Institute of Science, Bangalore
* Mini Balakrishnan, Indian Institute of Science, Bangalore
* Madhavi Ganapathiraju, Carnegie Mellon University, USA
* Eric Burns, Carnegie Mellon University, USA
* Krishna Konduru, Carnegie Mellon University, USA
* Kishore Madhav, Carnegie Mellon University, USA

* Walt Schearer, Carnegie Mellon University, USA
* Kiran Kumar

Partners

India

Coordination and Research Centre in India

* Indian Institute of Science, Bangalore

Academic Institutions

* Anna University, Chennai, Tamil Nadu
* Arulmigu Kalasligam College of Engineering (AKCE), Srivilliputur, Madurai, Tamil Nadu
* Goa University, Goa
* Indian Institute of Astrophysics, Bangalore,Karnataka
* Indian Institute of Information Technology, Allahabad, Uttar Pradesh
* International Institute of Information Technology, Hyderabad, Andhra Pradesh
* Osmania University, Hyderabad
* Punjab Technical University, Punjab
* Shanmugha Art, Science, Technology & Research Academy, Tanjavur, Tamil Nadu
* University Of Hyderabad, Hyderabad
* University of Pune, Pune, Maharashtra

Religious and Cultural Institutions

* Kanchi University, Kanchi, Tamil Nadu
* Poornapragna Vidyapeetha, Bangalore
* Salarjung Museum, Hyderabad
* Sringeri Mutt, Sringeri, Karnataka
* Tirumala Tirupati Devasthanams, Tirupati, Andhra Pradesh
* Tibetan Monasteries and Literature on Jainism

Government and Research Agencies

* Academy of Sanskrit Research , Melkote, Karnataka
* CDAC- Noida
* Indian Institute of Astrophysics, Bangalore,Karnataka
* Maharashtra Industrial Development Corporation (MIDC), Mumbai, Maharashtra
* Rashtrapathi Bhavan, New Delhi

United States of America

* Carnegie Mellon University

China

* Beijing University
* Chinese Academy of Science
* Fudan University
* Ministry of Education of China
* Nanjing University
* State Planning Commission of China
* Tsinghua University
* Zhejiang University

Funding Sources

Funding for the Million Book Project is coming from multiple sources.

The Office of the Principal Scientific Advisor to the Government of India is funding the project in the Indian Institute of Science.

The Ministry of Communication and Information Technology (MCIT) is funding the project at various partner centres of the Digital Library of India.

Various Centres have also pledged their local resources to make the Digital Library of India a reality.

The individual centres would acknowledge and provide more details about the agencies from which they have received support in their websites.

National Science Foundation is providing funding for Scanners and Software research and development.

Donations

Activities such as selection and acquisition of books, packing and shipping costs, and quality assurance of the content are unfunded, and would greatly benefit from your support.

Please contact for other details :

Prof. N. Balakrishnan

Chairman,

Division of Information Sciences,

Indian Institute of Science,

Bangalore - 560012,

Karnataka, India

balki@serc.iisc.ernet.in

Million Book Project

Information storage and management

The MBP when completed will produce approximately 250 million pages or 500 billion characters of information. The storage requirements for the image files will be approximately 50 petabytes ? an order of magnitude larger than any publicly available information base. Creating and managing such a vast information base poses many technological challenges and provides a fertile test bed for innovative research in many areas (described below). The MBP is a multi-agency, multi-national effort that will require the database to be globally distributed. For location independent access, this globally distributed database should appear to be a virtual central database from any place around the world. Mirroring the database in several countries will ensure security and availability. The network speeds at the various nodes would be different. Research in distributed caching and active networks would be needed to ensure that the look and feel of the database is the same from any location.

Search engines

The search engines of today work on the principle of keyword matching and perform searches in one language at a time. With a large corpus of multilingual data provided by the MBP, along with multilingual summarization and translation tools, a well-directed research effort would be needed to ensure concept- and content-based retrieval of knowledge from across multilingual data.

Image processing

The accuracy of Optical Character Recognition (OCR), even in some of the most developed languages, is hindered by the bad quality of the images. This is particularly true for older books and those that use ancient fonts for which the OCR is not tuned. Even the very best OCR accuracy of the order of 98% may not be acceptable in some cases. In order to obtain an improved accuracy close to 100%, advanced image processing research that will perform recognition beyond the character level will be needed. With the availability of large test data from the MBP and the exponentially increasing computing power of the microprocessors, well-directed image processing research would lead to near perfect optical recognizers.

Optical Character Recognition (OCR) in non-Romanic languages

The MBP will have considerable content in many Indian and Chinese languages. The development of OCR in many of the Indian Languages is far more complicated. For example, some of the problems in the development of OCR for Indian languages are:

* There are1500 spoken Indian languages and 17 scripts.
* Unlike English, where the number of characters to be recognized is less than 100, Indian scripts have several hundred characters to be recognized.
* Non-uniformity in the spacing of the characters within

a word because of the presence of Consonant Conjuncts (vowel + consonant) makes OCR more difficult. Also, the presence of Consonant Conjuncts results in improper line segmentation. Programs will have to do further processing to segment the lines.

* Consonants take modified shapes when attached with the vowels. Vowel modifiers can appear to the right, on the top or at the bottom of the base consonant. Such consonant-vowel combinations are called modified characters. In addition, two, three or four characters can combine to generate a new complex shapes called compound characters. These characters are very difficult for a machine to recognize.
* In scripts like Bangla and Devnagari, all the characters in a word are connected by a unique line called shirorekha (also called head line). In these scripts, character segmentation is especially difficult.
* In south Indian scripts, vowels occur only at the beginning of a word as against the vowels in Oriya, where they occur anywhere within a word. So, the language morphology for some groups of scripts is different from the others.
* There is no universally acceptable standard encoding scheme for Indian scripts. This necessitates a scheme where the output labels from the OCR system can be mapped to the labels used by the typesetter through a mapping table.

Because of the non-availability of quality-segmented data, the recognition rate of the Indian language OCR cannot be pushed beyond 90% using character level recognition. To obtain a higher recognition rate, word level information in the form of dictionary has to be used. A word corpus is essential, but such a word corpus for most of the Indian scripts is not available today. The MBP will be able to provide this important missing piece. Once such data is available, it will be possible to use advances in image recognition to develop the OCR in Indian and other non-Romanic languages.

Copyright laws and digital rights management

In the new digital economy, providing democratic access to information while suitably and reasonably rewarding the innovator is possible. The largest repertoire of free software available on the web in many cases has been the outcome of state supported research. This free availability of software has in fact contributed to more developments and hence an exponential growth of knowledge. Even in literary and scholarly publications, authors have experienced increase sales of their work whenever they are made freely available on the web. This is in tune with observations in the new economy that the companies that make more and more of their software freely available on the web, have their market capitalization enhanced. The MBP, with its proposed plans to make a large knowledge base freely available, will provide useful statistics for testing many economic and sociological models.

Language processing

The MBP will produce an extensive and rich test bed for use in further textual language processing research. It is hoped that at least 10,000 books among the million will be available in more than one language, providing a key testing area for problems in example based machine translation. In the last stage of the project, books in multiple languages will be reviewed to ensure that this test bed feature is accomplished.

Many believe that knowledge is now doubling at the rate of every two to three years. Machine summarization, intelligent indexing, and information mining are tools that will be needed for individuals to keep up in their discipline work, in their businesses, and in their personal interests. This large digitization project will support research in these areas. This will be of greater significance for the Indian languages where new tools for summarization, grammar and spell checking, thesaurus and translation dictionaries need to be developed.

The data provided by the MBP with the right research inputs will facilitate the development of language- and location-independent intelligence amplifiers for furthering information creation.

Blanket permission to digitize The MBP approach is to request permission for a range of years, for example, everything published prior to 1990. A publisher could specify the cut-off year or, alternatively, specify the list of titles for which they grant non-exclusive permission to digitize in the MBP.

Value-added: The MBP is not developing a for-profit system. All of the content will be available free-to-read on the Internet. Participating publishers will get copies of the digitized books and metadata, and can themselves provide or enable others to provide value-added services to access the digital books. Permission granted to the MBP is NON-exclusive.

Reading the case study of the National Academy Press's experience putting their books online free-to-read could facilitate understanding and appreciation of the benefits of this approach. The case study is available at: http://www.press.umich.edu/jep/04-04/pope.html (Journal of Electronic Publishing, Vol. 4, Issue 4, May 1999)

Participation of Presses

The National Academy Press has given us permission to digitize all of their books published prior to 1995. We are currently (July 2002) negotiating with MIT Press.

Accuracy in scanning

Carnegie Mellon has established a workflow (based on pilot ?100 book? and ?1000 book? projects) that includes steps to insure capture of high resolution images and essential metadata, post-processing to correct skewing and crop dark borders surrounding the page images, and OCRing to create searchable ASCII text with 98% accuracy.

Return of Documents after scanning

We expect/hope to return TIFF images to the publisher in about three months from the time permission is granted, but the time will depend on how long it takes us to locate copies of the books (after permission to digitize them is granted) and how many books are included in the group.

Print-On-Demand (POD) standards of Replica and Lightning Source

The MBP follows the standards and best practices supported in ?A Framework of Guidance for Building Good Digital Collections? developed by the Institute for Museum and Library Services in 2001 and endorsed by the Digital Library Federation in 2002. See:http://www.diglib.org/standards/imlsframe.htm, http://www.imls.gov/pubs/forumframework.htm

More specifically, our guidelines for data production (excerpted from the MBP NSF proposal and based on pilot projects) are:

* Bitonal images with a pixel depth of 1 bit-per-pixel scanned at a resolution of 600 dots per inch (DPI). Images will be stored as ?Intel? TIFF (Tagged Image File Format) files with the header content specified. The compression algorithm used is ITU (Formerly CCITT) Group 4.
* TIFF version 5.0 is acceptable. Subject to testing, version 6.0 (or later) may also be acceptable.
* The initial-capture system includes dynamic thresholding or a similar feature to capture variability of darkness in the imprint and possibly darker (e.g., foxed) backgrounds from decay. Images should be as readable as the original pages.
* Typical expected data will be provided for most TIFF tags (normally, the data supplied by software default settings). A specification for the TIFF header will be

produced to include scanner technical information, filename, and other data, but to be in no way a burden on the production service.

* Images will be written in sequential order, with corresponding 8.3 filenames, e.g., 00000001.tif as the first image in volume sequence and 00000341.tif as 341st image in volume sequence.
* Volumes provided to the MBP will be assigned unique identifiers that conform to 8.3 format. The images will be in directories named with the corresponding identifier (e.g., the volume identified as akf3435.001 will have a directory with the same name, and 00000001.tif through 0000000N.tif files within that directory).
* Images and directories (as specified above) will be written to gold CD-ROM according to agreed upon specifications and using ISO9660 format.
* Skew will be within a specified range of degrees allowed.

Compensation issues

No, neither the consortium nor participating publishers will have an administrative role in the MBP. Administrative responsibility for the MBP belongs to officials at participating universities.

At Indian Institute of Science, the administrative officials are:

Prof. N. Balakrishnan, Chairman, Division of Information Sciences

Determination of the pricing of value-added components of the MBP

The publishers or vendors who develop the value-added components will determine the pricing for the services they provide.

Collections

Books are available on the following subjects

* Engineering
* General
* Mathematics
* Sanskrit
* Science
* Classics
* Indian Institute of Science Collections
* Books From Other Centres
* Astro Physics and Astronomy
    * BioSciences
    * Bulletin of Material Science
    * Current Science
    * Indian Academy of Science - Section B
    * Journal of Chemical Science
    * Journal of Genetics
    * Journal of Earth and Planetary Science
    * Journal of Engineering Science Sadhana
    * Journal of Mathematical Science
    * Journal of Resonance
    * Proceeding of Indian Academy of Science
    * Pramana
    * Scientific Books

The Digital Library of India possesses many features that are common to the Universal Digital Library. Both are being actively supported by an eminent Indian scientist Dr. Raj Reddy, It is hoped that the Digital Library of India with its special characteristics of language processing as proposed will establish close links among the different geographical regions of the country having different languages apart from quenching the thirst of the knowledge seekers all over the world.

7
Networked Library Resources

The dramatic increase in information resources has revolutionized the use of resources in libraries. Libraries have previously functioned as repositories for collections, the collection is already moving well beyond the boundaries of library walls. The digitization of data sources and the production of electronic journals are precursors to new and rapidly developing forms of scholarly communication. Initiatives at scores of other academic institutions point the way to increased reliance on computers and networks for storage, access and manipulation of both primary and secondary sources of research.

Before the advent of the Internet, accessing the catalogues of other research institutions usually involved a trip to a library in another city. Technological advances in the organization and description of library materials have been translated into web-based products available to researchers throughout the world. Similarly, search tools have evolved for both stand-alone CD-ROM products and for direct access to network-accessible commercial information sources that index, abstract and, increasingly, provide access to full text.

A seamless transition between searching for and receiving the necessary information is not yet a reality. Information specialists are required to assess and select the best search tools (regardless of format) and to integrate these tools with local service. Instructing users to search using a wide range of tools is a formidable task during a time of transition. From developing computerized course packs in support of distance education to providing web guides for researchers, Information Resources staff will continue to devise and facilitate new forms of instruction to meet these challenges.

All disciplines are experiencing changes in scholarly communication in a variety of ways and at significantly different rates. Each discipline still relies on published journals for current awareness, but some disciplines have better access to electronic versions of both current and retrospective research materials than others. A few disciplines are creating resources that are not surrogates of paper products.

Effectively using electronic sources produced commercially or informally on the Internet has become a challenge for scholars. The library will provide guidance and instruction in the productive and effective use of these materials. For example, library staff will provide web-based guides, group instruction, or individual instruction.

As we enter the 21st century, libraries must continue to serve as intellectual and cultural centers for their communities by maintaining strong collections of books and periodicals. At the same time, they must also provide access to an expanding world of information and keep pace with changes in information technology. It is clear that libraries can and will play a critical role to meet the challenges of the future, but their ability to do so effectively will be determined by the a number of issues.

Libraries have undergone drastic changes in respect of their architecture, nature of holdings and also the services. All of them contribute to the change in the way of their functioning. It is not possible now for a single library to acquire or accommodate all the information resources being generated internationally, regionally or even in a given subject.

There is a sea change in respect of their holdings. Half a century ago, a well-funded academic, public, school, institutional or corporate library could reasonably expect to meet most of the needs of its users through a collection of materials housed within a single building. Since that time, the rapid growth in publishing and the accompanying dramatic increases in the variety and specialization of user needs have far outstripped the capacity of any library. During the last decade, however, library funding has failed to keep pace with these growing needs due to the combined effect of inflation and local budget cuts.

Now, libraries are well connected within their fore walls as well as with the outside world. They have responded to the crisis of increasing demands and limited resources through a greater reliance on regionalization, cooperation and networking. Two major initiatives in this area include the Regional Public Library Systems and the automated resource sharing networks, both of which provide libraries with expanded access to materials and information not available locally. However, the state supported regional library systems generally serve public libraries only, and while some of the automated resource sharing networks are multitype, they serve only one-tenth of all libraries in the Commonwealth. What is needed is a statewide structure to effectively link existing programs and extend the benefits of regionalization, cooperation, and networking to all libraries.

No single library can accumulate the information resources being generated internationally and even with a particular country. Now, individual libraries increasingly rely on cooperation and networking. It has become clear that libraries of all types need to work together much more closely if they are to meet all the information needs of users. Libraries are used more conveniently by varied type of users. They use public libraries as preschoolers, as students, as parents, as workers, and as lifelong learners. They use school and academic libraries as students, and institutional and corporate libraries as workers. If libraries are to meet the rapidly changing needs of residents in the future, they must have cooperative structures which allow them to connect users with the widest range of possible resources, regardless of which type of library provides this connection.

One library enters into contact with the other libraries on the basis of mutual understanding. Such a cooperation allows individual libraries to serve their users more effectively by offering them access to the resources of other libraries, but state support is required to make the full range of resources available to residents.

The Commonwealth has supported limited cooperation between public libraries since 1960's on a regional level, including some support for shared automated networks, and since 1970 has provided support for the maintenance of a research collection accessible to all residents. What is needed beyond these successful programs is an overall structure to promote cooperation and improved access to information among all libraries on a statewide basis.

State-supported programs for cooperation and networking among different types of libraries are currently in place in almost every other state, and are particularly well developed in states with technology-oriented economies. Without such a program, the Commonwealth is at a severe competitive disadvantage. While Massachusetts libraries hold a wealth of resources, access to many specialized resources of statewide importance is limited or nonexistent. A statewide structure for cooperation would make more of these specialized resources accessible through libraries to businesses and individuals who do not currently have ready access to them.

Currently, the quality and range of services offered by individual academic, public, school, institutional and corporate libraries varies from excellent to totally inadequate. Approximately one-fourth of all public libraries do not even meet minimum standards for library service, and many school libraries in the Commonwealth rank among the most poorly supported in the nation. Further serious inequities exist in the rural sections of the Commonwealth and in urban areas.

To help address these inequities, a commitment must be made by the Commonwealth, as it has already been made by most other states, to guarantee that every resident has a basic level of access to information.

A basic level of access to electronic information can be made available in every library throughout the Commonwealth at relatively low cost if provided on a statewide basis. Without this basic access, millions of residents will not have the information they need to achieve their personal and economic potential.

During the last two decades, advances in computer technology have stimulated dramatic growth in the number and variety of electronic information sources. As traditional printed catalogs are being replaced by computerized catalogs, many traditional reference sources and periodicals are being replaced by computerized databases. The impact of this growing world of electronic information is being felt in every library throughout the Commonwealth, along with strong growth in demand for electronic information services — a demand libraries are at present largely unable to meet.

Statewide access to computerized information requires an "information highway" which will link libraries and library users with online electronic information sources. Initiatives at the national level (the National Research and Education Network, or NREN) and the New England regional level provide the backbone telecommunications system (known collectively as the Internet) necessary for the provision of electronic information resources to libraries. However, a statewide network linking all libraries to these regional and national networks is essential in order to provide Massachusetts residents with the full range of electronic information resources. The current program of state support for telecommunications linkages among libraries currently reaches only 250 of the nearly 2800 libraries in the Commonwealth.

While new computer and telecommunications technologies offer exciting possibilities for students, businesses and researchers, the people of the Commonwealth cannot fully utilize these electronic information systems unless they are print, computer and information literate.

End users of these new electronic information systems will require considerable assistance and training. These users will also need knowledgeable librarians to assist them in locating information and learning new skills. User education must begin in public libraries with preschool children(when critical learning patterns are set) and continue through elementary and secondary school libraries. User education for adults must be provided through academic, institutional, corporate and public libraries. Given the rate of technological change, this training and assistance will need to be available on an ongoing basis.

Reduction in the number of print acquisitions has resulted in increasing reliance on the other documents containing information. Celluloid was once an effective medium for information, specially education and entertainment. The advent of video accelerated its use whereas the multimedia has overtaken it in about all the activities relating to the fulfillment of the information needs of the society.

Reference books are being published on the web for some years. Several hundred dictionaries are freely available. Many specialist encyclopedias and subject reference works have been converted to become experimental web services. This wave of reference publishing follows no concerted plan. There is no formal market for these services and perhaps there never was an expectation of profit. The early development of the web has been like this. Most of the notable achievements lacked a clear commercial motivation and this has led to the extraordinarily rich and varied choice that the web provides. But unfettered innovation has its downside. Although there are many good reference books on the web, the experimental and haphazard fashion in which they have been launched means that they are not as useful or as 'findable' as one might wish. The lack of system is particularly wasteful in the case of reference resources. The web could provide a more useful, reliable and consistent reference service.

A reference book is a book a reader will use while reading another book, a book that does not need to be read at a stretch. If we switch modes from the domain of bibliography and volumes printed on paper, a reference service on a network is liable to be needed throughout the network, its use will be episodic and somewhat unpredictable, but it is also liable to warrant centralized management. In network terms, reference works are resources most efficiently deployed on the server side. This is a pragmatic and behavioral definition but it is valuable in pointing us to the fact that reference works on the web need to be maintained and may need to be consulted from any context.

The commercial publishers see the potential of web delivery. Several of them have converted their most important reference works into web-based reference services, backed by professional promotion and customer support. There have already been some notable achievements: The Oxford English Dictionary, the Grove Dictionary of Art, and the large reference works published by the Gale Group are pioneers in this gradual mobilization of reference resources to the worldwide web. So far all the clear-cut commercial successes have been large books, which in their web implementation are offered to subscribers (mainly institutions with libraries) for an annual subscription. But most reference books are much too small, and individually of insufficient value to end-users, to warrant the investment and promotion needed to create a bespoke subscription service for web delivery.

The information is being published on the World Wide Web in greater quantity nowadays than in the print media for varied purposes and almost in all the disciplines of study. There are precedents for aggregating published reference works:

Infoplease and Bartleby are both examples of popular consumer-oriented web services pioneering a method of reference aggregation. But aggregation on its own may not be enough to create compelling user benefits. Aggregation becomes compelling when the user is able to use a web service to do things which cannot be done with the content in its traditional format: for example the best share price services offer powerful tools for charting share prices and customizing these charts. Nothing of the kind can be achieved with the traditional data distribution channels (wire service, teletext or ticker tape).

Network has become a very wide term now a days. It generally refers to the cooperative activity of man. There are as many networks in the society as are the fields of social activities. But the network we refer to here is about the coordination of the various information-providing agencies. Since the area we are dealing herewith relates to the education and research, we restrict to the networks in higher education only. Co-operation is a social activity as old as human civilization itself. The aim of any cooperation activity is to achieve what the members of the group cannot achieve individually. So library cooperation or network may be defined as a combined effort of two or more libraries to share their resources for providing better services to their user community.

Networking for sharing the library and information resources can be traced to 200BC when Alexandria Library shared its resources with Pergamon Library. According to Kraus, there existed library co-operation among monastery libraries in the 13th century. There were exchanges of agreements among the universities of Lund, Abo and Greifswald as early as 1740. The other examples of library cooperation include a projected union catalogue of the libraries ofWeimar and Jean and a proposal for a coordinated acquisition scheme for Walfenbuttel and Gottengen. The 'Catalogue of Manuscripts in various parts of India' complied by Whitney Stokes in 1868, and in 1863 Part I of Sanskrit manuscripts in private libraries of North-west provinces covering Varanasi was published. The first major union list entitled 'A Catalogue of Scientific and Technical Periodicals' was complied by Henry C. Bolton in 1885. With the advent of the 20th century, the Library of Congress started co-operative cataloguing projects and began working on the National Union Catalogue. Thereafter, in the 20th Century the compilations and publications of union catalogues of different types increased in number in most countries.

The first library cooperation activity in India is reported to be the Catalogue of Manuscripts complied by Whitney Stokes in 1868. Union catalogue development was one of major cooperative efforts in Indian libraries up to the 1960s. We can look at the following union catalogue development activities:

The 1960s also saw a large number of national seminars devoted to the concept of library cooperation. However, with the advent of computers in library work, a change occurred. It is reported that the first use of computer in library work for the production of the Union List of Serials in 1964 using the IBM/602 machine at INSDOC. Since then library automation has been a matter of primary importance in Indian Libraries. With the establishment of the National Informatics Center (NIC) in 1975 and the development of NICNET in 1977, networking and communication technology in India received a major boost. This as a whole had a major influence in resource sharing among various libraries and information centers through networks. The 1990s are said to be the golden period of library networking in India. There has been a plethora of publications and seminars on library networking during this period. Today besides INFLIBNET, there are various local library networks in India such as ADINET, BONET, BALNET, CALIBNET, DELNET, MALIBNET, MYLIBNET, and PUNENET etc.

The efforts made for library networking in the 20th century began with the compilation of union catalogues, as no co-operation could be effective without the knowledge of the resources of other libraries. The scope of co-operations soon took big leap. It became diversified and incorporated the various activities of the libraries such as Abstracting and Indexing, Acquisition, Bibliographic access, cataloguing, Circulations development, continuing education for staff and users, literature searching, management and accounting, microfilming, photo coping, processing, referral services, storage and union lists.

Resources sharing is sharing of library resources such as document collection, staff members, technical facilities and mechanical aids among the participating libraries on the basic principle of cooperation, "All for one and one for all". In this respect it is possible to consolidate the document collection of participating libraries, exchange their technical capabilities and share their services. In this way it is possible to share the resources to provide on access to the vast amount of library and information sources to a larger user community at the least-cost. The objective of resource sharing is obviously to make the greatest amount of best information available to the most users at the reasonable cost.

There has been a voluminous growth of published documents in the recent part. As a result no library in able to procure, process or store all documents that its users demand. According to Kent, it is difficult to anyone single library to acquire even one percent of the total document published in the world" due to one or more of the following reasons:

(i) Growth of Knowledge in different subjects

(ii) Rapid increase of literature and growth of publication

In the second half of the 20th century, the growth of new publication became unmanageable for traditional libraries. Its impact was felt primarily in major programs and later by the smaller libraries. In the field of Science and Technology alone about three million documents are published each year which includes articles, conference papers, books, technical reports and these the rate doubles every eight to ten years according to V.A. Kamath. There has been an alarming growth lately in journal articles.

Therefore some resource sharing is necessary between one library and another library to acquire more information in a specific subject with low cost as published records are increasing at on incredible rate and their prices are keeping pace, is such circumstances library cooperation will assume a pivotal role and resources sharing will become the focal point of cooperation.

Resource Sharing through Network

Earlier, the idea of resource sharing for a long time was restricted to the area of lending of books and periodicals now it has become diversified and incorporated the various activities of the libraries such as abstracting and indexing, acquisition, bibliographic access, Cataloging circulation, collection development continuing education for staff and user, literature searching management and accounting, microfilming photo coping, processing, referral services, storage and union lists. The resource sharing in modern times is helpful in the following four main activities.

The information on the web is growing and being updated every day. There are millions of web pages and there is a lot of great information. However, one of the most noticeable problems with the web today is the difficulty in finding a specific piece of information. Unlike a library, there is no central card catalog for the web and it follows no organizational standard. Instead, search tools are used to locate information on the web. For the most part, they are fast, easy to use and open 24 hours a day. A search tool performs searches of the Internet based upon input by the user. This input might include topics, keywords or phrases, or any other type of search criteria. Some of the difficulty in finding information is going away because the tools for locating information are maturing, becoming more powerful and sophisticated every day. Because of the enormous amount of information out there, search tools are indispensable.

There are numerous tools available for finding

information on the web, and each of these operates somewhat differently. Some of the tools use a comprehensive approach and try to include all of the information on the web. Other tools only cover a narrow subject matter, for example, there is a tool specific for finding conferences sponsored by the Microsoft Corporation. The results of your search will depend on the type of search tool you are using. Because there is such a wide range of tools available and we cannot cover each of them, this module will focus on two representative tools

The past few decades have witnessed knowledge and information explosion the world over and inadequate financial resources to do the best in terms of dissemination of knowledge and information. Under these circumstances, resource sharing and cooperative functioning of libraries and information centres through networking becomes vital. Efficient resource sharing can be achieved by using recent advances in Information Technology, i.e. networking of libraries and information centres through Local Area Networks, Metropolitan Area Networks, Wide Area Network and so on.

Network of information/Resource sharing is to use the computer and telecom link for transmission of information or data from one library to another. Keeping this concept in view, various library networks have been established for cooperation and resource sharing among libraries. They have grown mostly during the last thirty years in different geographical environments in order to cater to the specific needs of users. In the United States, there has been a proliferation of them. Library networks in other countries are also growing. Several models have emerged that provide specific services. Not all networks conform to the essential functions of library networks. However, it is noted that the essential functions should include:

* promotion of resource sharing,
* creation of resource sharing tools like bibliographic databases such as union lists of serials, union catalogue of books, periodicals, bibliographic databases of articles

and other types of materials such as CDs, Video recording, sound recording, theses, dissertations etc.,

* rationalization of acquisition,
* adoption of international standards for creation of records uniformly,
* delivery of documents, etc.

Economic pressures, growth of publications and emergence of subject specialization have compelled the libraries and information centres to think of sharing the information resources and optimizing the use of existing resources within India as well as from abroad through various networking systems. Some of the notable networks in India are NICNET, ERNET, SIRNET, INDONET and INET. In addition, there is a major initiative from the University Grants Commission called INFLIBNET, interconnecting universities, colleges and resource institutions countrywide.

National Level Resource Sharing

As stated earlier, INFLIBNET, a national level resource sharing of university libraries was set up in 1986 under Professor Yashpal, the Chairman of UGC, INFLIBNET is a multiple functions/service network with focus on resource sharing and cooperation through computer communication links. It is very useful to all libraries and their readers. For this purpose, it is possible to create data banks in different subject fields, produce a number of bibliographical tools and information services. It is also possible to conserve a lot of library resource avoiding duplication at the national level.

But under the present conditions, it is not congenial to initiate a network of libraries at the national level, because all universities in India depend on the finance from central and state governments. The various universities have their own district characteristics based on factors such as geographical, linguistic and political. Each university library is following its own pattern and procedure in its routine work. For this reason, there is no uniformity and standardization. However, such a networking can be initiated in a limited environment, regional or state level.

State Level Resource Sharing

In India, formation of a network of university libraries in all states is possible only if the concerned administrative and professional staff and supporting agency make a sincere attempt in this direction. They should plan to co-ordinate programmes of all universities in the state to form a uniform academic calendar. They have to establish a body like Council of Higher Education to initiate a network of libraries in the state say KAULIBNET (Karnataka State University Library Network) in the interest of larger academic community. They should bring all the affiliated colleges within the fold of state level library network and extend the services to colleges.

It is not difficult to bring uniformity and adopt a standard procedure in all participating libraries within the state. After achieving the success in running the network at the state level, it is possible to link all such state level networks to the national level network. Further, it will not be difficult to link university libraries network with specialized networks in the field of library and information in India, using sophisticated modern technology and satellite facilities.

City Level Resource Sharing

Specialized library networks have come up for individual cities like DELNET, CALIBNET, MALIBNET, PUNENET, BALNET, ADINET, BONET, MYLIBNET, etc. These networks are meant essentially for providing a centralized database of library information to be accessed by its user libraries, mostly in a particular city for the purpose of resource sharing.

In the present day of limited resources, it is imperative that an integrated view of these networks and National Information Systems and Centres on the possibility of sharing resources among them should be taken to explore avoiding duplication of efforts, materials and resources and maximizing the utilization as they form the base for successful networking. Access through any network in the globe can be obtained virtually through INTERNET which is widely used international network.

8
International Information Networks

1. ONLINE COMPUTER LIBRARY CENTER (OCLC)

Founded in 1967, OCLC is a nonprofit, membership, computer library service and research organization dedicated to the public purposes of furthering access to the world's information and reducing information costs. More than 45,000 libraries in 84 countries and territories around the world use OCLC services to locate, acquire, catalog, lend and preserve library materials.

OCLC's objectives are to:

Establish, maintain and operate a computerized library network and to promote the evolution of library use, of libraries themselves and of librarianship, and to provide processes and products for the benefit of library users and libraries, including such objectives as increasing availability of library resources to individual library patrons and reducing the rate-of-rise of library per-unit costs, all for the fundamental public purpose of furthering ease of access to and use of the ever-expanding body of worldwide scientific, literary and educational knowledge and information. It is a unique cooperative venture, giving your library access to a wide range of services and databases, including WorldCat. Together OCLC member libraries make up the world's largest consortium.

OCLC's first offices were in the Main Library on the campus of The Ohio State University (OSU), and its first computer room was housed in the OSU Research Center. It was from these academic roots that Frederick G. Kilgour,

OCLC's first president, oversaw the growth of OCLC from a regional computer system for 54 Ohio colleges into an international network.

In 1977, the Ohio members of OCLC adopted changes in the governance structure that enabled libraries outside Ohio to become members and participate in the election of the Board of Trustees; the Ohio College Library Center became OCLC, Inc. In 1981, the legal name of the corporation became OCLC Online Computer Library Center, Inc. Today, OCLC serves more than 45,000 libraries of all types in the U.S. and 84 countries and territories around the world.

Researchers, students, faculty, scholars, professional librarians and other information seekers use OCLC services to obtain bibliographic, abstract and full-text information when and where they need it. CLC and its member libraries cooperatively produce and maintain WorldCat—the OCLC Online Union Catalog. Membership in OCLC is a unique cooperative venture, giving your library access to a wide range of services and databases, including WorldCat. Together OCLC member libraries make up the world's largest consortium.

Products Services and eContent

OCLC offers full-service online cataloging, simple copy cataloging, MARC record collections, offline cataloging, customized OCLC cataloging from your materials vendor, automated copy cataloging for materials purchased and custom cataloging services. It also administers the Dewey Decimal Classification system, the most widely used library classification system in the world.

Collection Management

It offers collection development services to meet collection goals. Assess the strengths and gaps of collection with targeted analysis tools. Serve culturally diverse community with easy-to-order, shelf-ready collections of non-English materials.

Digital Collection and Preservation

OCLC's digitization, microfilm and archival services are designed to protect and share collections. Managees special collections, or turn to the skilled staff at our preservation centers.

EContent

Offers enhance your collections with eBooks from netLibrary, full-text electronic journals and a variety of online reference databases.

Reference

Through FirstSearch, OCLC offer online access to full-text documents, abstracts, indices and WorldCat, the world's most powerful bibliographic database. It is also a partner with the Library of Congress to provide a comprehensive virtual reference service.

1. Cataloguing and Metadata

Cataloguing and Metadata Services include Connexion CatExpress Dewey services Custom cataloging Batch processing PromptCat Cataloging partners program WorldCat Collection Sets GovDoc CJK Cataloging Arabic Cataloging CatME Z39.50 Cataloging Collection Management Digital Collection and Preservation eContent Reference Resource Sharing and ILL Services for Groups

Connexion

Integrated online cataloging

OCLC's flagship cataloging service. Connexion's flexible suite of tools aligns your bibliographic and authority record activities with WorldCat and the OCLC Authority File.

CatExpress

Simple copy cataloging. CatExpress is a Web-based tool for cataloging popular materials via an easy-to-learn interface, perfect for lower volumes and catalogers with less experience.

Dewey Services

Dewey Decimal Classification. The most widely used library classification system in the world. Order the new DDC22 print edition or subscribe to WebDewey, the online version that's continually updated.

Custom Cataloging

Comprehensive technical services. Improve access to materials and save library time, money and effort. Customized, expert solutions for your most difficult cataloging, conversion and authority control challenges.

Batch Processing

Records and holdings maintenance. Add, change or cancel large numbers of records or holdings—locally and in WorldCat—with a variety of offline options.

PromptCat

Automated copy cataloging. Save staff time and be ready to shelve materials faster. Materials ordered through participating material partners arrive with complete MARC records and your holdings set in WorldCat.

Cataloging Partners

Custom OCLC cataloging from material vendors. Receive high-quality, full MARC records for every title you order from participating vendors. Order materials and MARC records from one source, with one invoice, at a surprisingly low cost.

WorldCat Collection Sets

MARC record collections. Pre-packaged sets of full catalog records for microform, non-microform and electronic content purchased from vendors, ready to load into your local system.

GovDoc

Government document records. For federal depository institutions, delivery of up-to-date records for the government documents your library holds.

CJK Cataloging

Software for cataloging in Chinese, Japanese and Korean using vernacular characters. Ideal for libraries supporting Asian studies or communities.

Arabic Cataloging

Cataloging software for Arabic-language materials. This Windows-based application lets you catalog in basic and extended Arabic character sets.

CatME

Cataloging software. Create and edit new records and bibliographic information online or offline. Produce and update records in batch mode, and export records to local systems.

Z39.50 Cataloging Service

Z39.50 access to WorldCat. Search and retrieve MARC records from WorldCat using your Z39.50-compliant local system.

WorldCat

The power behind OCLC cataloging solutions is WorldCat, the authoritative source of cataloging records built by librarians.

Now available:

Connexion client version 1.10

Version 1.10 includes changes for set up options, editing records, a new macro recorder, and more. Learn more and download the client.

DDC 22

Dewey Decimal Classification 22 is now available in print (and online). One can order it at any time using the new Dewey Web Store. Learn more about the print version and the robust WebDewey online alternative.

The July 2003 edition of the OCLC Newsletter also offers a detailed look at DDC22; view the article online, or download the full issue (2.2MB PDF).

Watch WorldCat grow!

A new online counter lets you see the newest records added to WorldCat. The page, which refreshes every eight seconds, gives a glimpse at the variety of materials represented in WorldCat, the world's most comprehensive bibliographic database.

2. Collection Management

OCLC helps in analyzing collection to identify gaps and overlaps so that one can plan more effectively for the future and enhance collections with non-English materials or electronic resources.

Language Sets

Non-English collections. Preselected sets of non-English materials are delivered ready to shelve. It's a fast, affordable way to serve a multicultural community. Now available in 12 languages.

NetLibrary

Electronic books (eBooks). Full-text digital books, journals, newspapers and other published works in hundreds of subject areas. NetLibrary launched the eBook category and remains the worldwide leader.

Collection Analysis

Collection analysis and assessment. Coming in early 2005, the OCLC Collection Analysis service will provide libraries and library groups with WorldCat-based collection management tools accessed via the OCLC FirstSearch service.

Electronic Collections Online

Electronic journals. Easy Web access to thousands of full-text academic and professional journals from more than 70 publishers.

WorldCat

As your collection changes and grows, WorldCat evolves with it. Libraries use WorldCat, the world's most comprehensive bibliographic database, to analyze and augment their collections.

New Services

Six South Asian languages added to Language Sets

Serve your Indian, Pakistani and Bangladeshi communities with shelf-ready collections in six languages: Bengali, Gujarati, Hindi, Panjabi, Tamil and Urdu. Each set offers a mix of fiction and non-fiction titles for adults or children. Ordering Language Sets is easier than ever using the online store.

eBooks: 58,000 titles now available

NetLibrary, OCLC's eBook division, recent celebrated surpassing the 58,000-title milestone. Nearly 2,000 new eBook titles are added in one month, from some of the world's leading publishers. Learn more about NetLibrary eBooks.

3. Digital Collection and Preservation

Preserve and manage your digital collections with microfilming, digitizing and archiving services. Learn more about best practices and funding, and discover outsourcing opportunities that let you manage your digital collection's life cycle as successfully as you do your print collection.

CONTENTdm

Digital collection management for special collections. Build and manage a digital collection on your own with CONTENTdm, an affordable, scalable solution that's easy to use.

Olive

Digital collection management for newspapers. A solution for digitizing and managing historical newspapers that preserves cultural context while providing powerful indexing and searching.

Preservation Services

Custom, expert preservation. Let OCLC preserve a collection for you with film, digitization and other services performed by skilled teams with the newest technology.

Digital Archive

Storage, access and retrieval of digital assets. Capture Web pages and other digital-only assets and maintain them for tomorrow in the Digital Archive. You choose how information is harvested and how your users find it.

Education and Planning

Comprehensive front-end help. We understand the challenges of planning for and developing digital collections. From grant-writing assistance to technology training, OCLC is a resource center designed around your needs.

Why OCLC?

OCLC is uniquely qualified to assist. As a library technology leader, OCLC understands the challenges faced by community members when planning for and developing digital collections. The value and benefit of shared resources—through cataloging and now through digitization and archiving—drives everything we do.

WorldCat

WorldCat is the world's largest bibliographic database. It makes easy to catalog the digital assets in WorldCat, so libraries and users worldwide can benefit from such unique collection.

4. eContent

These Web-based digital resources occupy no shelf space, but offer patrons a wealth of full-text content. Choose from the world's largest collection of eBook titles and a suite of reference databases that connect users with thousands of abstracts, journal articles and more.

NetLibrary

Electronic books (eBooks). Full-text digital books, journals, newspapers and other published works in hundreds of subject areas. NetLibrary launched the eBook category and remains the worldwide leader.

Electronic Collections Online

Electronic journals. Easy Web access to thousands of full-text academic and professional journals from more than 70 publishers.

PAIS International

Public affairs database. An unparalleled resource for users who research public policy and world affairs. Accessible through FirstSearch, it covers politics, human rights, health, energy, science and many other topics.

OCLC Databases

In addition to the hundreds of third-party databases accessible through FirstSearch, a number of databases are owned and managed by OCLC—and many are included with the FirstSearch Base Package.

WorldCat

Records for nearly all OCLC eContent resources are included in WorldCat, the world's most comprehensive bibliographic database.

5. Reference

Reference services that tap dozens of leading databases and leverage your library's own assets more effectively. These online services help your users with accuracy, speed and convenience.

FirstSearch

Online reference. Powerful and highly customizable,

FirstSearch is a key reference tool for any library, and the most intuitive access available to the WorldCat bibliographic database. Your patrons will marvel at how quickly they locate the right resources.

QuestionPoint

Virtual reference. Add this Web-based tool to your library's Web site and give users access to quality online reference assistance at any time. QuestionPoint is brought to you by the Library of Congress and OCLC.

PAIS International

Public affairs database. An unparalleled resource for users who research public policy and world affairs. Accessible through FirstSearch, it covers politics, human rights, health, energy, science and many other topics.

OCLC Databases

In addition to the dozens of third-party databases accessible through FirstSearch, a number of databases are owned and managed by OCLC—and many are included with the FirstSearch Base Package.

WorldCat

The power behind FirstSearch is WorldCat, the most comprehensive bibliographic database anywhere.

6. Resource Sharing and ILL

Create, track and send integrated Interlibrary Loan requests via the Web to participating libraries and document suppliers. ILLiad, our management system, helps you streamline your resource sharing.

OCLC Interlibrary Loan

Resoource sharing solutions. Resources your users need for borrowing and lending. Regionally or globally, OCLC ILL lets you share your collection and offers convenient access to materials at thousands of participating libraries.

ILLiad

Interlibrary Loan management software. Reduce resource-sharing paperwork and let your users track their own loan requests with software that consolidates all ILL functions in one place.

Union List

Holdings for serials and more. Greatly improve users' access to serials and similar materials while lowering your borrowing costs. Union List gives you access to shared holdings information via more than 200 groups and other online resources.

WorldCat

Our Interlibrary Loan service is faciliated by WorldCat, the world's most comprehensive bibliographic database.

Services for Groups

With OCLC Services for Groups, your library consortium can have its own union catalog in WorldCat that offers a single, unified view of your collections. Eliminate duplicate spending. Gain maximum use of your most valuable materials by sharing resources. And do it economically. Using a unique modular approach, OCLC builds a custom solution based on search tools and infrastructure you've already put in place, so implementation is accelerated and the end result is completely familiar.

What's included and who can join

OCLC Services for Groups include a centralized union catalog, unlimited access to cataloging and resource sharing, plus a customized FirstSearch interface. OCLC hosts the solution while you maintain control over all operations. Every library in your group and subgroups—regardless of size, type or current OCLC membership status—can participate in the group catalog.

Group catalog is already started

Many library groups already have millions of holdings in WorldCat, so OCLC can get you set up with a union catalog quickly. Rollout is fast, because every library that uses WorldCat already has the necessary infrastructure in place. Your group will provide users ready access to all its resources, and will be taking full advantage of investments already made in other OCLC services—such as cataloging, resource sharing and reference.

The added benefit of WorldCat

When group's catalog has its foundation in WorldCat, the world's largest bibliographic database, your users get the advantage of high-quality indexing, access to their own libraries' holdings and to the holdings of libraries worldwide.

Encourages users to start searching locally

OCLC creates group catalog from holdings set in WorldCat, including only those resources held by the libraries in your group. Users can start with local resources first, then expand outward to regional, consortium-wide and worldwide listings in WorldCat. For circulation and item availability information, materials can link at the record level to the home catalogs of all participating libraries.

Your savings begin at once

One can start saving immediately, without having to finance new hardware, software or staff training. Hosted by OCLC, these group services continue to make good financial sense for the long term. When each member library has access to all the holdings within the group, user satisfaction increases and libraries will lower acquisition costs by increasing opportunities for resource sharing. And with unlimited access and subscription-based purchase, you can continue to expand your capabilities while managing your budget with predictable pricing.

2. CONSORTIUM OF UNIVERSITY RESEARCH LIBRARIES (CURL)

CURL was established in 1983 to promote co-operation between academic research libraries in Great Britain and Ireland. The rich holdings of the CURL libraries are represented by catalogue records of varying types and quality, and there is a need to take the manual records, which are limited to local use, and make them universally available through electronic databases. This process is known in the library world as retrospective conversion.

When the CURL Strategic Directions for 2000-2004 were published, there were 21 university libraries in full membership of the Consortium. By March 2002 the number of full members had risen to 25, including 22 university libraries, as well as the British Library, the National Library of Scotland and the National Library of Wales. The change in the three national libraries' status from associate to full member, together with the British Library's commitment to working in close collaboration with the HE sector, has greatly increased CURL' s potential for improving information resources and service provision for research and research-led learning and teaching across the British Isles.

Other factors have led to a significant change in the information and library environment since 2002. To name only a few, by July 2002, all UK CURL libraries had experienced close working collaboration with other CURL and non-CURL

libraries through participation in the highly successful UK-wide Research Support Libraries Programme (RSLP). 2002 was also the year when the Consortium actively participated in the debates generated by the Research Support Library Group

(RSLG), including the implications of the electronic media on the national research infrastructure. The expected resulting establishment of the Research Libraries Network represents a significant shift in the landscape for CURL.

Given the importance of these developments, both internal and external, CURL believes that, rather than wait until 2004, it must review its mission and strategic goals now. Within this updated framework, CURL can seize the opportunities created by this new environment and work towards enhancing library and information provision for the research community as a whole.

Mission

CURL's mission is to increase the ability of research libraries to share resources for the benefit of the local, national and international research community.

Vision

CURL will make a difference for researchers by helping to build the Distributed and Hybrid Research Library of the future. Researchers, wherever in the world and whatever their disciplines, will be able to:

* Search, locate and request all resources, whatever their format, easily and quickly from the desktop
* Have quick and easy access to an increasing amount of electronic resources, both born-digital and digitized
* Have physical access to manuscripts, archives or printed items that have not been digitized and cannot be moved, wherever these are held
* Have other printed items from outside their own institutions delivered to them efficiently

CURL is committed to:

* Provide strong leadership to find research-centred solutions to common problems
* Influence change and provide a seedbed for innovative projects and services
* Provide practical tools for finding information
* Engage its membership to improve support for researchers

- Foster synergies through strategic alliances and collaborative partnerships that will benefit research support in the UK, Ireland and worldwide
- Help to shape the wider debate at national and international levels

Databases

The Consortium of University Research Libraries (CURL) has established a database for bibliographic records. This record retrieval service offers UKMARC records at competitive rates. The database currently contains some 38 million records, and the number is growing constantly. The records include those from member libraries and also from LC (Roman script monograph records 1968- and CJK records) and from the BNB (1985-). As libraries progress their retrospective conversion programmes the number of records for older material and for non book material is increasing. The records are of good quality and CURL has established Bibliographic Standards for contributors and records are flagged to indicate standard.

The service is open to any non-profit organization. There is a flat-rate for searching and no other charges. A month's free trial is available if required. Access is subject to signing licence agreements.

Other Database links and projects

- MARC21 Project
- National Online Public-Access Catalogue (COPAC)
- CURL feasibility study of Z39.50 technology
- CURL Database Project: A Feasibility Study for a National Programme of Retrospective Conversion of Catalogue Records
- CURL Minimum Standards for Bibliographic Records
- National Union Catalogue Feasibility Study

MARC21 Project

In August 2002, CURL appointed Nicholas Syrotiuk to

be its MARC21 Officer. The MARC21 Officer is based in Manchester, working alongside the MIMAS COPAC team. The brief of the MARC21 Officer is to write the specification for the new database structures that will be put in place in July 2003 in order to effect the transition of the CURL Database to MARC21.

Test Database

With efforts at MIMAS, a MARC 21 database system consisting of data-handling programs, a database and a Z39.50 target was made open to testing by CURL cataloguers on 19 May 03. This test database has benefited from the work done by MIMAS on the inclusion of both MARC-8 and Unicode UTF-8 encoded records, which means that the database already enables the searching, retrieval and display of some non-Roman script. Testing came to an end on 20 June 03.

MIMAS has been invited to prepare a costed proposal, to be submitted first to the RD&D SG and then to the Board in the Autumn 03, that will concentrate on the development of a web interface and of a clustering system for the display of search results.

Meanwhile, some collaboration will be taking place between CURL and RLG. Durham, as the principal CURL user of the Eureka MARC export facility, has agreed to act as the tester of the new RLG interface and to share its finding with MIMAS by the end of 03, in line with RLG's own timeframe and testing. The point of the exercise is to find out to what extent the software developed by RLG can be adapted to the CURL MARC 21 database.

'Interim' Database

An interim version of the CURL database, containing MARC21 records, was released on 28 July 03. Given that it will be several months before the new CURL MARC 21 gets big enough to become useful, MARC 21 versions of recently loaded catalogues have been preserved in a form which is compatible with the existing CURL UKMARC database. It has now been made possible to release this 'Interim' version of the CURL database for access via Z39.50. (Telnet access will continue to be to the UKMARC database only).

At present the MARC21content is only from a small number of CURL libraries, though this will grow as we progress with the reloading schedule. The remainder is held in UKMARC.

Stage 2 of the MARC21 Project.

After the completion of the indexes for the new database, outlined in the original MARC21 specification, we enter stage 2 of the MARC21 project. MIMAS's proposal to develop a clustering mechanism for the new MARC21 database has now been approved by the CURL Board. From January 2004, MIMAS will be working on a new algorithm for delivery in June 2004. MIMAS has underlined its commitment to deliver a service modelled closely on the consultation with CURL staff in the autumn of 2002, especially with regard to defining a primary cluster member according to local priorities. MIMAS has also noted that the clustering mechanism would be compatible with Members' proprietary Z-clients.

Strategic aims

For the next three years CURL will pursue five main strategic aims:

National Strategies for Research Support

CURL will actively contribute to the development and implementation of appropriately funded national strategies aimed at coordinating the provision of research information and generating sustainable solutions to the information needs of the research communities. This objective will be at the heart of CURL's activity in a number of areas, including resource management and discovery, digitisation and scholarly communications. CURL will also seek to make a significant contribution to the success of the Research Libraries Network, the new body recommended by the Research Support Libraries Group.

Collaborative Resource Management

In the light of the widely recognised fact that no research library can cater for all the needs of its researchers, CURL will continue to explore, test and implement procedures enabling research information providers to engage in deep collaboration with one another in all areas of resource management. This will involve furthering the collection mapping agenda and developing strategies aimed at facilitating the sharing of responsibilities in the areas of acquisition, preservation, digitisation and retention, e.g. as initiated by the CURL-CoFoR project.

Resource Discovery

CURL will adopt a two-pronged strategy to further the development of electronic resource discovery tools in the light of recent and future technological developments.

It will (a) continue to enhance existing activities, such as the CURL record retrieval database and the COPAC resource discovery service, and to contribute to the development of the Archives Hub and the e-prints SHERPA project; (b) revisit the whole resource discovery landscape with a view to identifying innovative, inclusive and sustainable solutions, in particular, in terms of models (types of data, technology, quality control) and services. CURL will also actively contribute to other national initiatives, in particular, Full Disclosure.

Digital Content Creation and Curation

CURL will develop and implement a digitisation strategy aimed at facilitating digitisation and digital preservation work at institutional level within a coherent and coordinated national framework. In order to do this, it will identify what is already being done by other organisations and what needs to be done by CURL, on its own or in collaboration with other bodies, particularly in the areas of repositories for born-digital content, digitisation of library material, preservation and long-term access of digital content.

Communication & Working Methods

CURL will develop and implement a communication strategy and working methods within the Consortium aimed at providing a framework for greater engagement from the Members in order to increase consortial debate, networking and co-operation. It will also seek to provide a framework conducive to appropriate involvement across sectors and domains, as well as to the development of strategic alliances and collaborative partnerships with other stakeholders and sister organisations both in the UK, Ireland and worldwide.

CURL Projects and Services

Ongoing Projects

Archives Hub

The Archives Hub is a collaborative service which provides a single point of access to descriptions of archive collections held in universities and colleges throughout the United Kingdom. Over 60 institutions are contributing high-quality information to the Hub, which will cover over 20,000 archives by July 2003. The website is free to use and contains information relevant to a wide range of research areas. The service is funded by the Joint Information Systems Committee (JISC) and is overseen by CURL. MIMAS runs the service at the University of Manchester and development work on the Archives Hub software is undertaken by the Cheshire Development Team at the University of Liverpool.

Britain in Print

The Britain in Print project involves the participation of eight CURL libraries as well as that of the Edinburgh Royal College of Physicians and the Mitchell Library in Glasgow. All ten libraries have significant collections of pre-1700 British books which are not yet catalogued in electronic form and the aim of the project is to enhance electronic access to this wealth of heritage material for the benefit of the general public.

This work will also embrace the creation of a subject-based interpretative resource which will add value to the discovery information on COPAC by identifying key materials of importance to special interest groups, in particular school-age learners, local history groups, genealogical societies, life-long learners.

CURL-CoFoR

A CURL project to promote collaborative collection management. CoFoR (Collaboration For Research) is a new CURL initiative, set up to provide its members and other research libraries with practical tools (templates, guidelines and recommendations) for collaborative acquisition and retention. It will also give special attention to techniques for serial deduplication and to the mapping of relationships between research activity and library provision.

The 21-month project builds on work already carried out by the RSLP COCOREES project (Collaborative Collection Management for Russian and East European Studies) and by the CURL Task Force on Resource Management. The service offered by the COCOREES database, with its large set of collection descriptions and massive finding list for Russian and East European serials will be maintained.

Monograph Inter-lending Project

Project Brief

The purpose of this one-year project is to explore further and take forward the principal recommendation made in the report "Monograph Inter-lending for the Higher Education Research Community", which was jointly commissioned by CURL and the British Library in 2003.

The report recommends the adoption and implementation of a 'BLDSC Plus' option that would involve the British Library forming a consortium with a range of partner libraries willing to provide monograph inter-lending services to defined service standards and charges.

The project will aim:

(a) To scope the prior implementation phase for BLDSC Plus, as recommended by the Report, including making specific recommendations on the following issues: governance mechanisms; criteria and terms of conditions for participation in the scheme; specification of service levels; pricing and payment policy and mechanisms; IT specifications; future funding requirements; relationship of the service to the soon to be created Research Libraries Network (RLN).

(b) To discuss and agree the prior implementation scoping recommendations with:

* the key organisations involved, including the British Library, the other national libraries, CURL, the RLN and a sample of research librarians (including CURL librarians);
* with the wider information community via a broad cross-sectoral consultation exercise, with a view to gaining commitment to the new scheme from as broad a base as possible;

(c) To prepare an implementation plan for the agreed scheme, by making specific recommendations on the following: membership and terms of reference of the scheme's Management Board; identification of partner libraries; a detailed and timed work plan for implementation.

(d) To liaise closely with the CURL Resource Management Task Force on progress with implementation.

Access to CURL Libraries

The Libraries in *membership* of CURL (both full members and associate members) recognise their obligations as the major research libraries of the UK and Ireland in the support of research both at a national and international level.

Their combined holdings represent a major resource in the support of research.

The CURL member libraries are committed to:

* Making their holdings available (in the case of full members) through COPAC nationally and internationally
* Providing access to their collections to all *bona fide* researchers

Access is defined as:

Access to print collections, special collections and archives and other material for consultation purposes during normal library opening hours

* It may not include access to electronic material and computer networks where the conditions of site licences do not permit this

Some CURL libraries may offer services to external researchers on payment of a fee. Each member library of CURL will publish on its web site details of opening hours, a description of its special collections and archives, requirements for access (e.g. proof of identity) and details of any charged services.

Researchers intending to apply for access to a CURL library are urged to consult that library's web site before making a visit. Contact details and a summary of the requirements for access to each library can be found at

All of these libraries welcome visits by academic staff or graduate students from other universities who are undertaking research for which the collections in the library to be visited will be valuable. In some cases prior arrangement is necessary by writing or telephoning, in order that the host library staff may be able to notify you if there is any difficulty about access to the collection you require on the day of your visit. On arrival at the library you wish to visit, please indicate that you are a visitor from another CURL institution, showing any form of identification that the host library may require.

Further information about all of the libraries listed here (collections, opening hours, etc.) may be obtained on the World Wide Web. There are links to the pages of each library included below.

* University of Aberdeen Directorate of Information Systems & Services
* University of Birmingham Information Services
* University of Bristol Information Services
* British Library
* Cambridge University Library
* Durham University Library
* Edinburgh University Library
* Glasgow University Library
* Imperial College London Library
* John Rylands University Library of Manchester
* King's College London Information Services & Systems
* Leeds University Library
* University of Liverpool Library
* University of London Library
* Library of The London School of Economics and Political Science (LSE)
* National Library of Scotland
* National Library of Wales
* Newcastle University Library
* University of Nottingham Information Services
* University of Oxford Libraries
* School of Advanced Study
* The University of Sheffield Library

* University of Southampton Libraries
* Trinity College Library Dublin
* UCL (University College London) Library Services
* University of Warwick Library
* Wellcome Library for the History and Understanding of Medicine

3. LIBRARY INFORMATION NETWORKS (RLG) RESEARCH

RLG is an international, not-for-profit membership organization of over 150 universities, libraries, archives, historical societies and other institutions with collections for research and learning. Founded in 1974 by The New York Public Library and Columbia, Harvard, and Yale universities, RLG provides solutions to the challenges presented by information access and management in the digital era.

RLG is governed and run by its members, staff and board of directors. It is headquartered in Mountain View, California. It supports researchers and learners worldwide by expanding access to research materials held in libraries, archives, and museums.

RLG works with and for its member organizations enhancing their ability to provide research resources. RLG designs and delivers innovative information discovery services, organizes collaborative programs, and takes an active role in creating and promoting relevant standards and practices. As a result, RLG offers a variety of information resources useful to institutions and individuals.

Mission & Goals

RLG is a not-for-profit membership corporation of universities, archives, historical societies, museums, and other institutions devoted to improving access to information that supports research and learning.

RLG exists to support its members in containing costs,

improving local services, and contributing to the world's collective access to scholarly materials. The mechanisms applied in pursuit of these goals take many shapes but have one thing in common—cooperative action.

RLG has been working with research collections and their communities for nearly three decades. Work underway addresses three primary goals shared by RLG's international membership:

— The fullest online access to research resources
— Effective, global resource sharing on new models
— Enduring access to resources through digital preservation

Organization

In the early 1970s, three US universities and the New York Public Library created a new kind of practical resource-sharing consortium, which incorporated in 1975 as The Research Libraries Group, Inc. (RLG). Since then, RLG has grown to include virtually every type of cultural memory institution—universities, national libraries, archives, historical societies, museums—all with remarkable collections for research and learning. Given our increasingly comprehensive membership mix, we use "RLG" to identify the organization and our projects and products. RLG has offices in Mountain View, California, approximately seven miles south of Stanford University (where our data center is housed) and in New York City.

RLG staff, numbering approximately 90, are organized into the following departments:

— General Administration
— Member Programs and Initiatives
— Integrated Information Services
— (Technology) Development
— Customer and Operations Support

— Finance and Administration

Projects

How do institutions of research and learning provide online access to information about their collections, share the actual materials, and ensure access over the long term? RLG has been helping its international members solve these problems over the past three decades.

Projects by Goal

The three large and interlocking goals listed here have guided a wide range of current and past efforts. The lists they link to demonstrate that one project can advance more than one goal. Members and staff seek projects that are results-oriented and respond to shared institutional objectives.

* Expanded Online Access to Research Resources
* Global Resource Sharing
* Digital Preservation & Ensured Long-term Access

Expanded Online Access to Research Resources

Bringing information about materials for research and learning onto the Internet is both a primary RLG goal and a defining strength of the organization. This page indexes both current projects and past work to increase online access through new databases, enabling standards, and shared expertise. More results are demonstrated in Products & Services:

Global Resource Sharing

RLG was born from the will of major research institutions to share their collections with each other's scholars and students in new and cost-effective ways. In this arena, the SHARES partnership of RLG members has been the driving force for innovative protocols, technology, and partnerships.

Digital Preservation & Ensured Long-term Access

Guides & Tools

RLG projects have produced a number of guides and tools useful both to members and to the larger community. Additional printed reports and symposium proceedings, as well as resources like RLG DigiNews, are under Publications.

* Description Guidelines for RLG Cultural Materials
* Digital Preservation Needs and Requirements in RLG Member Institutions
* EAD Best Practice Guidelines
* EAD Conversion Service
* Guides to Quality in Visual Resource Imaging
* Guidelines for Microfilming to Support Digitization (pdf)
* Preparing Digital Surrogates for RLG Cultural Materials
* Preservation Metadata and the OAIS Information Model (pdf)
* Preserving Digital Information (pdf)
* Tools for Digital Imaging
* Trusted Digital Repositories—Attributes & Responsibilities (pdf)
* Trusted Digital Repositories—Draft (pdf)

Products & Services

RLG's complementary databases support access to research collections around the world. Its consortial partnership and Windows®-based software set the standard for cost-effective, peer-to-peer interlibrary loan. Any institution can take advantage of the wealth of online data available from RLG to meet local reference and cataloging needs. It also encourages to join in expanding these unique resources with contributions of an institution's records through file transfers or online record creation in RLG catalogs. Everyone is welcome and encouraged to make use of

RedLightGreen (redlightgreen.com), a free site that mines the RLG Union Catalog to give any Web user a better, faster research tool.

Free Use at Accredited Schools of Library & Information Science

There is a provision of free searches of a variety of RLG databases to ALA-accredited schools of library and information science in North America and to recognized schools on other continents. This access is limited to use for instructional purposes. As part of the special arrangement, OCLC does not charge for network connections.

This program includes:

* The AMICO Library™from RLG
* RLG Archival Resources
* RLG Cultural Materials
* English Short Title Catalogue
* Hand Press Book Database
* SCIPIO: Art and Rare Book Sales Catalogs
* RLG Union Catalog
* Authority Files (LC/NACO & LC/SACO)

Access is through RLG's Eureka® searching interface or the special digital objects interface used for The AMICO Library and RLG Cultural Materials.

With SCIPIO, the RLG Union Catalog, and the Authority Files one students can also use the RLIN21™searching interface. This enables them to locate and export records in MARC format for cataloging and other collection management activities.

To arrange free instructional access for faculty and students, determine which databases want to use in your courses and then contact the RLG Information Center. Short-term access to other RLG databases besides the ones listed here may also be arranged.

Online Databases

RLG'c Web-accessible databases contain a wealth of information and resources: Traditional library materials, including books, journals, music, and maps; indexes to archival collections; art and rare book auction catalogs; even digital images of works of art and cultural artifacts.

Which database for which kinds of research? Index to each database for features, sample records, and more:

* RLG Union Catalog
* The AMICO Library™from RLG
* Anthropological Index, Royal Anthropological Institute
* Anthropological Literature
* Anthropology Plus
* RLG Archival Resources
* Avery Index to Architectural Periodicals
* Bibliography of the History of Art
* Chicano Database
* RLG Cultural Materials
* English Short Title Catalogue (ESTC)
* FRANCIS
* Hand Press Book Database
* Handbook of Latin American Studies
* History of Science, Technology, and Medicine
* Index to Foreign Legal Periodicals
* Index to Hispanic Legislation (World Law Index, Part 1)
* Index to 19th-Century American Art Periodicals
* Inside Information Plus
* Russian Academy of Sciences Bibliographies
* SCIPIO: Art and Rare Book Sales Catalogs
* Authority Files

Resource Sharing & Interlending

Effective, global resource sharing is central to RLG's mission. For this, our members' SHARES partnership and RLG's cutting-edge, distributed ILL management software are essential.

SHARES

This program for a partnership of RLG members fosters expedited request and delivery, powerful supporting software, and ongoing improvements. SHARES participants save thousands of dollars annually in reduced lending charges and overhead.

ILL Manager

RLG's Windows®-based, state-of-the-art software eliminates dependence on multiple legacy systems for interlibrary loan, reduces operating costs, streamlines workflows, and empowers your library patrons.

Record creation

RLG's RLIN21™Windows®-based software enables to do record creation directly in the RLG Union Catalog—as well as in the SCIPIO database and the LC/NACO Authority File.**Record supply**

One can take advantage of the wealth of cataloging already done by RLG members and contributors as copy for its systems. We offer record supply through a Z39.50 connection that lets you use your own local system to search and retrieve records, or through its specially designed RLIN21 Web interface.

Marcadia® cataloging

Marcadia is a fully automated and customizable cataloging service that lets one set the highest standards for copy from the RLG Union Catalog.

* Creating Records in the RLG Union Catalog with
* Creating Records in the SCIPIO Database with RLIN21™

- Creating Records in the LC/NACO Authority File with RLIN21™
- Record Supply Through a Z39.50 Connection
- Record Supply Through the RLIN21™Web Interface
- Marcadia® Cataloging Service from Backstage Library Works

Freely Available Databases

The RLG Resources gives access to records of books, journal titles, manuscripts and archival material, music scores, maps, government publications, audiovisual material, art, and rare book auction catalogues and computer files. The material is contributed by over 200 research libraries, archives and museums, public and corporate libraries and learned societies. The RLG Resources include: - the RLG union catalogue for books (RLIN), artifacts and electronic material: Citation Resources (CitaDel), which includes a number of databases and covers mostly journal articles, but includes sales catalogues (SCIPIO) as well as the English Short Title Catalogue.

The RLG individual databases listed below do not require a password if you are accessing on campus or accessing via dial-up but DO need a password if accessing off-campus via an alternative ISP

Anthropology Plus: brings together into one resource the highly respected Anthropological Literature from Harvard University and Anthropological Index, Royal Anthropological Institute from the UK. Anthropology Plus provides extensive worldwide indexing of journal articles, reports, commentaries, edited works, and obituaries in the fields of social, cultural, physical, biological, and linguistic anthropology, ethnology, archaeology, folklore, material culture, and interdisciplinary studies. The index offers excellent coverage of all core periodicals in the field in addition to local and lesser-known journals. Coverage is from the late 19th century to the present

RLG's Archival Resources: provide centralized access

for searching and retrieval of archival finding aids that have been encoded using SGML [Standard General Markup Language] and the emerging standard for Encoded Archival Description (EAD). The finding aids are indexed centrally at RLG but are supported in a distributed environment. Some reside on a server at RLG, others are located on other servers around the world. Archival Resources also includes access to RLG's AMC (Archival and Mixed Collections) file. AMC provides researchers with timely and comprehensive access to brief, high-level information for nearly half a million collections of manuscripts and archives, and has greatly enhanced the dissemination of information about the holdings in repositories around the world.

Index to Periodical Literature: The only comprehensive American index to the current periodical literature of architecture and design. The Avery surveys more than 2000 US and foreign journals, 75 percent of which are not indexed in any other source. It covers not only the international scholarly and popular literature, but also the publications of professional associations, US state and regional periodicals, and major serial publications in the architecture and design of Europe, Asia, Latin America, and Australia.

Art History Bibliography: The most comprehensive and up-to-date art history bibliography available, this file covers European and American art from late antiquity to the present, indexing art-related books, conference proceedings, dissertations, exhibition and dealer's catalogs, and articles in more than 2,500 periodicals from 1973 to the present.

This file covers Mexican-American topics and the broader Latino experience of Puerto Ricans, Cuban Americans, and Central American immigrants; it indexes all types of materials including journal articles, books, and newspaper articles published from the 1960s to the present, with selective coverage dating back to the early 1900s.

Descriptions and holdings information for letterpress

materials printed in England or its dependencies (in any language) or in English (anywhere in the world) from 1473 to 1800.

Humanities & Social Sciences: An index to multilingual, multidisciplinary information in the humanities, social sciences, economics, religion, the history of art, and literature from 1984 to the present.

Scholarly evaluations of books, book chapters, articles, and conference papers in the field of Latin American studies published worldwide from 1990 to the present, indexed by the Hispanic Division, Library of Congress.

The definitive international bibliography for the history of science, technology, and medicine and its influence on culture from pre-history to the present. Journal articles, conference proceedings, books, book reviews, and dissertations from 1975 to the present are indexed in this file, which combines the Isis Current Bibliography of the History of Science, Current Bibliography in the History of Technology, the Bibliografia Italiana di Storia della Scienza and the Welcome Library for the History and Understanding of Medicine.

The only online index to art periodicals that were published in the United States during the 19th century. Since entire journal contents are indexed — articles, art notes, illustrations, stories, poems, and advertisements — the index is a valuable source of information on popular culture and industry, as well as artists and illustrators, painting, sculpture, drawing, photography, architecture and design, exhibitions and sales, decoration, and collecting.

This file cites and abstracts books, manuscripts, dissertations, and articles from more than 19,000 periodicals covering Slavic studies and social sciences published primarily in Russia, the republics of the former Soviet Union and countries in Eastern Europe from 1986 to the present. Records are provided by INION: the Institute of Scientific Information on Social Sciences, Russian Academy of Sciences.

RLG Cultural Materials: is a collaborative effort from RLG member institutions, bringing together primary source materials in high-quality digital form. It contains maps, photographs, objects, documents, art, sound, and motion. Archives, libraries, and museums from around the world are making their treasured collections available through RLG Cultural Materials. The content reflects the richness of the human experience through time, high-quality digital versions of ancient maps, medieval manuscripts, handwritten letters, drawings, paintings, sound recordings, books, and moving images? from prestigious memory institutions. Bringing these exceptional materials together encourages new kinds of multidisciplinary research. This database has separate password

The RLG Serials File: is a comprehensive database of primarily textual material such as journals, magazines, periodicals, newspapers, monographic series, some conference proceedings, annuals, yearbooks, annual reports, looseleaf, and electronic journals. Some formats and materials issued serially such as maps and computer files may be included.

9
Indian Information Networks

1. INFORMATION AND LIBRARY NETWORK (INFLIBNET)

Information and Library Network (INFLIBNET) is regarded as a landmark in the information scenario of higher education. It is the brainchild of Prof. Yashpal, an eminent scientist and the former Chairman of the University Grants Commission. Incepted in the year 1988, INFLIBNET became operational in 1991 and got the status of an autonomous body in 1996.

INFLIBNET is now an Inter-University Centre of the University Grants Commission (UGC) of India. It is a major National Programme initiated by the UGC with its Head Quarters at Gujarat University Campus, Ahmedabad. Initially started as a project under the IUCAA, INFLIBNET is involved in modernizing university libraries in India and connecting them as well as information centres in the country through a nation-wide high speed data network using the state-of-art technologies for the optimum utilization of information. INFLIBNET is set out to be a major player in promoting scholarly communication among academicians and researchers in India.

OBJECTIVES OF INFLIBNET

The objectives of INFLIBNET as envisaged in Memorandum of Association are:

* To promote and establish communication facilities to improve capability in information transfer and access,

that provide support to scholarship, learning, research and academic pursuit through cooperation and involvement of agencies concerned.

* **To establish INFLIBNET :** Information and Library Network a computer communication network for linking libraries and information centres in universities, deemed to be universities, colleges, UGC information centres, institutions of national importance and R&D institutions, etc. avoiding duplication of efforts.

FUNCTIONS OF INFLIBNET

In order to fulfill the broad objectives, INFLIBNET will:

* Promote and implement computerization of operations and services in the libraries and information centres of the country, following a uniform standard.
* Evolve standards and uniform guidelines in techniques, methods, procedures, computer hardware and software, services and promote their adoption in actual practice by all libraries, in order to facilitate pooling, sharing and exchange of information towards optimal use of resources and facilities.
* Evolve a national network interconnecting various libraries and information centres in the country and to improve capability in information handling and service.
* Provide reliable access to document collection of libraries by creating on-line union catalogue of serials, theses/dissertations, books, monographs and non-book materials (manuscripts, audio-visuals, computer data, multimedia, etc.) in various libraries in India.
* Provide access to bibliographic information sources with citations, abstracts etc. through indigenously created databases of the Sectoral Information Centres of NISSAT, UGC Information Centres, City Networks and such others and by establishing gateways for on-line accessing of national and international databases held

by national and international information networks and centres respectively.

* Develop new methods and techniques for archival of valuable information available as manuscripts and information documents in different Indian Languages, in the form of digital images using high density storage media.
* Optimize information resource utilization through shared cataloguing, inter-library loan service, catalogue production, collection development and thus avoiding duplication in acquisition to the extent possible.
* Enable the users dispersed all over the country, irrespective of location and distance, to have access to information regarding serials, theses/dissertations, books, monographs and non-book materials by locating the sources wherefrom available and to obtain it through the facilities of INFLIBNET and union catalogue of documents.
* Create databases of projects, institutions, specialists, etc. for providing on-line information service.
* Encourage co-operation among libraries, documentation centres and information centres in the country, so that the resources can be pooled for the benefit of helping the weaker resource centres by stronger ones.
* Train and develop human resources in the field of computerized library operations and networking to establish, manage and sustain INFLIBNET.
* Facilitate academic communication amongst scientists, engineers, social scientists, academics, faculties, researchers and students through electronic mail, file transfer, computer/audio/video conferencing, etc.
* Undertake system design and studies in the field of communications, computer networking, information handling and data management.

* Establish appropriate control and monitoring system for the communication network and organize maintenance.
* Collaborate with institutions, libraries, information centres and other organizations in India and abroad in the field relevant to the objectives of the Centre.
* Create and promote R&D and other facilities and technical positions for realizing the objectives of the Centre.
* Generate revenue by providing consultancies and information services.
* Do all other such things as may be necessary, incidental or conducive to the attainment of all or any of the above objectives.

ACTIVITIES OF INFLIBNET

DATABASE DEVELOPMENT AND MANAGEMENT

* Provide reliable access to document collection of libraries i.e. Union Catalogues etc.
* Provide access to world wide bibliographical information.
* To maintain consistency and quality in databases created by the participating libraries
* Evolve standards, uniform guidelines, methods, and procedures, both for data capturing as well as Hardware and Software.

Major Activities

Development, managing and updating of Union databases is one of the major activities of this group. Eight databases have been developed and are continuously growing. Following is the list of databases:

* Books - Represents holding of participant libraries under the programme

* Theses - Doctoral theses submitted to various Indian universities till date
* Serial Holdings - Holdings information of various university libraries about the serial
* Current Serials - Currently subscribed journals by the universities
* Secondary Serials/CD-ROMs
* DDC Serials - Currently subscribed journals by the six universities identified as DDC
* Experts - Useful data about specialists in various disciplines
* Research Projects - Information about ongoing projects
* NISSAT Project - Experts Database (Science & Technology)

Group also proposes to create and develop other databases of national importance viz.

* Patents
* Manuscripts
* Technical Reports
* Non-Books Materials

Standards and Formats required for creation of Databases

1. Guidelines for Data Capturing a user manual

To maintain consistency and quality in databases prepared by the libraries and INFLIBNET, INFLIBNET Centre had constituted a taskforce consistency experts in this area. This taskforce has brought out a 100 pages documents entitled GUIDELINES FOR DATA CAPTURING : A USER MANUAL. This documents is prepared based on Common Communication Format (CCF), 1992 edition and same has been given participating libraries for adoption. Taskforce also studies other standard required for this activity and according recommended that the following may also be used

1. Anglo American Catalogue Rules. Edition 2nd revised
2. Library of Congress Subject Heading

2. SOUL Guidelines for Data Capturing: A user manual for books

This is designed to be a handy manual to create records in SOUL. The user guide lists all bibliographical elements covered in the SOUL, with complete description of each field and subfields. It also provides guidelines as per AACR - 2 as to how to render the information in each field and subfield with examples.

Creation and Maintenance of Authority File

INFLIBNET is suggesting libraries to use Library of Congress Subject Headings as LCSH as a standard for providing subject headings, INFLIBNET is going create and maintain the authority files of names and subject headings in the machine readable form and it will be linked with the Union Catalog and Library Automation S/w SOUL developed by INFLIBNET.

A few more standards required for the participating libraries and INFLIBNET Centre are being developed.

Infrastructure

Well equipped laboratory with latest Pentium/RISC computers running on different operating systems like DOS, Windows 95/2000

Development tools: CDS/ISIS Ver. 3.08 (DOS version)

RDBMS: Databases were loaded on Microsoft SQL Servers on SYBASE Adaptive server.

DATABASE RESEARCH AND DEVELOPMENT

Creation of union databases of books, serials, theses etc has been one of the major objectives of INFLIBNET and the Database Research and development group has been setup to address the problems involved in the development, maintenance, updating of these union databases.

Development of software tools for converting data from one format to another, effective retrieval and managing the databases are the major areas of work undertaken by this group. Future planned activities include research and development of retrieval software for multilingual, multimedia and full text databases. Distribution of databases through the medium of CDROM is also going to become a thrust area for database research and development group.

Major Activities

* Database design, analysis and technical support.
* Assisting participating libraries in database development.
* Development of utilities for database creation, conversion and maintenance in different formats like CCF and MARC 21 etc.
* Development of retrieval software for CD-ROM based bibliographic Databases.
* Development of Utility tools for Retrospective conversion of union catalogues.
* Development of software tools for Multilingual Database of union catalogues.
* Administration (routine jobs like backup, tuning and implementation of security policies etc) of Union Database servers in the Centre.

Future areas of research and development

Further research and development in the areas of

* Retrieval software for CDROM databases
* Retrieval software for multilingual databases
* Retrieval software for textual and non textual databases
* Software for effectively managing union database systems
* Retrieval software for union databases

* Software for automatic backup, performance tuning
* Algorithms for effective searching and sorting and compressing data.

Infrastructure

Well-equipped lab with latest Pentium/RISC computers running different operating systems like Windows 95/98/2000/XP, LINUX, HP UNIX.

Development tools: Microsoft Visual studio, SDK.

RDBMS: Microsoft ACCESS, Microsoft SQLSERVER 7.0/2000, ORACLE 8i/9i, SYBASE Adaptive Server.

3. LIBRARY AUTOMATION

The automation of university libraries is a pre-requisite for networking and resource sharing. INFLIBNET Centre, through UGC, has been providing the required support to universities in phases.

Till 1999-2000, 123 universities have been given initial grant of Rs. 6.5 lakhs each to develop infrastructure for automation. By the end of IXth plan period, rest of the universities will also be included. After installation of the systems, further financial support is provided for the first five years to take care of recurring expenditure.

These Libraries on receipt of initial grant sign a Memorandum of Understanding with INFLIBNET. An integrated software for the automation of in-house functions called SOUL has been developed. It has been well received by the University Libraries. SOUL has been installed at 15 Libraries. Many more libraries have shown desire to procure and install SOUL.

Currently libraries funded under the programme are advised to subscribe to one of the following networks, depending on the availability in the respective locations:

* ERNET
* VSNL

* NICNET
* Other ISPs

Wide Area Network

It is planned to setup a Wide Area Network "UGCNET" linking more than 170 universities and other academic institutes in the country.

Local Area Network

INFLIBNET Centre has suggested all the funded universities to set up LANs using HUB/SWITCH and CAT V cables within their libraries for successful installation of SOUL software. Since SOUL is based on client/server architecture, It is essential that the server and all other nodes be connected by LAN.

INFLIBNET Centre desires that each university should establish a LAN in it's campus linking all the departments including library. This LAN in turn will be connected to the WAN.

E- EDUCATION

E-Education Group is concerned with the R & D and keeps abreast with latest technological changes in the area of computer technology. This group was established sometime in August 2001 and is responsible to implement Web-Based Training (WBT) to technocrats and Professionals. Various e-learning training courses will be launched with the help of HRD group of the Centre. This group will provide the necessary tools and technologies to deliver the e-learning courses.

This group is promoting R & D activities in area of e-learning. One of the major objective of this group is to collaborate with Universities/colleges for setting / managing e-learning lab for various training/e- courses. Consultancy is provided for starting the e-learning activities and also to selecting the H/W, Software combinations etc. Guidelines and suggestions for effective and optimized use, administration, maintenance and timely starting the Web-Based Training are also can be obtained from the Group.

Major Activities

* The Group is concerned with all the technical and non-technical issues related to e-learning in general and Web Based Training in particular.
* Plan, evaluate, implementation, review of e-learning policies, models, soft wares and technology.
* Setting up e-learning Lab at INFLIBNET premises. Development of retrieval software for CD-ROM based bibliographic Databases.
* Exploring various options regarding e-learning.
* Preparation of analysis, and minimum critical resources.
* Development of various disaster scenarios and formulation of a framework for the plan coverage.
* Assessment, preparation and recommendation of system requirements for e-learning set up.
* Analysis of proposals from Techno-major (e-learning vendors) and recommendations for selection of the solution.
* Discussions with technocrats on technical and feasibility issues.
* Planning, preparation and recommendations for e-learning preparation work and infrastructure for the set up.
* Preparation of road map for e-learning activities for the coming next few years.
* Further area of research and development
* Implementing e-Learning at all levels at INFLIBNET.
* Collaboration with subject-matter-expert from colleges/universities for contents to be made available free to academic communities from content sever at INFLIBNET
* Setting up and starting e-learning software R & D facility equipped with state-of-the art technology at the centre.

* Providing consultancy and Guidance to the R & D Institutions/ universities / colleges wishing to work with INFLIBNET.
* Design and Development of e-learning Model.
* Knowledge Management techniques and sharing, manage knowledge with other national organizations.
* Exploring technology to implementing Digital Library (DL) and Knowledge Management (KM).

HUMAN RESOURCE DEVELOPMENT

To enhance the skills of University Library staff for implementation of INFLIBNET Programme, following training courses are conducted.

One month Training Programme

This is mainly meant for operational staff of libraries. They are given exhaustive training on application of computers to library and information services. Eighteen such programmes were held covering most of the universities, and around 350 persons have been trained.

On-site Training

Staff from INFLIBNET Centre visited 31 universities, and conducted training for the library staff members for a week initiating automation process.

ILMS Training

Ten Librarians from different universities spent a week at INFLIBNET to solve their problems in using ILMS.

SOUL Training

Soul was installed at 66 Libraries and onsite training of one week to the library staff was provided at each site.

CALIBER

It is an annual convention held every year in collaboration with a university in different region on a theme related to library automation. Nine such conventions have been held so far.

Works Resource Sharing through Network

Workshops

Six workshops for senior level staff viz, University Librarians and Deputy Librarians were conducted.

NETWORKING OF UNIVERSITY LIBRARIES

PRESENT NETWORKING ENVIRONMENT

Currently libraries funded under the programme are advised to subscribe to one of the following networks, depending on the availability in the respective locations:

* ERNET
* VSNL
* NICNET
* Other ISPs

Wide Area Network

It is planned to setup a Wide Area Network "UGCNET" linking more than 170 universities and other academic institutes in the country.

Local Area Network

INFLIBNET Centre has suggested all the funded universities to set up LANs using HUB/SWITCH and CAT V cables within their libraries for successful installation of SOUL software. Since SOUL is based on client/server architecture, It is essential that the server and all other nodes be connected by LAN.

INFLIBNET Centre desires that each university should establish a LAN in it's campus linking all the departments including library. This LAN in turn will be connected to the WAN.

Library Management Software:

For the automation of in-house functions of participating university libraries, INFLIBNET Centre has developed a user friendly state of the art GUI based software named ' SOUL' Software for University Libraries. This is based on Client/Server Architecture. It uses an robust RDBMS as back end tool. This works on Windows and Windows NT environment with a number of new features.

LIBRARY SOFTWARE MANAGEMENT

Utility Software:

Following utility software developed at the Centre are available to the universities on request.

* To search the data from union databases (OPAC).
* Catalogue card generation.
* Duplicate checking of records.
* Customized software for Books, Theses, Serials.
* Data Conversion from Dbase, Foxpro and text file to ISO-2709 format.

Major objective of this group is to develop software for Library automation and other supporting tools for library automation. This group is also involved in supporting all other activities of the center by providing adequate software help time to time. The mission of this group is to provide technological support to all activities of the center with software developments using latest technologies and available development tools.

Major Activities

Development, managing and updating of Union databases is one of the major activities of this group. Eight databases have been developed and are continuously growing. Following is the list of databases:

* Development of SOUL

* Incorporation of Various Bibliographic standards in SOUL
* Constant Update of Current version based on user requirements
* Trouble Shooting and Customer support for SOUL users

Future Plans

* Development of fully web based library management system
* Incorporation of Multilingual Interface (To be developed by Database R & D Group) in SOUL
* Incorporation of Data Conversion Utilities (To be developed by Database R & D Group) for conversion of Various Bibliographic format including MARC and CCF in to SOUL
* Development of MARC 21 based database creation tool.

Infrastructure

Working Platforms of this group:

Operating Systems

Windows 95,Windows 98,Windows NT 4.0, Windows 2000

RDBMS

MSSQL Server 6.5,MS SQL Server 7.0, MS SQL Server 2000, Sybase 11.5,Oracle 9i

Development Tools

PowerBuilder 6.0, Microsoft Visual Studio 6.0,Microsoft Visual Studio. Net (beta), Oracle Internet developer suite.

WEB DEVELOPMENT

Organization of vast information present on the Centre's website and making the website a resource gateway and a knowledge hub, to the user community is one of the main objectives of the INFLIBNET Centre. The web development group setup in promoting the access to the information in the field of research and academic pursuit by using latest web technologies is working towards in implementing this objective. The major areas of work undertaken by this group are to select, organize and present the quality resources of the Centre in a meaningful way that will be useful for the user community.

Major Activities

* INFLIBNET Site design and updating.
* Promoting the website of the centre and provide a complete tracking reports of users accessing the website.
* Maintenance of various web services running at the site.
* Identifying the Hardware, Software requirements in improving the Centre's Infrastructure with the latest available technologies.
* To install and provide support for the available software at the Centre and advice the participating libraries with regard to hardware and software requirement.
* Bringing out SOUL software CD's for all the versions i.e. SOUL network version, SOUL Standalone version & SOUL Demo version.

Future areas of development

Setting up an Intranet for managing the internal information of the Centre.

Infrastructure

Well equipped with Pentium-IV systems running windows 98/2000 and Linux operating systems. The web server is hosted on a Pentium-IV system and is likely to switch over to a rack-mount machine. There is one CD writer to burn the SOUL software CD's.

This group has been created for promoting R & D activities in area of Networking and Quality management. Major responsibility of this group is to manage, maintain and timely update the campus wide Network. One of the major objective of this group is to coordinate with UGC-NETWORK, the proposed wide area network connecting all academic institutions under University Grants Commission for setting/ managing data centre for various databases of INFLIBNET, Indian universities, Information Centres. This group is working progressively for implementing Total Quality Control (TQC) for in-house developed software. Training /workshop in the area of network management, security design and state-of-the-art technologies for library professionals across the country is being initiated by the group. Consultancy work in the area of networking, network security of universities/ colleges library is also going to become thrust area of this group.

Major Activities

* LAN/WAN Setup and maintenance at INFLIBNET.
* Assisting Universities/colleges for Campus LAN.
* Design network security policy.
* Network Traffic management.
* Network resources allocation to the other groups.
* System administration, configuration and tuning.
* Database administration and tuning.
* Disaster recovery plan for e-resources.
* System maintenance at Centre.
* Testing and Quality control of software developed at the centre.
* Guidelines, suggestions and standards to all development groups for maintaining quality.

Future areas of research and development

Further research and development in the areas of

* Upgrading Local Area Network (LAN) with FC backbone, Layer-2, Layer-3 switches.
* Collaboration with UGC-NETWORK for setting / managing data centre for various databases of

INFLIBNET, Indian universities and Information Centers.

* Setting up network R & D and quality control Lab. equipped with state-of-the-art technology at the Centre.
* Offering consultancy service to the universities / colleges for computer sing the libraries including H/W, Local Area Network (LAN).
* Designing the Network security and disaster recovery plan for data servers.
* Knowledge sharing with different national and international organization.
* Promoting Linux operating system in universities.
* Insuring implementation of different standards for software development and management.
* Software testing using advanced software available in the market.

Infrastructure

Well-equipped server lab. with P3 and P4 Servers running on Windows NT / 2000 Advance Server. Separate mail server is running on Linux. Network is protected by firewall running on Linux. Centre has 128 kbps-leased lines Internet connectivity. Currently LAN at Centre is based on Radio Modem, CISCO 2610 router, hubs. New high End RISC server is being added to the existing infrastructure.

2. INFONET

Indian Universities constitute one of the largest higher education systems in the world. With 325 universities/ institutions, 15000 affiliated colleges, 100.00 lakh students and 4.27 lakh teachers; it is a great challenge to ensure effective coordination and communication.

Fast changing curricula and frequent introducing of new subjects impose a great demand on the system in general. Indian Universities need to be given the required thrust to entire the third millennium with a leading edge.

Technology is a driving force in the contemporary education systems. University Grant Commission has launched an ambitious programme to bring about a qualitative change in the academic infrastructure, especially for higher education. Under this initiative UGC is modernizing the University Campuses with State-of-the-art campus wide networks and setting up its own nationwide communication network named UGC-Infonet.

ERNET India, scientific society under the Ministry of Communications and Information Technology, in partnership with the University Grants Commission is setting up UGC-Infonet. Under this programme it is proposed to use information and communication Technology (ICT) and Internet to transform learning environment from a mono-dimensional one to a multi-dimensional one. UGC-Infonet will be a boon to the higher education systems in several ways:

* UGC-Infonet will become a vehicle for distance learning to facilitate spread of quality education all over the country.
* UGC-Infonet will be a tool to distribute education material and journals to the remotest of areas.
* UGC-Infonet will be a resource for researchers and scholars for tapping the most up-to-date information.
* UGC-Infonet will form a medium for collaboration among teachers and students, not only within the country but also all over the world.
* UGC-Infonet will be an Intranet for University Automation.
* UGC-Infonet will encompass entire University Systems for most efficient utilization of precious network resources.
* UGC-Infonet will establish a channel for Globalization of Education and facilitate the universities in marketing their services and developments.

Intranet for Universities

Availability of Reliable and Stable network infrastructure will facilitate increased usage of computers in the University Campuses. Campus Management will be more efficient and student friendly. Interlinking of the universities will expand the reach of students and faculty to other universities providing them with better avenues for wider horizontal growth.

UGC-Infonet will establish a seamless link between the UGC and the universities. This will help to provide a more accurate and up-to-date picture of the Universities, while at the same time it will enable universities to have timely information about the various schemes of the UGC. Consequently, this will bring a qualitative change in the UGC-Universities interaction. The huge and multifaceted Indian Education Systems would achieve greatest efficiency through e-governance of UGC.

Technology Partnership

Information Technology is evolving at a rapid pace worldwide to cater to the need for providing information in any form, at any anywhere. The trend is to set up networks, which are device independent, thus enabling flexibility of access, and also meet the requirements arising out of codependence technologies. Regular technology inputs would be required to upgrade the network infrastructure to ensure delivery of upcoming applications and contents to the education and research community in the country. UGC and ERNET have come together to meet the challengers that may face the education community with respect to real time information.

Implementation Methodology

The UGC-Infonet will be overlaid on ERNET Infrastructure in a manner so as to provide assured quality of service and optimal utilization of bandwidth resources. The network will be run and managed by ERNET India. The project will be funded by UGC with 100% capital investment and up to 90% of recurring costs. Towards this end, a MoU has been signed between UGC and ERNET India for implementation of UGC-Infonet and also for long-term technology partnership. A joint technical and tariff committee, consisting of leading experts in the country has also been setup to guide and monitor the design, implementation and operations of UGC-Infonet. INFLIBNET, an autonomous IUC of the UGC, would be the nodal agency for coordination of the UGC-Infonet and facilitate linkage between ERNET and the Universities. In the long run, each University will become a hub for the colleges affiliated to it.

Network Architecture

UGC Infonet is based on open IP platform, employing state-of-the-art technologies like IP or TV, enabling on-line response to queries. Open system architecture will ensure support for current and future applications. Users from educational Institutions would enjoy high data rates while accessing Intranet and Internet resources.

Main features of the UGC-Infonet are:

* Scaleable Architecture to grow from Universities to affiliated Colleges
* Nation-wide Terrestrial Backbone using Fiber Optic links
* Integrated Satellite WAN supporting broadband and SCPC VSAT technology
* Comprehensive Network Management Systems for overall monitoring of the network, down to each and every device.
* Linkage with other Academic and Research Networks all over the world.
* Data security and virus protection using firewalls and Intrusion Detection Systems
* Dedicated Data Center for Web hosting, e-Journals and Mail Boxes.

* Mirror sites spread all over the country for content hosting.
* Broadband Multimedia and Video Channels for Distance Learning

Data Center

A data center with large server capacity is being set up for the UGC-Infonet., Content of common interest will be maintained at this data center. Each University will have the option of hosting their website and the journals subscribed through University Consortia.

The data center will be:

* dedicated for the UGC-Info Net
* comprising of Email, Web, News and Proxy Servers
* protected with firewalls and IDS
* co-located with Satellite Hub
* within single hop access to the Universities over VSAT
* hosting a Portal on Higher Education in India

Electronic Subscription of Journals

With globalization of education and competitive research, demand for journals has increased over the years. Due to insufficient funds, libraries have been force to cut subscriptions of journals.

UGC has turned towards the Internet to cover the gap between demand and supply by way of e-journals that can be subscribed online. Most of the journals are available in electronic form.

UGC is also exploring the possibilities of alliances with publishers for adapting a consortia-based approach for e-subscription of journals. These journals will be available over UGC-Infonet to all the universities. Much of the new research publications are also available on the net as free ware, thereby, making quality information accessible to a wider academic scholar base spread across the country at an affordable price.

Connectivity Options for the Universities

UGC-Infonet is overlaid on ERNET Infrastructure including a nation wide terrestrial backbone and a complimentary satellite Wide Area Network (WAN). As such ERNET can provide a complete range of connectivity options to the universities depending upon their location and bandwidth requirements. Since terrestrial media offers greater scalability and performance, efforts will be made to connect the universities on terrestrial media. Alternately a Satellite connection will be provided through VSAT.

Digital Leased Lines

In the localities where telecom network is well developed, dedicated leased lines will be hired from basic telecom service providers. Such links are primarily for 64 Kbps and 2 Mbps speeds. Since fiber optic connections facilitate better connectivity, efforts will be made to bring the fiber links as near to the universities as possible. Most of the universities have the potential to become hubs of communication for affiliated colleges. Therefore, basic service providers will be locating their terminal within the university premises.

The universities, located within 30 kms of the ERNET PoPs, will be provided with dedicated radio links operating from 64 Kbps to 2 Mbps speeds. These links require line of sight clearance between the network node and the concerned university. Radio links are very reliable and their operational cost includes only maintenance of the equipment and Radio Link a nominal license fee.

Satellite based Wide Area Network

ERNET operates a Satellite based Wide Are Network (SATWAN) using C-Band transponder on INSAT-3C. SATWAN hub, located at Bangalore, supports Broadband VSATs with up to 45 Mbps shared bandwidth and Single Channel Per Carrier (SCPC) VSATs capable of providing up to 2 Mbps dedicated bandwidth.

Broadband VSAT

Most of the remote universities will be served using BroadbandVSATs. TheseVSATs operate in a shared bandwidth mode for optimal utilization of the precious satellite resources. Since Internet traffic is asymmetric in nature BroadbandVSATs are optimized to receive high bandwidth (shared beam of up to 45 Mbps) and relatively smaller capacity for outgoing traffic (shared channel of up to 307 Kbps) from a University.

SCPC VSATs

Single channel Per Carrier (SCPC) VSATs will be used for establishing dedicated tow-way channels of 64 Kbps to 2 Mbps from Hub. SCPC VSATs are ideal for those universities which are located in remote areas but wish top host their own internet server for providing access to their information through internet all over the world.

Campus LANs at Universities

Infrastructure at the University campus is also critical to take full advantage of the UGC-Infonet. Campus LAN technology is evolving rapidly and many universities may not have the expertise to setup the most modern and cost effective LANs. ERNET India has participated with many institutions in the planning and implementation of their campus computing facilities. The expertise generated thus will be extended to the Universities so that every university can have a state of the art infrastructure.

Network Access Center

For maximum benefits of UGC-Infonet, Universities should preferably set up a campus wide network and ensure uniform access all over the campus. Wherever campus LAN is not in place, it is suggested that the university sets up a network access center, which is open to all students at the university. This will work on lines similar to the terminal in traditional computer centers.

Network-Trained Manpower

Trained manpower is one of the most critical resources for successful implementation of high-tech programmes like UGC-Infonet. ERNET India has setup a modern training laboratory to train network system managers and users of UGC-Infonet. Technical staff from each of the participating universities will be trained to take maximum advantage of the infrastructure.

University Grants Commission

The University Grants Commission (UGC) is a statutory organization established by an act of Parliament. This is a national body for the coordination, determination and maintenance of standards of University education. The UGC serves as a vital link between the Union and State Governments and the institutions of higher training. In addition to its role of giving grants to universities and colleges, the UGC also advises Central and State Governments on the measures necessary for the improvement of university education. It also frames regulations on various issues like the minimum standards of instruction and minimum qualifications of teachers, on the advice of subject specialists and academicians with whom it frequently interacts in connection with the formulation, monitoring, and evaluation of programmes.

294 Universities/institutions in the country are directly under the preview of UGC. The universities are uniformly spread all over the country from metropolitan cities to very remote areas.

Implementation and operation of UGC-Infonet will be coordinated by INFLIBENT, an autonomous Inter-University Center of the University Grants Commission of India. INFLIBENT is providing a variety of services to the academic community of the country and is helping libraries in their automation efforts. About 142 University libraries are on the way to computerization.

3. Developing Library Network (DELNET)

Delnet started as a network of libraries in Delhi in 1988 and was named as Delhi Library Network. It is the first operational library network in India. It was initiated as a project of the India International Centre with the financial and technical assistance by National Information System for Science and Technology (NISSAT), Department of Scientific and Industrial Research, Govt. of India. It was registered as a society in June 1992 under the Societies Registration Act of 1860 and is currently being promoted by the National Informatics Centre (NIC), Planning Commission, Govt. of India and India International Centre, New Delhi.

Delhi is growing as a major centre of information resources in India. These resources cater both to the specialized and the general users. They are located in activities, information and documentation centres, institutional libraries, research libraries, government libraries, public libraries, department libraries besides the libraries of the universities, colleges and schools.

During the recent years, increase in information has led to increase in the demands of the users. It has been noticed that in this area of information explosion, libraries in India are generally ill-equipped to handle and retrieve information effectively, the financial resources and the space requirement for housing library collection are limited in almost all of the libraries. No a single library can afford to house every necessary document even in the area of its interest. Resource sharing, thus assumes great importance at this juncture the option left with the forward looking librarians has been to promote the sharing of resources by automation and networking. With this objective, in January 1988, the India International Centre initiated efforts for the establishment of Delhi Library Network (Now Developing Library Network).

The following are DELNET's main objectives:

* to promote sharing of resources among the libraries by

developing a network of libraries, by collecting, storing and disseminating information and by offering computerized services to the users.

* to offer guidance to the member libraries on cataloguing database services, circulation, acquisition, serials control, online services, selection of hardware and software, etc.
* to coordinate efforts for suitable collection development and reduce unnecessary duplication wherever possible.
* to establish a referral centre, to monitor and/or facilitate catalogue search and maintain a central online union catalogue of books, serials, and non-book materials of all the participating libraries.
* to facilitate and promote delivery of documents manually and mechanically.
* to develop specialist bibliographic database of books, serials and non-book materials.
* to develop a database of projects, specialists and institutions.
* to possess and maintain electronic and mechanical equipment for fast communication of information and delivery of electronic mail.
* to coordinate with other regional, national and international networks for exchange of information and documents.
* To undertake facilitate and provide for the publication of newsletters/journals devoted to networking and sharing of resources.

Membership

At present, DELNET has Two Hundred and Forty Three libraries as its members, including both institutional and associate-institutional members: in India 235 and outside India 8.

Fees Details: Following are the fees details for its members

Admission Fee : Rs.5,000

Institutional membership : Rs.7500/- per year (For libraries with 10,000 or more book collection)

Associate institutional membership : Rs.10,000/- per year (For libraries with less than 10,000 books)

Overseas Institutions : Admission fee : US $100/-

Annual Membership fee : US $500/-

The membership is progressively increasing and includes universities, diplomatic missions, college, government department, institutions and public libraries. Some institutions from far off places like Shimla, Bhopal, Punjab, Andhra Pradesh, Lucknow and Pondicherry in India have also joined DELNET as members. DELNET's membership has increased from 103 in Feb'99 to 243 to date (August, 2001).

DELNET Activities/Services

(I) Promotion of Database Creation

For effective networking, standard bibliographic data should be available in machine readable form with the libraries. So, efforts were made from the very beginning to promote the standardization of databases in the DELNET libraries. Experts were sent to the libraries to solves day-to-day problems. A panel of experts was seeing maintained for this purpose. Regular meetings of the librarians and computer specialists were organized to discuss mutual problems and the areas of cooperation. Nevertheless, there have been some libraries in Delhi that took keen interest in database creation on their own. But the practice of regular meetings for database creation and resource sharing continue. DELNET provides technical assistance to member libraries in the following areas:

* creation and maintenance of bibliographic databases
* serials controls
* user services

* hardware and software requirements
* union catalogue preparation
* current awareness and SDI services
* authority data compilation
* subject profiles construction
* abstracting services
* inter-library loan and user services
* document transfer/copying facilities
* access to local, national and international databases

II. Resource Sharing

DELNET saved foreign exchange worth Rs. 10 million by rationalizing subscriptions to foreign periodicals during 1991, 1992 and 1993 through resource sharing. This was mainly achieved in the fields of physical science, medical science and agricultural sciences. It is hoped that in the years to come, DELNET would be able to save more foreign exchange for India through sharing of periodical resources. In 1991, a courier service was started on contract basis will a private agency for inter library lending among the participating libraries but it was not very effective. Later, DELNET has introduced its own courier service with the financial help of NIC. The service is well used.

III. Standardization

A standardization committee of DELNET has been meeting from time to time. The standardization committee takes into account the following areas:

* Communication format for interchanging bibliographic data
* Input output format
* Bibliographic description: Mandatory and optional data elements
* Classification scheme and subject headings

* Thesaurus
* Authority files
* Language scripts into roman script
* Forms of heading
* Identification numbers, codes and abbreviations
* Data input for abstracting and indexing
* Search/command language

It was noticed that colon classification, universal Decimal classification and Dewey Decimal classification were mostly used in Indian libraries and therefore, it would be almost impossible to impose a standard classification scheme on all libraries. It was decided to use Dewey Class Number. As searching by class numbers was done by very few librarians, it was decided that the participating libraries could search by the classification numbers or they could pass on such requests to DELNET central office for necessary action. With regard to the standardization of subject headings and to usage DELNET recommends the use of LCSM. Specialized libraries may use additional thesauri that are available in each major discipline such as social sciences, humanities and science and technology.

IV. Online databases:

DELNET has around twenty databases available online for its users. These are:

* Union Catalogue of Books : UCF
* Union Catalogue of Books : MARC Format
* Union List of Current Periodicals
* Union Catalogue of Periodicals
* Database of Periodic Articles
* Indian Specialists Database
* CD-ROM database
* Union list of Video recordings
* Union List of Sound Recordings

* Union List of Newspapers
* Union List of Serials of Management Libraries
* Union Catalogue of Hindi Books
* Multilingual Books : Sample database
* Urdu Manuscripts Database
* Database of Theses and Dissertations
* DEVINSA Database
* Serials : Petroleum and Natural Gas
* Books in-Print Database
* Jain Database
* Directory of Libraries

The Other Services

ILL Online

DELNET members can place their inter-library loan requests through our ILL online facility, which is available on the union catalogue of books database. The member requests appear on the main server, which are monitored by DELNET staff at regular intervals and the books are acquired and supplied to the requesting library through the courier. Photocopying charges for journal articles etc. and courier charges for sending books to member libraries outside Delhi are extra.

DEL-LISTSERV

DELNET has created a Listserv service called DEL-LISTSERV to provide the current awareness service to users and allow the member libraries to receive the latest daily information from the INTERNET automatically in the form of electronic mail. The following listservs have been created and are available online through DELNET:

* **Net-happenings** – This Listserv appraises the users about the latest new sites along with their web addresses on the INTERNET and has proved to be a major source of information for the users on the INTERNET.

* **Med-clips** – This medical clippings listing discusses the various topics of medical interest like AIDI, cancer, etc. and is informative in nature.
* **IFLA** – This Listserv allows the users to get the latest information from the International Federation of Library Associations and Institutions, which includes the issues of concern to library and information professionals.
* **LIBJOBS** – Through this Listserv, the library professionals are able to find out daily, the jobs/ vacancies available throughout the world.

Book : New Arrivals

This is a new service through internet giving a list of recent publications in all subjects. The service covers education, management and physical sciences. Other subjects can be introduced on demand.

Book Reviews from INTERNET

This is an INTERNET service of reviews of latest published books covering different subjects. The service covers in the field of Arts and Music, INTERNET and military history. From time to time, other subjects will come into this fold.

Current Contents

This service gives the current contents of the latest issues of journals. It is particularly useful for rationalization of periodicals and resources sharing in member libraries.

Index to Hindu

DELNET has started offering Index to Hindu online to its members. Indexed news items are available on the system covering different periods of the Chennai edition. More updates and archival data is being added into the system regularly.

Retro-Conversion

DELNET offers retro conversion facilities to the libraries through specialized agencies and also facilitates the use of modern tools such as CO-ROM's and online facilities for retro-conversion.

Referral Services

DELNET maintains a referral centre that provides reference facilities to participating libraries. The referral centre also looks after the access to the central databases and monitors access to international databases.

Document Transfer/Copy facilities

DELNET provides the facility for transferring or copying of the documents to its users.

Training Programmes

DELNET conducts training programmes in the use of DELNET services, software, E-mail, AACR II and LC subject headings, Internet, etc. from time to time. Information about future training programmes is available on request.

Lectures and Workshops

DELNET organizes lectures by networking specialists working in different parts of the world. The lectures are open to members, specialists and users in general. DELNET also organizes national workshops, seminars and meets on library networking from time to time. DELNET had organized National Annual convention on Library and Information Networking (NACLIN) in 1998 & 1999.

Newsletter

DELNET publishes a newsletter in order to spread the message and increase the awareness about library networking in India. Through this Newsletter, DELNET communicates to its members the progress, it is making in various fields. The Newsletter is also a forum for communication on the advances, achievements and needs of the libraries and their services.

VI. INTERNET

* Electronic Mail

DELNET provides RENNIC Email facility to its member libraries, which is introduced by National Informatics Centre. This gives them access to both national and international E-mail users and also to INTERNET users. DELNET Email reaches the libraries, institutions and individuals in India as well as abroad having E-mail connection. Email is being used not only for communication between institutions but also for inter-library-loan requests.

Subscription rates for E-mails are as follows:

RENNIC of NIC: Rs. 2750/- per year for 5 MB data transfer

* Full INTERNET (TCP/IP) connectivity

DELNET is providing full INTERNET SLIP/PPP dial up access at a concessional rate of Rs. 8,500/- per annum for Rs. 500 hours of connect time through NIC to the member libraries. Also the shell account facility for INTERNET access is available for Rs.4,000 per annum for 500 hrs of connect time. A number of DELNET member libraries are already availing these facilities. These rates are subject to change by NIC.

* Web Page

DELNET has a web page (http://www.delnet.nic.in/) on INTERNET . This enables all INTERNET users the world over to know about DELNET and its activities. The web page also includes a list of Member-libraries along with their E-mail addresses. The Web page is being updated from time to time.

VII. Products

* DELSIS

A major breakthrough has been achieved by DELNET with the launch of DELSIS, a powerful library networking software. DELSIS (DELNET System for Information Services) is an integrated modular system, which supports DELNET online databases.

It has been developed by DELNET on a Relational Database management System called BASIC plus, a product of Information Dimension Inc. of USA, which has been provided to DELNET courtesy National Informatics Centre, New Delhi. It handles not only the Online Public Access Catalogue (OPAC) but also has the administrative tools for building up the union catalogues on BASISplus. It provides powerful and extensive facilities for online enquiries for books, serials, biographical details about the specialists and supports the cataloguing of books in Indian languages.

Features of DELSIS:

- DELSIS is a user friendly menu driven package
- Its versatile options allow the users to retrieve the information quickly.
- It contains the modules for Online Public Access Catalogue as well as the modules for the creation of databases e.g. addition, deletion, inserting of records etc.
- The Online Public Access Catalogue (OPAC) components of DELSIS can meet the needs of the users, irrespective of whether the user has little computer experience or is familiar with using computers to perform various library tasks.

* **DEL-WINDOWS**

DELNET has released the DEL-WINDOWS version 1.0 after the successful creation and implementation of DELSIS Unix version. It is an efficient tool for creating and retrieving bibliographic databases and catalogues.

DEL-WINDOWS can convert the simple PC into a powerful management information system. Some of the **salient features** are:

- It is simple and easy to use. The novice library professionals and end users can interact with the software without any prior training.

- It is user-friendly with adequate windows-menus for data inputting and search capabilities.
- It provides the option for creating the bibliographic records either using ECF or the MARC format.

* **DELSEARCH**

DELNET has opened a new chapter in the information retrieval procedure by devising a new database access mechanism through DELSEARCH. It is an off-line remote database access system through E-mail. It is the first of its kind and is the most economical and user-friendly remote database access system. It helps institutions, information specialists, research scholars, librarians and users interested in bibliographies and tutorial information on South Asia. It allows them to search the DELNET union catalogues through E-mail and is a great tool for research scholars. The software is developed on UNIX platform and allows the users to send their search requests through E-mail. As soon as the query is received by the system in the form of an E-mail, the respective databases are searched for the query word and the results are returned to the addressee immediately. The searching of the database does not require any human intervention and the searches are done by the system automatically.

The Future of DELNET

The future of DELNET is very promising. Its membership with India and outside India is going to take a quantum jump. The DELNET databases are growing in number and size and as a variety of information on South Asia is becoming available through DELNET, it is expected that all institutions outside India specializing in South Asian studies to take DELNET membership. DELNET databases are going to be accessible through INTERNET which will made accessibility very fast. INTERNET users in India are increasing and it will increase DELNET presence in different parts of India. DELNET has already created software, viz. DELDOS and DEL-WINDOWS for creating MARC records.

These software will so on be developed to perform library operations as well. There developments are likely to give more revenue to DELNET and provide justification for more and more libraries to join DELNET. As a resource, it is hoped the DELNET will grow faster as a service based resource sharing model in India.

4. Calcutta Library Network (CALIBNET)

It was the first library network visualized and started by NISSAT. At a meeting in 1986 in Calcutta, DSIR initiated action for preparation of a feasibility study for networking about 40 libraries in Calcutta. CALIBNET now is a society under West Bengal Societies Registration Act 1961 and responsible for Calcutta Library Network, a project sponsored and supported by NISSAT. NISSAT also contributed to the development of MAITRAYEE software package based on INGRESS 5.2 for CALIBNET. This package was developed through CMC Ltd. And given to CALIBNET. So far, no data has been created in machine readable from using MAITRAYEE. At present, CALIBNET has become a centre for CD-ROM databases.

Objectives

CALIBNET has made significant studies towards fulfilling its dual objectives:

* Launching its library network programs, facilitating remote online access to the holding data of Calcutta libraries and other specialized databases as well – a significant step towards bibliographic resource sharing amongst Calcutta libraries; and
* Providing electronic access to globally available information, imbibing its information centre approach.

Both are essential for advanced learning and scholarship. In the process, CALIBNET aims at covering a wide panorama of information end-user interests, with diffusion of new electronic information technology as the primary concern.

Software Developed and Library Network Launched:

Intense in-house research and development efforts have now achieved the Library Network capability by three significant studies:

* A multi-user storage and retrieval software 'SANJUKTA' to support CALIBNET's centralized Database (CDB) and to provide online access to its from remote locations.
* A conversion software package 'PARAPAR' to support interchange of bibliographic data between USMARC, UNIMARC and CCF files and also from non-standard formats to standard ones.
* Evaluation of a centralized Database (CDB) of holdings data of Calcutta libraries, and specialized databases as well.

These apart, CALIBNET'S pioneering study and research led to its publication of the "Guidelines for Implementation of UNIMARC in Indian Libraries". This will be an invaluable aid for the national database development programme under consideration, that favors adoption of UNIMARC format.

With the support of SANJUKTA, the centralized database hosted on CALIBNET server and located at the Network Service Centre, can be accessed and searched online by any one from a remote location, provided one is equipped with a computer, a telephone, a modem and a password from CALIBNET. The efficacy of SANJUKTA has been tested by successful remote logging of the CALIBNET server at Jadavpur, hosting the CDB from a workshop venue at Great Eastern Hotel, Calcutta. Online access to the locational information of bibliographic resources via the CDB and sharing up such resources amongst the libraries of this metropolis is now a reality.

The capability of PARAPAR was established through exercises and tests on sample records furnished by a major library in New Delhi and conducted in-house at Calcutta at their instance and eventually demonstrated at a workshop-cum-meeting in New Delhi.

The Centralized Database

Since library network capability has been established, the most crucial and indispensable activity is to develop the basic resource – the Centralized Database (CDB), that constitute the very backbone of any library network – by inputting the holding data of Calcutta libraries. The centralized database, launched only recently, currently held around 30,000 record covering:-

- conference documents held by Calcutta and contiguous libraries.
- social science management and economics, behavioral sciences, quantitative methods, computer science, etc. including predominantly journals held by management libraries in South Asia libraries of Indian Statistical Institute and the Indian Institute of management, Calcutta and
- Index to contents of serials published by Asiatic Society in previous two centuries.

Library Network

The Centralized Database (CDB) is the bedrock of CALIBNET and its development essentially calls for a cooperative movement, whereby each library par rakes in the movement by contributing its own holdings data to be incorporated in the CDB and thereby enrich it. The CDB needs to be now augmented by inputting holdings data of as many libraries as possible and getting the data continuously updated. Optimum coverage of libraries, which alone will progressively transform the CDB into a truly resourceful online searchable central pool of Calcutta's bibliographic holding data, is now on with the cooperation of libraries.

The participating libraries

The responses from institutional libraries are very encouraging. The libraries of following institutions have extended co-operation by way of furnishing their respective machine-readable database and current journal subscription lists:

1. Calcutta University
2. Jadavpur University
3. Indian Statistical Institute
4. Indian Institute of Management
5. Central Research Institute for Jute and Allied Fibres
6. Anthropological Survey of India
7. Botanical Survey of India
8. Geological Survey of India
9. Zoological Survey of India
10. Bengal Engineering College (a deemed university)
11. National Atlas and Thematic Mapping Organization
12. Bose Institute
13. University College of Medicine (Calcutta University)

These are being now inputted into the CDB. In coming years, holding data of many more libraries are expected to go into the CDB. Priority is being accorded to holding data relating to current journals subscribed and new additions from January 1, 1999.

Electronic Access to Global Information

In addition with its library network programme, CALIBNET has added to itself under to information centre approach, a new dimension that of a purveyor of global information, a phenomenon that now pervades international information market.

With online access to Internet and in-house CD-ROM resources, CALIBNET can explore a wide spectrum of the knowledge base and cooperate and professional enterprises, and meet the information requirements of researchers, academics and other scholars, professional and any other practitioners engaged in a wide gamut of subject interest.

CALIBNET

Services Activities

(i) On-demand Information services

CALIBNET has several attractive information packages:

* **Confile Service** – CALIBNET's Confile service reaches at one's desk contents of any journal of one's choice out of over 20,000 high-impact journals. Libraries can now prune their journal subscription list or even forego subscribing to new ones, when budgetary constraints so demand, and still get expressed to their contents from ConFile. ConFile helps libraries in economizing on journal subscription and reducing the drain on precious foreign exchange resources.
* **Caliborder** – On demand, caliborder offers the requisite back-up service by way of delivery of full text of any article and even patents.
* **ConAlert** – Through ConAlert service CALIBNET gives current and tailored bibliographic information. One can leave with CALIBNET just keywords defining his subject interest and get at regular intervals, the current information related to his interest at his desk.
* **RetroFile** – This service offers latest status and trend of research on any specific topic.

ConFile, ConAlert and RetroFile, in combination, offers the latest information and advances in the entire spectrum of the subject interest.

(ii) CALIBLINK

A special feature of CALIBNET is the Caliblink, a email connectivity (from its ERNET hub) installed and working fine at four institutions.

(iii) Institutional Resources Development Services

Some of the key institutional resources development services offered are:

(a) Retrospective conversion of existing card catalogue in libraries into computerized local databases via electronic mode by down loading from international databases;

(b) Consultative services on LIS automation

(c) Manpower development for operating and manning automated LIS environment through a wide range of graded training programmes, and customized courses for individuals or group at client's site.

(iv) SANJUKTA & PARAPAR Software

SANJUKTA

A multi-user storage and retrieval software has been developed in-house to support CALIBNET's Centralized Database and to provide online access from remote locations. SANJUKTA has been designed and implemented by A Mukhopadhyay, Technical Consultant, CALIBNET and his associates based on MOD+, a software he developed earlier to support management of small/medium-size libraries. The software has been developed, using 4 GL Code and designed to provide the user with options and flexibility in generating records, organizing and searching information viewing the search outputs, and interchanging data files with external databases with least manual interference.

PARAPAR

A conversion software package, PARAPAR has been developed in CALIBNET to support interchange of bibliographic data between USMARC, UNIMARC and CCF Files and also from non-standard formats to standard ones. Its primary objective is to convert data files, received from the participating libraries in variant formats, into a ISO-2709 compliant implementation through which the files are merged into the centralized Database of CALIBNET.

(v) Guidelines for Implementation of UNIMARC

It has been brought out by CALIBNET to provide the

library professionals in India with a working tool for developing their databases in a mutually exchangeable format. The document has been prepared in 1994, based on UNIMARC Manual (1987), by A Mukhopadhyay, Technical Consultant, under a project sponsored by the National Information System for Science and Technology (NISSAT), Department of Scientific and Industrial Research, Government of India. The guidelines have made an attempt to take care of the special requirements of the Indian libraries. They are expected to serve the Indian libraries in upgrading their databases to the international standard.

Immediate Focus

(i) Indian Resources Database

Development of Indian Resources Database on historical value covering manuscripts and rare books, and personal collections, has already been initiated with porting on the CDB and index to serials published by Asiatic Society during the last two countries.

(ii) CALIBNET on INTERNET

The design of CALIBNET web page is complete and is available on the Net. The web page(http: / /www.calibnet.org/) facilitates access to bibliographic information resources available through hosting of CALIBNET's centralized database. The **CALIBNET web site** provides:

a. Active link to access
   * Indian Library and Network Resources
   * Overseas Library Resources on India, including rare documents – printed and manuscripts.
   * Worldwide Library Catalogues
   * National Libraries of the world
   * Newspapers and journals
   * Electronic Reference tools
   * Factual Information sources

- * Book Trade Databases

b. Varied CALIBNET programs for

- * On-demand Information services
- * Electronic-mail connections
- * Consultative services for Library Automation
- * Manpower Development
- * R&D in IT Application

10
Digital Sources of Information

A source is defined as any document that provides information sought by a writer, researcher, library user, or person searching an online catalog or bibliographic database. Also refers to a document that provides information copied or reproduced in another document, for example, a quotation or excerpt. In literature, the story, legend, or work that inspires or provides elements of plot or characterization for another literary work, for example, the chronicles of English history on which Shakespeare based some of his history plays.

Traditional sources of information are printed: books, serial publications, journals, articles, theses, meeting publications, standards, patent publications, reference books and sources of official information. Some of the printed sources are also published in electronic format.

Now, CD ROM databases and Internet form a distinguished part of the reference collection since they accommodate a larger body of information comparing with their print counterpart. The vastness of the Internet resources may be viewed with the fact that its two popular engines, namely google.com and yahoo.com provide access to 4.3 and 3.1 billion pages (as per the figures in March 2004).

Here we are providing details of some widely consulted reference tools. About all these sources of information are available online are they are in the active process of being uploaded to Internet to facilitate easy access.

1. Abstracts

Abstract is a brief objective summary of the essential content of a book, article, speech, report, dissertation, or other work, which presents the main points in the same order as the original, but has no independent literary value. An abstract can be indicative, informative, critical, or written from a particular point of view.

The following are some of the most popular abstracting publications which are available now online or on CD ROMs in addition to their print versions:

Chemical Abstracts

Chemical Abstract is a very comprehensive and exhaustive source of information and is very useful for research scholars, scientists, teachers and librarians.

Chemical Abstracts is the largest abstracting service of the world in chemistry and Chemical Engineering. It is published by the American Chemical Society on weekly basis. About 1,20,000 pages are published annually covering more than 2,50.000 abstracts. It is international in scope. It enlists entries covering about 12,000 scientific periodicals. All the abstracts are classified according to the specialized subjects and one section each is provided for each the subject.

Psychological Abstracts

Psychological Abstracts (PA) is the print version of the PsycINFO database. It's produced monthly and contains summaries (abstracts, bibliographic information, and indexing) of English-language journal articles, technical reports, book chapters, and books in the field of psychology.

PA is organized by subject area according to the PsycINFO Classification Codes for easy browsing, and monthly author, brief subject, and book title indices and annual author and subject indices are included with the subscription.

Asian Recorder

The Asian Recorder Group is a company that represents

a few foreign publications in India. These publications include reports by E.I.U and Financial Times (FT) ,New York and E.I.U. online media products available via the internet and on CD-ROM. To find out more please browse our site and feel free to clarify any doubts with us.

Index Chemicus

Index Chemicus focuses on current awareness of new compounds and reports over 200,000 new compounds and synthetic intermediates each year, with coverage of over 1 million structures published in the literature since 1991. Covering the world's leading organic chemistry journals, Index Chemicus is a text- and substructure-searchable database. It serves as both a compound database and a current awareness tool, providing full graphical summaries, complete bibliographic information, and author abstracts for the papers it covers.

With Index Chemicus, a user can:

* keep up with the latest research
* find new ideas for projects
* track the work of other research groups
* save time in the laboratory and the library

Formats Available:

* Print
* CD-ROM
* Magnetic tape

Excerpta Medica

Excerpta Medica has built up an international reputation for the quality of its abstracting services. In addition, EM can provide access to highly respected scientific resources such as EMBASE, MEDLINE and BIOSIS.

Combining access to EMBASE with unique MEDLINE records provides an essential tool to help experts keep up to date with important new developments in healthcare.

Branding through added sponsorship modules provides an excellent profiling opportunity.

* EMBASE - the leading biomedical/pharmaceutical abstracts service supplemented with unique MEDLINE records
* ALERTS - simpler, faster, more general abstracting service
* LITERA - specific abstracts on diskette or CD-ROM using scientific databases

Dissertation Abstracts

Dissertation Abstracts contains selective indexing of masters theses and dissertations on academic topics accepted at accredited institutions since 1861. Abstracts are available from 1980 forward. Coverage includes the U.S., Canadian, British, and other European dissertations and theses. Please note that complete theses and dissertations are often difficult to obtain through interlibrary loan, as many times only the graduating institution has a copy and may not be willing to loan it. You may use the books interlibrary loan request form to request a theses or dissertation if you feel this is the most appropriate resource for your research.

Medicinal and Aromatic Plants Abstracts (MAPA)

It is a bimonthly abstracting journal covering global current literature on all aspects of medicinal, aromatic and allied plants. It is produced by scanning, selecting and abstracting relevant papers from about 600 primary journals published from about 65 countries and in 25 languages, research reports, conference proceedings and patents. Each of the 700 or so abstracts selected for every issue contains names of author(s), their affiliation, title of the paper, bibliographical details, article language, number of references and an informative abstract. Each issue and volume of MAPA is supported by a keyword index. From 1988 onwards, MAPA is available on CD-ROM also.

The abstracts in MAPA are provided under the following broad subject groups:

Agronomy

* Analytical & Processing Techniques
* Antimicrobial Activity
* Botany (General & Systematic)
* Breeding & Genetics
* Chemotaxonomy
* Clinical Studies
* Diseases & Pests
* Ethnomedicine

Insecticidal & Piscicidal Activity

* Marketing & Trade
* Miscellaneous
* New Publications
* Patents
* Physiology & Biochemistry
* Pharmacognosy
* Pharmacology & Toxicology
* Phytochemistr

Dissertation Abstracts International

Abstracts covers 1861+ Indexes dissertations accepted for doctoral degrees by accredited North American educational institutions and over 200 other institutions. Also contains citations and abstracts to masters' theses. Covers approximately 3,000 subject areas. Includes bibliographic citations with abstracts; abstracts are included since 1980. Subject Covered are Architecture; All Subjects; Composition; General Indexes (All Subjects); Multidisciplinary Databases (All Subjects); Dissertations; Planning; Rhetoric. Types of Materials Covered are doctoral dissertations and masters' theses; masters' theses are included since 1988.

* Dissertation abstracts international. A: The humanities and social sciences; see the ASU Libraries' Catalog for volume availability and location.
* Dissertation abstracts international. B: The sciences and engineering; see the ASU Libraries' Catalog for volume availability and location.
* Dissertation abstracts international. C: Worldwide; see the ASU Libraries' Catalog for volume availability and location.
* American Doctoral Dissertations; see the ASU Libraries' Catalog for volume availability and location.
* Comprehensive Dissertation Index; see the ASU Libraries' Catalog for volume availability and location.

Library and Information Science Abstracts (LISA)

Library and Information Science Abstracts (LISA) is a valuable reference tool for current awareness in information sciences. Comprehensive coverage allows access to past, present, and ongoing developments in librarianship, information science, online retrieval, new information technologies, and publishing. LISA on SilverPlatter includes abstracting and indexing of 500 periodicals (dating from 1969) from over 60 countries along with unpublished academic and institutional research from the Current Research in Library and Information Science Database (since 1981). This is a SilverPlatter database, and can be searched individually or in combination with other SilverPlatter databases.

Sociological Abstracts

Sociological Abstracts, 1963-date. Publisher: Cambridge Scientific Abstracts, P.O. Box 22206, San Diego, Sociological Abstracts (SA) indexes and abstracts scholarly literature in the field of sociology and related disciplines. The database provides abstracts only—no full-text—of articles from over 2,500 journals, book chapters, conference papers presented at association meetings, dissertation citations from

Dissertations Abstracts International, and book reviews. Social Planning/Policy & Development Abstracts (SOPODA) is a subfile of the database and includes literature on policy issues such as aging, health, environment, and violence.

Journals that contain the word "sociology" in the titles are considered core journals and are abstracted fully. Noncore journals include priority journals and selective sources. Priority journals are those in which sociologists regularly publish. They are chosen according to their relationship to the social sciences and their relevance to sociological topics. More than 50% of the substantive articles in these journals are included in the database. Selective sources are those in which sociologists sometimes publish and have some relationship to the social sciences. Less than 50% of the articles appearing in this type of he articles appearing in this type of journal are included in Sociological Abstracts. Articles are screened by senior editors with backgrounds in the social sciences; as a result, the publication has remained consistent.

Biological Abstracts

Introduction. Biological Abstracts encompasses the entire field of life sciences and provides comprehensive coverage of the world's published biological and biomedical research. Ohio University students and faculty have direct access to BA on CD (1990-present) from their own desks or from SearchNet terminals in the OU libraries through OhioLINK.

In addition to teaching biology instructors conduct research in many different areas. An important research area in biology at OU is vertebrate locomotion.

Other Popular Abstracts Available on the Internet

Aids and Cancer Research Abstracts

America: History & Life

Aquatic Sciences & Fisheries Abstracts

ArticleFirst

Arts & Humanities Search
BasicBIOSIS [Biology]
Biological Sciences Database
Computer & Information Systems Abstracts
Computer Science & Engineering Databases
Dissertation Abstracts
Electronics & Communications Systems Abs.
Environmental Sciences & Pollution Mgmt.
ERIC [Education]
Historical Abstracts
Internet & Personal Computing Abstracts
Linguistics & Language Behavior Abstracts
Monthly Catalog of US Govt. Publications
Oceanic Abstracts
Social Services Abstracts [Social Work]
Sociological Abstracts
Water Resources Abstracts

2. Indexes

Index is defined as a list of citations to journal articles and/or books arranged by subject, author, or title; indexes may be in print format, electronic format, or both. Also, a list of subjects covered in a book, usually published at the end of the book.

An index is a specific kind of tool for finding information. Whether an index is used by a human being or by a machine, its essence is a list of index entries. Each index entry leads to an indexed item somewhere outside the index; for instance, to a record in a database, to a folder in a file drawer, or a book on a library shelf. The entries are in some recognizable order, usually alphabetical. A back-of-the book index is alphabetical by subject and points to a page number(s) in the work with information about that subject.

The following are some of the popular indexes being published at international as well as national levels:

Index Chemicus

Index Chemicus focuses on current awareness of new compounds and reports over 200,000 new compounds and synthetic intermediates each year, with coverage of over 1 million structures published in the literature since 1991. Covering the world's leading organic chemistry journals, Index Chemicus is a text- and substructure-searchable database. It serves as both a compound database and a current awareness tool, providing full graphical summaries, complete bibliographic information, and author abstracts for the papers it covers.

With Index Chemicus, a user can:

* keep up with the latest research
* find new ideas for projects
* track the work of other research groups
* save time in the laboratory and the library

Formats Available: Print, CD ROM and Magnetic tape Social Sciences Citation Index

The Social Sciences Citation Index® (SSCI®) and Social SciSearch® provide access to current and retrospective bibliographic information, author abstracts, and cited references found in over 1,700 of the world's leading scholarly social sciences journals covering more than 50 disciplines. They also cover individually selected, relevant items from approximately 3,300 of the world's leading science and technology journals.

Key Advantages & Capabilities

* Allows researchers to conduct comprehensive searches that uncover all the relevant information they need
* Provides cited reference searching, the unique ISI search and retrieval feature that lets users track the literature

forward, backward, and through the database, breaking through disciplinary and geographic boundaries

* Enables users to conduct multidisciplinary searches to discover hidden subject relationships

British Humanities Index

An international abstracting and indexing tool for research in the humanities, BHI indexes over 320 internationally respected humanities journals and weekly magazines published in the UK and other English speaking countries, as well as quality newspapers published in the UK.

Regular monthly updates ensure subscribers can retrieve the latest material on a wide range of arts and humanities subjects, aided by a completely interactive thesaurus and the capability to link to electronic fulltext of many journal articles.

Subject Coverage

Major areas of coverage include:

* Architecture
* Archaeology
* Art
* Antiques
* Cinema
* Current Affairs
* Education
* Economics
* Environment
* Foreign Affairs
* Gender Studies
* History
* Language
* Law
* Linguistics

* Literature
* Music
* Painting
* Philosophy
* Poetry
* Political Science
* Religion
* Theatre

Biological and Agricultural Index Plus

Biological & Agricultural Index Plus offers researchers convenient online access to the core literature of biology and agriculture—much of it from peer-reviewed journals—plus full text. Full text citations also link to PDF page images, featuring graphs, charts, diagrams, photos, and illustrations indispensable to science research.

* High quality indexing of periodicals as far back as 1983.
* In-depth—50 to 300 words—abstracts written by Wilson staff for every article indexed.
* Full text of articles from journals as far back as 1997.
* Search using the Wilson subject thesaurus developed specifically for this product.
* Up-to-date subject headings keep pace with the latest developments.
* Graphical content adds a key dimension to scientific research—PDF page images accompany full text articles, offering both words and images.
* Search using the Wilson subject thesaurus developed specifically for this product.
* Broad coverage includes a wide range of scientific journals, from popular to professional. About 45 percent of the focus is on agriculture.
* Search by keyword, subject, personal names, title words,

publication, year, type of article or any combination to find exactly what you need.

* Library holdings indicator links to your OPAC, lets users know if they'll find cited issues on your shelves.
* Links to websites cited by articles help users find related information and images.
* Acquire articles easily through document delivery links built right into the database.
* Uniform name authority control (Details) makes searching easy and reliable.
* Daily updates on WilsonWeb bring users current information (monthly on WilsonDisc).
* Wilson quality indexing—done by professionals with advanced degrees in science—guarantees user satisfaction with results.

Index Translationum

The Index Translationum is a list of books translated in the world, i.e. an international bibliography of translations. The data base contains cumulative bibliographical information on books translated and published in about one hundred of the UNESCO Member States since 1979 and totalling more than 1,400.000 entries in all disciplines : literature, social and human sciences, natural and exact sciences, art, history and so forth. It is planned to update the work every quarter.

By publishing this list, to serve as a reference work, UNESCO provides the general public with an irreplaceable tool for making bibliographical inventories of translations on worldwide scale. International cooperation makes the "Index Translationum" a work tool that is unique in the world.

Each year, the bibliography centres or national libraries in the participating countries send to UNESCO Secretariat the bibliographical data concerning translated books in all fields of knowledge. Periodicals, articles from periodicals, patents and brochures are not included.

Indian Science Index

Indian Science Index is a subject index to articles, research papers, research notes, conference/seminar, symposia, proceedings, transactions of societies, significant editorials, news and book reviews from selected Indian journals in all disciplines of science, technology and medicine. The second volume of the Index covers about 300 periodicals and lists over 16,000 entries. The entries are arranged alphabetically.

Applied Sciences and Technology Index

This index covers thousands of scientific journals (computer technology, etc.). For communications students, the index includes appropriate subject headings: telecommunications, television, computer, and radio, among others. Each volume includes a main subject section; there is a separate book review citation index. Covers SMPTE Journal, among others. It was published first from New York By H. W. Wilson Company in 1958.

Bibliographic Index

A "bibliography of bibliographies" (issued quarterly and annually); includes those published in books, periodicals, pamphlets, or issued separately (with 50 or more citations). Relevant subject search terms: mass media (psychological aspects, social aspects, etc.), speech, communication (business communication, research, psychological aspects, social aspects, audiences, television and children), and telecommunication. The Index was first published in 1942 by H. W. Wilson Company.

Business Periodicals Index

This index is arranged alphabetically by subject and covers many important journals in business (radio, television, newspapers) and marketing (advertising). Covers important trade magazines: Broadcasting, Editor and Publisher, Advertising Age, Journal of Advertising Research, etc. Typical search terms include: television, etc. The Index was published by H. W. Wilson Company in 1958.

Current Index to Journals in Education (CIJE)

Published by Oryx Press from Phoenix in 1969, this Index provides selective covering of more than 750 journals in education and related areas (communication). It's issued monthly and cumulated twice a year. One must use the Thesaurus of ERIC Descriptors, the subject index, then the article description section of each volume to locate abstracts. A "must" for most communication, telecommunication, journalism, and mass media searches. Use with Resources In Education. Indexes Journal of Communication and Journal of Broadcasting and Electronic Media, among others.

The Education Index

It was first published in 1929 from New York by New York: H.W. Wilson. Issued monthly, with annual cumulations. Like Current Index to Journals in Education, this includes more than 350 monographs, yearbook, and periodical listings in educational and related areas (communication). Includes subject and author indexes, and a separate book review listing. Subject headings include: television—audiences, psychological aspects, social aspects, children, and teaching, television in education, etc.

Humanities Index.

A "must" for communications research. Comprehensive, interdisciplinary, this index covers more than 300 periodicals. It was called Social Sciences and Humanities Index until 1974. It's issued quarterly, with annual cumulations, subject/author indexes, and a separate book review section. Indexes Journal of Broadcasting and Electronic Media, Journalism Quarterly, and Columbia Journalism Review, among others. It was first published in 1975 from New York by H. W. Wilson Company.

The New York Times Index

Published by New York Times in 1913, this index "of

record," is a semimonthly (with quarterly/annual cumulations) service uses a subject index to organize stories, editorial condensations, and headlines of all material printed in the daily newspaper. Helpful for tracing the development/ progress of media issues, technology, etc.

Resources in Education

Publishes monthly, semiannual, and cumulative indexes. Includes abstracts and indexes for educational documents (including mass media-related material) published by Education Resources Information Center (ERIC). Included are curricula, conference papers, project/research reports, bibliographies, etc. Publishes a Thesaurus of ERIC Descriptors and subject index. One must ultimately locate the documents on microfiche (ERIC). Use with CIJE. Indexes Journalism Monographs, among others. It was first published in 1966 from Washington, D.C. U.S. Government Printing Office.

Social Sciences Index

Was part of Humanities Index (Social Science and Humanities Index) until 1974. Issued quarterly, with annual cumulations. Covers more than 300 periodicals; includes subject/author and book review indexes in each volume. Relevant mass media subject headings include: television (and children, and youth, audiences, psychological aspects, social aspects, etc.), mass media (psychological aspect, social aspects, and children, and youth, research, etc.), etc. Indexes Public Opinion Quarterly, among others.

3. Dictionaries

Dictionaries are a vital source of information in libraries, offices, establishments and at home. They have become an integral part of not only library collections but also a common feature on the desk of all literate persons. The cooperative activities at the national as well as international have further necessitated the use of dictionaries to maintain contacts, usually within the groups of persons who do not know each other's language. Dictionaries are taken as authoritative work for pronunciation, meanings, spellings and usage of words and terms.

The details about some popular dictionaries are given below:

The Oxford English Dictionary

The Oxford English Dictionary is extensively referred by scholars. It has been regarded as the last word on words for over a century. But, as with a respected professor or admired parent, we count on its wisdom and authority without thinking much about how it was acquired. What is the history of the Oxford English Dictionary? Exploring its origins and development will give new insight into this extraordinary, living document.

The new dictionary was planned as a four-volume, 6,400-page work that would include all English language vocabulary from the Early Middle English period (1150 AD) onward, plus some earlier words if they had continued to be used into Middle English.

It was estimated that the project would be finished in approximately ten years. Five years down the road, when Murray and his colleagues had only reached as far as the word 'ant', they realized it was time to reconsider their schedule. It was not surprising that the project was taking longer than anticipated. Not only are the complexities of the English language formidable, but it also never stops evolving. Murray and his Dictionary colleagues had to keep track of new words and new meanings of existing words at the same time that they were trying to examine the previous seven centuries of the language's development.

In Oxford John Simpson and Edmund Weiner with a core group of lexicographers reviewed, corrected, and edited this new electronic dictionary, as well as adding 5,000 new words and senses to 400,000 definitions previously expressed in

60,000,000 words. In all, the Project team succeeded in accomplishing around 85 per cent of its work by software, but the remaining 15 per cent required the critical eye of the editors. The culmination of this mammoth task was the setting in type and subsequent printing of the Oxford English Dictionary, Second Edition. In 1989 this was published on time, to great acclaim. The finished work, edited by Simpson and Weiner, fills 22,000 pages which are bound in twenty substantial volumes.

Webster's New International Dictionary of the English Language

Webster's New International Dictionary is based on the international dictionary of 1890 and 1900," and is "now completely revised in all departments including also a dictionary of geography and biography, being the latest authentic quarto edition of the Merriam Series. W.T. Harris, Ph.D., Ll.D., Editor in Chief; F. Sturges Allen, General Editor. Springfield, Mass., U.S.A. Published by G. & C. Merriam Company. 1924."

Roget's International Thesaurus

Based on the original by Peter Roget, this is the standard, classic thesaurus updated with 3,000 new words. It the only thesaurus based on Peter Roget's original classic first published in 1859, this edition is the most definitive, up-to-date, and comprehensive reference of its kind. Not an A-Z listing, this all-time bestseller retains Roget's unique and brilliant category-based organizing system, an innovative ordering of the English language designed to organize readers' thoughts and stimulate ideas. Here all synonyms, antonyms, and related words are grouped together for quick and easy comparison. without all the needless repetition and cross-referencing of alphabetical thesauri. With a 20% revision, including edits to reflect the very latest trends and technologies—and nearly 3,000 new words—Roget's International Thesaurus, 6th Edition is an essential reference for every home library.

Merriam-Webster's Collegiate Dictionary

The new Eleventh Edition of America's best-selling dictionary merges print, CD-ROM, and Internet-based formats to deliver unprecedented accessibility and flexibility at one affordable price. Fully revised print content features more than 225,000 clear and precise definitions and more than 10,000 words and meanings. Includes easily installable CD-ROM and free one-year subscription to new Collegiate Web site.

The 10th Collegiate appeared in 1994, and is cited in Guide to Reference Books. The 11th contains another 70 pages and another 10,000 words (e.g. World Wide Web, post-structuralism, netizen, McJob and phat) derived from a lexical archive of over 15.5 million words (the 10th's archive was 14.5 million). Many dates of first use have been pushed back in time based on new evidence: the 10th had the date of postmodern at 1949 while the 11th has 1925 (the definition has been expanded as well). Finally, the following change of appearance: main entries and guidewords are now sans serif, further distinguishing them from explanatory matter. As in other Collegiate editions, all images are line drawings, and biographical and geographical names garner their own sections. The 11th includes a CD-ROM and a year subscription to the online version. Annotation ©2003 Book News, Inc., Portland.

yourDictionary.com

yourDictionary.com is an online dictionary. It is a language products and services company that maintains the most comprehensive and authoritative language portal on the web with more than 2500 dictionaries and grammars in over 300 languages, games that build language skills, and a forum (The Agora) for discussing language issues with the logophile community. More than 1,000,000 people a month visit its website.

In its short existence, the website, yourDictionary.com, has become the most authoritative and comprehensive website specializing in information about language—any language in the world. Come here to look up general or specialized words in literally thousands of English and foreign-language dictionaries or ask us and we will create a customized dictionary, spellchecker or word filter expressly for your application in any language.

yourDictionary is a company based on the linguistic sciences by professional linguists and businessmen combining their expertise. The authority and academic rigor of the yourDictionary.com site is provided by our **Advisory Council of Experts** (ACE), which comprises some two dozen of the world's most accomplished linguists. The distinguished members of the Council provide indispensable guidance in the development, acquisition, and maintenance of the dictionaries under their purview, and help ensure the integrity of their respective areas of linguistic specialization. Members of the Council also contribute original articles to the **YDC Library**.

Online Dictionary of Library and Information Science

ODLIS began at the Haas Library in 1994 as a five-page photocopied handout intended for undergraduates not fluent in English, and students with limited exposure to library terminology. In 1996, it was expanded and converted to HTML format for installation on the WCSU Libraries HomePage under the title Hypertext Library Lingo: A Glossary of Library Terminology. In 1997, many more hypertext links were added and the format improved in response to suggestions from users. During the summer of 1999, several hundred terms and definitions were added, and a generic version created which omitted all references to the specific conditions and practices at the Haas Library. In the fall of 1999, the glossary was expanded to 1,800 terms, renamed to reflect its extended scope, and copyrighted. In February, 2000, ODLIS was indexed in Yahoo! under "Reference - Dictionaries - Subject." It is also indexed in the WorldCat database in OCLC FirstSearch. During the year 2000, the dictionary was expanded to 2,600 terms. On average, it has received over 6,200 visits per month since January 2, 2000.

Specialized Dictionaries

There are more and more books being printed all the time; but among the most important are the references we call dictionaries and/or lexicons

Here are just a few samples of dictionary/lexicon titles that show the extent of dictionary specializations:

Merriam-Webster Unabridged Dictionary

* On line new and updated databases.
* Includes headwords, definitions, and etymologies.

Merriam-Webster Collegiate Dictionary

* New Eleventh Edition
* Includes 225,000 definitions and more than 700 illustrations.

The American Heritage Dictionary of the English Language

* Derived from a complex, highly versatile structured database.
* Considerable attention is devoted to the history of words.

Oxford English Dictionary

* Actual size is 20 volumes, 21,730 pages.
* Number of words in entire text is 59 million.

Encarta World English Dictionary

* Compiled by over 320 scholars in 20 nations, working simultaneously for almost three years.
* This "first-time partnership among global scholars is, for North Americans, a comprehensive record of English—but one with a world view."

Dorland's Illustrated Medical Dictionary

* Medical terms with extensive definitions.

* Etymologies of words with many illustrations.

Stedman's Medical Dictionary

* A comprehensive, current, and medical lexicon for medical and health professionals.
* Critically reviewed and revised by consultants representing 52 medical specialities.

Taber's Cyclopedic Medical Dictionary

* Offers 55,000 entries for nursing and allied health services.
* Encyclopedic entries offer detailed explanations of important concepts.

Psychiatric Dictionary

* Records words that are used in the field of psychiatry to keep pace with its new developments.
* Strives to make each definition comprehensible not only to those active in the behavioral sciences but also to readers whose primary work, training, or major interest is not in the area being defined.

The Barnhart Dictionary of Etymology

* Presents recordings of the roots of English and shows their many points of contact with other cultures from which they have absorbed new words and new ideas.
* Aim has been to make examples of the development of English an understandable subject for those with no specialized knowledge of language study.

A Comprehensive Etymological Dictionary of the English Language

* Dealing with the origins of words and their sense developments thus illustrating the history of civilization and culture.
* "Since my youth I have devoted myself to philology, with special regard to etymology." —Dr. Ernest Klein, compiler of this two-volume dictionary.

International Dictionary of Medicine and Biology, in Three Volumes

* Contains more than 151 000 terms and more than 159 000 definitions.
* Eighty-one advisory editors, 10 co-advisory editors, and 90 contributors wrote the definitions for 70 different subjects.

Dictionary of Plant Virology

* Common names of plant viroids of higher plants.
* Order of diseases according to contemporary scientific names of the most important host plant.

Dictionary of Edible Mushrooms

* Botanical and common names in various languages of the world.
* For amateur mushroom hunters and growers.

Dictionary of Wild and Cultivated plants

* Scientific names of wild and cultivated plants found in Europe.
* Multilingual dictionary.

Dictionary of Geosciences

* Terms used in geochemistry and physical chemistry, geology and tectonics, meteorology, et al.
* Bilingual Russian-English dictionary.

Dictionary of Aquaculture

* Terms related to the various types of aquaculture; such as, hatchery, nursery, and growout production for fish culture, crustacean and mollusc culture, algal culture, reptile culture, amphibian culture, and echinoderm culture.
* Includes terms for pathology, prophylaxis, breeding, nutrition, genetics, hydrology, engineering, marketing,

biology, systems behavior, chemicals, and water chemistry.

4. Encylcopedias

An encyclopedia may be defined as a reference source containing information on a variety of topics. The information may be supplied in short paragraphs or in lengthy articles that include citations to other works on the same topic. Encyclopedias can be general - covering all topics, or specialized - focusing on a particular discipline such as art or philosophy.

Nowadays, encyclopedias have become a vital tool for locating information on any subject. They have varying scope ranging from the general coverage of knowledge to the specific areas of human activities. Encyclopedias have become so popular that they are regarded as substitute to a number of information tools.

General Encyclopedias

Encyclopedia Britannica

Encyclopedia Britannica was first published in Edinburgh in 3 volumes during 1768-1771 under the tilte Dictionary of Arts and Sciences by Society of Gentlemen. It grew to 10 volumes in the second edition and the third edition published in 1810 was in 20 volumes. The IX edition of the Encyclopedia was published between 1875-1889 was in 25 volumes. The XV edition is brought significant change. In fact it brought a revolution in encyclopedia making by combining reference and educational functions. It became an effective tool for research providing references from one part of it to the other through its 30 volumes set. The encyclopedia is divided into three main parts i.e. propedia, micropedia and macropedia.

The venerable Encyclopedia Britannica has launched the Britannica Internet Directory, where the encyclopedic editors use their razor-sharp skills to cut through the chaff of the Net. In Netsurfing terms this is known as the "human filter," which doesn't rely on the preprogrammed search engine spiders and key word databases, but instead the EB actually categorizes Websites by hand. This filtering is, in part, much like that of the famous YAHOO directory, but with an even more exclusive and discriminating hand. Recently released as a preview, Netresearchers can find the free Britannica Internet Guide at this Internet address:

http://www.ebig.com/

Each listed Website has been "chosen, reviewed and rated by Britannica editors," said an EB spokeswoman. So far, about 65,000 Websites have been indexed.

The Britannica Directory allows users to search by key word, name, or by phrase, or they can peruse the topical table of contents. This subject outline includes such informational categories as Art and Literature; Health and Medicine; News and Current Events; Science, Technology and Mathematics; and Social Science. In all there are 14 categories. In addition to its new Internet Directory, the Britannica has a fee-based service which allows journalists to access most of the contents of its famed encylopedia. A limited search can be performed free. Address of this site:

http://www.ebig.com/search/

Collier's Encyclopedia. 24v. 1997. Collier's.

The first edition of Collier's was published in 1950-51 in 20 volumes. There was a major revision in 1962 increasing the number of volumes to 24. It is considered one of the "big three" encyclopedias (Americana and Britannica are the other two) in terms of depth of coverage and amount of text. The number of entries in the 1997 edition remains at 23,000. Collier's continues to have many broad subject articles such as the heavily revised 19-page marine biology article and more than 100 pages for United States of America. The majority of articles are signed, even those consisting of a few sentences, such as Legume. Contributors of revised articles include Barry

Kernfeld, the editor of The New Grove Dictionary of Jazz; Richard Marchi of Airports Council International; John J. O'Connor, television critic of the New York Times; and Bob Verdi, sportswriter for the Chicago Tribune.

Collier's has replaced its black-and-white illustrations, with 412 four-color illustrations new in 1997, including a beautiful color drawing of the borage plant, a photograph of an urban skateboarder, and a number of photographs in the revised Fashion and Clothing. Since 1991, more than 4,500 new four-color illustrations have been added; 49 percent of the illustrations are now in color. This is a high percentage compared to Americana and Britannica. There are still a few portraits that are gray and fuzzy, and the black-and-white photograph of Cleveland is certainly not a good advertisement for the revival of a city. Although no new maps have been added to the 1997 edition, 62 maps were revised. Color maps of Asia and China were changed to note the incorporation of Hong Kong into the People's Republic of China.

For the most part, bibliographies are found in volume 24, along with the index. However, bibliographies are also being added to revised articles-Air Pollution lists articles and books from the early 1990s. Glossaries and biographies at the ends of longer articles continue to be extremely useful. For example, the newly revised Football has a glossary of 45 entries and short biographies of players and coaches from Wilbur ("Fats") Henry to Emmitt Smith. An old black-and-white photograph of the Princeton "V trick" detracts from the new look of the article. The index in volume 24 is reliable, with 450,000 entries for articles, maps, illustrations, and bibliographies. More than 15,000 of these index entries are new or revised.

Collier's increased the number of new and revised entries compared to the 1996 edition. This year's edition has 57 new entries and 78 rewritten articles. An additional 42 articles were substantially revised. New articles cover such diverse entries as Fairy Tale; Gates, Bill; National Geographic Society; Rolling Stones; Suicide; and Winterthur Museum and Gardens. There is a new article called Internet and Other Computer Networks, with a current bibliography at the end of the entry. Opera was heavily revised and now has a short biography and a color photograph of Cecilia Bartoli. It also mentions newer opera festivals such as the Metropolitan Opera in the Parks Program and Glimmerglass Opera in Cooperstown, New York. A section of Black Americans was replaced and now has a photograph of Marion Wright Edelman and President Clinton (with only Edelman identified). This article, as well as Automobile, could be drastically improved by adding color photographs.

Gymnastics was replaced and mentions the 1996 Olympics. The winners of events from the 1996 Summer Olympics are included in Olympic Games, but there is nothing on the bombing in Centennial Park. Other events of 1996 that are mentioned include the 1996 U.S. elections, Nobel Prize and World Series winners, Boris Yeltsin's reelection and illness, events in Chechnya, and the deaths of Spiro Agnew, Gene Kelly, and Edmund Muskie.

Articles that warrant updating include Consumerism (nothing mentioned after the late 1970s); College and Universities (college costs are for 1991-92); and Foundations and Trusts (MacArthur Foundation assets are listed as close to $2 billion, but as of December 1995, they were $3 billion). Periodic Table does not mention elements 110-112, Refugees mentions nothing about problems in the 1990s, and Food has no statistics later than the mid-1980s. A text-only version on CD-ROM was first released in 1996. New this year is a multimedia CD-ROM.

Collier's remains a good, comprehensive encyclopedia for secondary-school, public, and academic libraries. The many color photographs may even make it a more palatable source for students who would rather use electronic resources. It made a late entry into an already crowded CD-ROM encyclopedia market (Britannica, Compton's, Grolier's, IBM World Book, Microsoft Encarta). Sierra developed and markets this 3 CD-ROM multimedia encyclopedia which includes an atlas, dictionary, and several interactive simulations.

Netscape Communicator 4.0 is used as the interface. The toolbar at the top of the screen is from Netscape and provides the useful forward and backward buttons, as well as bookmark and printing functions. If you are already familiar with a web browser, the basic operation of the program is straight forward. But most of this toolbar is irrelevant to the encyclopedia.

Down the left side is a toolbar specific to Collier's. This lets you access the major parts of product: Encyclopedia, Atlas, Dictionary, Simulations, Timeline, Internet, and Help for Collier's (the Help menu at the top of the screen is specific to Netscape).

Encyclopedia Americana

The Encyclopedia Americana was first published during 1827-29. It was based on the seventh edition of the German encyclopedia "Brockhaus Konversations Lexicon'. In 1903, it wad published as entirely a new work. Encyclopedia Americana is considered as as one of the most significant reference tools. The set is designed to serve as a "bridge between the worlds of the specialist and the general reader" (editor's preface). Some 52,000 articles, contributed by in-house editorial staff and 6,500 academics primarily from the U.S. and Canada, are written in a clear, straightforward style with an emphasis on accuracy, impartiality, and objectivity. While the set is international in scope and covers all major areas of knowledge, it has traditionally centered on North American people, places, and history. Its strong coverage of scientific and technical topics is also well established. Drawbacks to the set include its slow pace of revision, outdated bibliographies, lackluster illustrations, and unattractive format.

Long a standard in school, academic, and public library collections, the Encyclopedia Americana is now available on the World Wide Web, blending the depth and accuracy of the print edition with the currency expected of an online reference work. Its 45,000 articles and more than 25 million words have been contributed by over 6,500 specialists in their respective disciplines and cover all academic fields and curriculum topics. Updated quarterly, the Americana Online can be used either as a stand-alone source of current information on almost any topic or as a guide to the resources of the World Wide Web.

SPECIAL ENCYCLOPEDIAS

McGraw-Hill Encyclopedia of Science and Technology

The McGraw-Hill Encyclopedia of Science & Technology (MEST) was first published in 1960, It serves as an excellent resource for those who need an authoritative overview of a subject within the major disciplines of science and technology. Contributed by 5000 internationally known researchers (1500 more than in the eighth edition), the 7100 articles are well written and well organized. The excellent Illustrations, primarily drawings with some black-and-white photographs and color plates, are central to the text. The topical index groups article titles under broad subject categories, while the 500-page analytical index provides more specific indexing. The set is updated every five years, with this edition's comprehensive revisions emphasizing industrial engineering, information technology and computing, chemistry and chemical engineering, physics and astronomy, the biomedical sciences, and the environmental, earth, and climate sciences. The short bibliographies at the end of each article have been revised, and the study guides have been expanded to cover 15 major scientific disciplines such as agriculture, electronics, and environmental science. Aside from this, very little is changed from the eighth edition. Both MEST and the recent Encyclopedia of Physical Science and Technology (EPST) are excellent science encyclopedias and complement each other. Although the sets are comparable in size, EPST has only 790 articles, a difference that results from MEST's breaking up a topic into several individual articles. In contrast, EPST organizes the information into fewer chapter-length articles, making it better suited for self-study. Because MEST has slightly broader coverage and costs about $1000 less than EPST, most libraries would probably prefer to purchase this set if they have to make a choice

No other single resource provides such a sweeping look or in-depth coverage of the major scientific and technological developments than The McGraw-Hill Encyclopedia of Science & Technology. This time-honored reading tradition is the most authoritative and comprehensive guide available to both known and new science. It offers well-illustrated, detailed coverage of the discoveries, breakthroughs, and milestones that have and continue to shape our lives and times.

* 7,500 articles covering more than 80 fields of science
* Hundreds of new contributors from around the world, more than 9,000 in all, including 25 Nobel Prize winners
* Extensively revised bibliographies for further study
* More than 12,000 digitally prepared illustrations, 16% brand new Study Guides, a Topical Index, and a 500+ page Analytical Index for fast access to information

MEST Online

McGraw-Hill's AccessScience is an online gateway to an unparalleled library of science and technology information. Updated daily, AccessScience delivers the latest content of the trusted McGraw-Hill Encyclopedia of Science & Technology, 9th Edition, and the McGraw-Hill Dictionary of Scientific and Technical Terms, 6th Edition.

On can search our database containing more than 8,000 articles written by the leading figures in their fields—including 30 Nobel Prize winners—edited and illustrated with the non-specialist in mind. Find late breaking news biographies of famous scientists, a Student Center, and much more—all brought to life by 13,000 high-quality illustrations.

AccessScience® is easily navigable, providing users with many searching and browsing options, including Boolean operators, the ability to limit to specific content categories (e.g., dictionary entries, biographies, encyclopedia articles), or to topical categories (e.g., medicine, paleontology, mathematics). The articles are easy to read on-screen, have internal navigation links, and contain high quality graphics.

AccessScience@McGraw-Hill is the online counterpart. . .McGraw-Hill's Encyclopedia of Science & Technology, with a slew of additional material. Among that additional material are three or four weekly news stories and a News Archive browsable by topic and/or chronology. There is also full-text access to 8000-plus articles, with hundreds of Research Updates not available in the print format. AccessScience also includes 115,000 dictionary definitions; 2000 in-depth biographies of leading scientists from throughout history, including Nobel prize and Fields Medal winners; and 11,000 illustrations, now searchable as a separate collection. A Student Center contains study guides, essay topics, reading materials, and a Q&A archive. Rounding out the compilation of resources is a Data, Tables & Tools section, with an impressive collection of links to scientific and technical tables and tools...

International Encyclopedia of Social and Behavioral Sciences

The Encyclopedia is the first attempt in a generation to map the social and behavioral sciences on a grand scale. It is the largest reference work ever published for the social and behavioral sciences and will be the first to appear in both print and electronic formats.

The Encyclopedia includes:

3,842 signed articles

15 million words of text

90,000 bibliographic references

150 biographical entries

The printed edition runs to 24 volumes plus 2 index volumes. It is alphabetically organized and extensively cross-referenced throughout and is supported by a comprehensive name index and multi-level, hierarchical subject index. It also includes a classified list of entries. The electronic edition will offer all of this and much more: the vast database of articles will be enhanced by flexible search-and-retrieval facilities and by a rich variety of electronic reference links.

The IESBS aims to capture the "state of the art" of the social and behavioral sciences, as the 1968 International Encyclopedia of the Social Sciences (David L. Sills, ed.) did in its generation. Expands its focus to include related biological fields, such as evolutionary science, genetics, cognitive neuroscience, psychiatry, and health. Includes Anthropology, Archaeology, Demography, Economics, Education, Geography, History, Law, Linguistics, Philosophy, Political Science, Psychiatry, Psychology, Sociology. Related disciplines include: Gender Studies, Religious Studies, Expressive forms (in Art and Literature), Environmental/Ecological Studies, Science and Technology, Mathematics and Computer Sciences, Statistics, and International Studies. Applications include: Management Studies, Media Studies, Urban Studies and Public Policy.

Every article in the electronic edition will be supported by an abstract prepared specifically for the online publication. These abstracts will be posted to this website as they become available, offering an extended preview of the content of the Encyclopedia in advance of full publication. With annual updates planned for release from 2004, the online version of the International Encyclopedia of the Social & Behavioral Sciences will be a dynamic resource for students and faculty alike.

Encyclopedia of Library and Information Science

Second Edition, Revised and Expanded in 4 volumes

Edited by Miriam Drake, Encyclopedia of Library and Information Science has been published in 2003 in print and online simultaneously. It comprises 3600 pages and encompasses topics providing an excellent overview of the Library and Information Science field, and authored by a roster of highly-respected researchers in the field, the second edition of the Encyclopedia of Library and Information Science contains a wealth of well-written, comprehensive overviews concerning a plethora of LIS-related topics, including both pure library science and pure information science articles. With appropriate sources liberally cited in the bibliographies, this new edition makes an excellent addition to any academic/ research or large public library collection."

The Encyclopedia of Library and Information Science, Second Edition is an extraordinarily comprehensive work of geographic, technological, and professional scope. From the Albanian Library Association to the Wayne State University Libraries, from Boolean algebra to voice recognition, and from acquisitions to wireless services in public libraries, this volume covers it all. Edited by Miriam Drake, an icon in the world of libraries and information services, the Encyclopedia serves as a valuable teaching and reference source for professionals as well as people with only a casual interest in the field. The articles, authored by highly regarded experts in the field, are readable, informative, and each contains sizable bibliographies to more detailed sources of information.

The Encyclopedia of Library and Information Science is an authoritative source for consultation and reference for almost any library or information profession related issue. It includes thorough articles not only of traditional professional values and ideas such as intellectual freedom, censorship, rare book collections, and the theory of classification, but also such recent urgent issues as SFX, print-on-demand, metadata and the Open Archives Initiative. ELIS has captured the core body of knowledge of our rapidly evolving profession in a complete, up-to-date, manner that serves the needs of both novice and expert."

The second edition of the Encyclopedia of Library and Information Science is useful to both the general public and to librarians. An impressive range of topics is covered that goes beyond what is expected to include such topics as "The Future of Primary Records" and "Metadata on the World Wide Web." The articles are written by known experts and strike just the right balance in the amount and depth of information provided."

Description

It contains more than 10,000 references for additional, more detailed information. New topics covered in the revitalized Second Edition:

* Competitive intelligence
* Decision support systems
* Digital library projects
* Electronic records preservation
* Ethical issues in information
* Online library instruction
* Telecommuting
* Software reliability
* The user-centered revolution

Targets new and dynamic movements in the distribution, acquisition, and development of print and online media—addressing recruitment, program planning in the digital era, information management, advances in digital technology and encoding, intellectual property issues, and hardware, software, and database selection and design.

5 Biographies

The Oxford English Dictionary defines biography as "the history of the lives of individual man". Louis Shores defined it as "essentially a directory of notable persons usually arranged alphabetically by surnames, with biographical identifications that range from brief outline to extended narrative".

Biographies have been maintained compiled in helpful sequences to fulfills man's desire to know about the other great lives in order to get light from them. The details in biographies include dates of birth and death, education, position held, family lives, achievements and contribution, address for correspondence etc of the individuals.

Biographical information can be found in books, dictionaries, directories, manuals, encyclopedias (general and subject), journals/magazines, newspapers (obituaries), and specialized biographical sources. This information may be divided into three categories - "current" (people included are still living), "retrospective" (people included are dead), and those sources which include both living and dead persons. In addition, there are "general" biographical sources as well as those for specific subject areas.

General Biographical Sources

* Biography.com - Search over 25,000 lives of the greatest people, past and present. This site is sponsored by the A&E Television Network.
* Lives, the Biography Resource - Links to thousands of biographies, autobiographies, memoirs, diaries, letters, narratives, oral histories and more. Individual lives of the famous, the infamous, and the not so famous can be found in alphabetical index. Group biographies about people who share a common profession, historical era or geography can be located in Collections. Also general collections includes resources on biographical criticism and special collections. However, this site does not include biographies of living people.
* Infoplease - Biography - More than 30,000 biographies are included for the Infoplease almanacs, dictionary, and encyclopedia.
* Biographical Dictionary - This dictionary covers more than 28,000 notable men and women who have shaped our world from ancient times to the present day. The dictionary can be searched by birth years, death years, positions held, professions, literary and artistic works, achievements, and other keywords.

* Biography Center - Indexes other biographical sites. This site has the ability to search in multiple languages.

Specialized Biographical Sources

* TIME Magazine's 100 Most Important People of the 20th Century - Profiles of those individuals who have most influenced the last 100 years. They are grouped in five areas: Leaders & Revolutionaries, Artists & Entertainers, Builders & Titans, Scientists & Thinkers, and Heroes & Icons. TIME's Person of the Century is also presented.
* Distinguished Women of Past and Present - This site has biographies of women who contributed to our culture in many different ways. There are writers, educators, scientists, heads of state, politicians, civil rights crusaders, artists, entertainers, and others. Some were alive hundreds of years ago and some are living today.
* The Literary Web - Authors - This page lists the best digest sites of authors with many links to authors from the past and present.

Biography Indexes

* Homework Center - Biographies - Biography links organized by fields such as scientists, authors, musicians, etc. are presented by the Multnomah County Library in Oregon.
* Internet Public Library General/Reference: Biographies - Links to general biographical resources which also includes specialized biography links: Authors & Architects, Authors, Entertainers, Musicians & Composers, Politicians & Rulers, and Scientists & Inventors.
* Penn Library - Reference Shelf/General Biography - Great college site that has links to general biography sites but includes links for African-Americans, Award Winners, Business and Economics, Celebrities, Musicians, Government & Politics, Religion, Science &

Technology, and Women. librarian know if you are looking for an obituary.

Indian Sources

Directory of National Biography. Edited by S. P. Sen, Calcutta, Institute of Historical Studies, 1972-74. 4 vols.

This publication covers prominent persons from all walks of life who have made significant contribution to the national life, from the beginning of XIX century to the time of independence. The area covered is the whole of independent India. It enlists about 1400 biographies in alphabetical order by surname according to their English spelling.

India: Who's Who. New Delhi, INFA Publications, 1969- Annual

It aims at providing basic information about the living Indians who have gained recognition by virtue of their contribution to the society. The publication is brought out annually. The biographical sketches are short as every entry generally covers present position, date of birth, place of birth, name of father, mother and wife, number of sons and daughters, educational qualification, career, publications, office and residential address, telephone numbers etc. The publication is divided into sections and a general section at the end of it.

National Biographical Dictionary of India. Compiled by Jagdish S. Sharma. New Delhi, Sterling, 1972.

This source covers biographical information about the persons who played significant role in the history of the country. It covers a period of about 5,000 years from the remote past to the present time. A brief biographical sketch has been provided for each person giving dates of bith and death, profession, important activities of their lives and publications. The entries have been arranges alphabetically by surname. An index has also been provide at the end.

Other Bibliographies

Biography Index

http://www.lib.iastate.edu/

scholar/db/biognx.html

Available under "Indexes, abstracts" on the ISU Library Homepage. Indexes articles, books, critical studies, fiction, drama, pictorial works, poetry, juvenile literature, obituaries, book reviews, interviews and more. 1984 to present.

Marquis Who's Who

http://www.lib.iastate.edu/

scholar/db/whowho.html

Biographical information on a wide variety of people: historical figures, newsmakers, the infamous, pop culture personalities, and more. An interactive site with games, polls, historical features, news groups, etc. Published by A&E television network.

Biographical Directory of the United States Congress: A biographical directory of everyone that has served in the United States Congress, 1774 to present. Includes members of the Continental Congress and congressional delegates from U.S. Territories. Searchable by name, by position, and by state.

World Biographical Index: An extensive site for information on people from all over the world, past and present. Content provided by the renown German publishing group, K. G. Saur Publishing. In part, the value of this site is due to the fact that there is, presumably, little or no American (or English language) bias present. Site offers a variety of search strategies and limiters, including the choice of number of foreign archives.

http://www.biblio.tu-bs.de/

acwww25u/wbi_neu_en/

Biography Index. (1949 to date) A guide to biographical material appearing in approximately 2,200 periodicals, obituaries published in the New York Times, "current books of individual and collective biography" and more. Each quarterly issue indexes biographies for persons, present and past, in every occupation and from all over the world. An index by occupation is included. Available online via the ISU Library Homepage under Indexes, abstracts, 1984 to present.

Biography and Genealogy Master Index. (1980) 2nd Ed. w/supplements This consolidated Index enables the user to locate more than 4 million biographical entries on persons from the beginning of time through the present, in current and retrospective biographical dictionaries. Supplements from 1981 to 1990 add more citations. Available online via the ISU Library Homepage under Indexes, abstracts

Business Biographies Master Index. (1987) A selection of current and retrospective biographies of people in the field of business and finance.

Artist Biographies Master Index. (1986) Biographies of people in both the fine and applied arts. This index includes: painters, sculptors, illustrators, designers, graphic artists, craftsmen, architects and photographers.

Performing Arts Biography Master Index. (1981) A consolidated index to biographical sketches of persons, both present and past, involved with performing arts. This index is a revision of Theatre, Film and Television biographies Master Index.

Historical Biographical Dictionaries Master Index. (1980) Consolidated index to information in the principal biographical dictionaries. Includes people from the beginning of recorded history. Emphasis in this index is on people who have been prominent in United States history.

Author Biographies Master Index. (1st through 5th editions)Index to more than 845,000 biographical sketches concerning authors present and past.

Childrens' Authors and Illustrators: An Index to Biographical Dictionaries. (1981)A research aid for anyone interested in the study of children's literature. An index to approximately 20,000 persons, past and present.

Current Biography Yearbook. (1940 to date) A monthly compilation of short biographies of individuals prominent in the news. Photographs are frequently included, and it has a classification-of-profession index and citations to obituary notices. Updated by monthly issues entitled Current Biography

Newsmakers. (1988 to date) Newsmaker's provides biographical profiles on the people making current headlines. Each volume contains cumulative subject, name and nationality indexes.

Pseudonyms and Nicknames Dictionary. (1987, 2 vols.) Guide to pen names, stage names, pseudonyms and nicknames of individuals of all nations and ages.

Webster's Biographical Dictionary. (1976) Brief biographies of living and past persons from around the world, with pronunciation of each name indicated. Tables of presidents, popes, and rulers are included. (Note: there is a 1980 edition in Special Collections - on the 4th floor)

Dictionary of National Biography. (1885-1900, vols.1-63) & 10 supplements to 1985. Most important scholarly dictionary of the British Isles and its colonies. Long, authoritative articles with bibliographies. Covers from about ce. 500 to 1990. Includes index.

Dictionary of American Biography. (1928 - 1996) vols. 1 -22, (vols. 21 & 22 are Supplements 1 & 2) Also: DAB Supplements 3 - 10. Comprehensive index. Important scholarly dictionary of American biography, with long, authoritative articles and bibliographies. Covers Colonial America to 1980, in the original 20 vols. plus the supplements. Note: there is also a set in General Collections; missing vol. 8, including only Supplements 1 & 3. There is also a set in Special Collections.

International Who's Who. (Current edition) This annual gives short biographies of living persons who have earned international recognition for achievements and contributions in their country's political, economic, cultural, or social life. Editions back to 1951 are in the General Collection.

Who's Who in America. (Current edition) With Index Brief biographies of distinguished living Americans, listing personal history, publications, and current address. Editions back to 1899 are in the General Collection. Specific regional volumes are available for the East Midwest, South and Southwest, West, and World. Volumes organized by occupation have been produced for Government, Finance and Industry, Religion, and American Law.

Who's Who. (Current edition) This annual directory constitutes a comprehensive biographical directory with emphasis on the United Kingdom, includes important world leaders in other countries.

Dictionary of American Biography: Outstanding lengthy biographies of notable Americans. (30 vols.)

Dictionary of National Biography: Extensive scholarly biographies of eminent residents (men and women) of the British Commonwealth in the area of social and cultural history. Includes portraits and sources for further reading.

6. Geographical Sources

The advancement in communication technology has turned the entire world into a 'global village'. There is more and more demand for information on geography mainly for the purpose of travel and tourism. Geographical sources present an array of the sources introducing the land and people at regional, national and international level.

Geographical information may include name of a place, pronunciation, location, area, population, geographical and physical description, economic and historical data, etc. There are some common problems that hinder the retrieval of geographical information such as the frequent changes in names of place, changes in political boundaries of the countries etc.

The following are the common types of geographical sources of information available. Some example have also been provided of the most important or representative titles of each type. It is not intended to be a complete list of geographical reference materials

Guides to Sources
Bibliography
Dictionaries and Encyclopedias
Biographies
Gazetteers
Names and Terms
Atlases
Travel Guides

GUIDES TO SOURCES

American Library Association, Map & Geography Round Table. Base Line. 1980- . Bimonthly. Newsletter with current information on cartographic materials and issues of interest to map and geography librarians.

American Library Association, Map & Geography Round Table. Meridian. 1988- . Semiannual. Provides reviewed articles, book reviews, and news of interests to map and geography librarians. Companion publication to Base Line.

Campbell, John. Map Use and Analysis, 2nd ed. University of Wisconsin-Parkside: Wm. C. Brown Publishers, 1993. Explains and analyzes map use.

Cobb, David A., comp. Guide to U.S. Map Resources. 2nd ed. Chicago, IL: American Library Association, 1990. Comprehensive information on nation's map collections, including analysis. Indexed by library/institution, collection strengths, and names/numbers.

Durrenberger, Robert W. Geographical Research and Writing. New York: Crowell, 1971. A basic guide for students. Part I conveys the nature of geography and Part II contains a bibliography and subject index.

Goddard, Stephen, ed. A Guide to Information Sources in the Geographical Sciences. London: Croom Helm; Totowa, N.J.: Barnes and Noble, 1983. Bibliographical reviews of the geographical literature by region, thematic focus, and type of information source. Lacks an index.

Harris, Chauncy D. Bibliography of Geography. Chicago: Univ. of Chicago, Dept. of Geography, 1976-84. Includes annotated bibliographies covering the geographical literature. Updates Wright and Platt. A basic source for serious work in this area.

Larsgaard, Mary L. Map Librarianship: An Introduction. 2nd ed. Littleton, CO: Libraries Unlimited, 1987. Includes information on collection development, cataloging, technical services, reference, and preservation of maps.

Makower, Joel, ed. The Map Catalog: Every Kind of Map and Chart on Earth and Even Some Above It. 3rd ed., newly rev. New York: Vintage Books, 1992; Provides information about the many types of maps available, sources of map types, and descriptions of map products which are available.

Monmonier, Mark and George A. Schnell. Map Appreciation. Englewood-Cliffs, NJ: Prentice-Hall, 1988. Provides clear explanations of various types of maps.

Monmonier, Mark S. Mapping It Out: Expository Cartography for the Humanities and Social Sciences. Chicago, IL: University of Chicago Press, 1993. Describes cartography graphic methods for the humanities and social sciences.

Parry, R.B. and C.R. Perkins. World Mapping Today. London: Butterworths, 1987. Puts together various kinds of information for finding out about and acquiring modern topographic/thematic maps, and current available maps. Includes glossary, geographic index, and a publishers index.

Perkins, C.R. and R.B. Parry. Information Sources in Cartography. London; New York: Bowker-Saur, 1990. Covers international materials; both retrospective and current; 30 chapters with references. (Listed in Supplement to the Tenth

Edition, Guide to Reference Books, Covering Materials from 1985–1990, edited by Robert Balay, p. 360, 1992).

Sellers, John R. and Patricia Molen Van Ee, comp. Maps and Charts of North America and the West Indies, 1750–1789: A Guide to the Collections in the Library of Congress. Washington, DC: Library of Congress: for sale by the US GPO, 1981. Contains North America and West Indies maps; bibliographies; cartography.

Special Libraries Association, Geography and Map Division. Bulletin. 1947 . Three times per year. Includes research articles and information of interest to map and geography librarians.

Western Association of Map Libraries. Information Bulletin. A significant journal containing feature articles pertaining to geography, maps, and map librarianship; book reviews.

Murray's Ghide or Handbook for Travelers in India, Pakistan, Burma and Ceylon. London, Murray, 1961. It is a travel guide which provides details through maps, lists of terms and list of books for further reading so as to enable a traveler to plan the tour programme.

Fodor's India: A handbook of Republic of India. Edited by Eugene Fodor and William Curtis, London, Hodder and Stoughton, 1984. Annually published, Fodor's Guide is an excellent handbook for travelers to India. It gives maps, and other illustrations. It provides information on various aspects of the country including physical features, constitution,, population, religion etc. It also contains articles by well known authors on history, literature, arts, philosophy and public life of India.

Bibliographies

There are a number of bibliographical sources which present geographical information. They can be conveniently put in the following two categories :

(i) Retrospective bibliographies

(ii) Current bibliographies

Retrospective

Encyclopedia of Geographic Information Sources, International Volume. 4th ed. Detroit: Gale Research, 1988 Focus is on economic and financial materials including trade directories, newsletters, and analytical reports. Subtitle: A Bibliographic Guide to Approximately 13,000 Citations for Publications and Organizations of Interest to Business Personnel, Covering More Than 160 Cities, Countries and Regions.

Geo Abstracts. Norwich, Eng.: University of East Anglia, 1972-1989. (Published 6 times a year with annual indexes. Issued in seven parts: landforms and the quaternary; climatology and hydrology; economic geography; social and historical geography; sedimentology; regional and community planning; and remote sensing, photogrammetry, and cartography. Subject arrangement.

Grim, Ronald E. Historical Geography of the United States; A Guide to Information Sources. Detroit: Gale Research, 1982. A volume of the Geography and Travel Guide Information Series. Includes annotated bibliographies on cartographic sources, archival and historical materials, and secondary topics literature published since 1965. Complements McManis.

Harris, Chauncy D., ed. A Geographical Bibliography for American College Libraries. Washington, D.C.: Association of American Geographers; National Geographic Society, 1985. The basic guide for collection development of sources published prior to 1970. Presents a core collection for

American undergraduate libraries within a classed arrangement with annotations. Author index.

McManis, Douglas R. Historical Geography of the United States: A Bibliography, Excluding Alaska and Hawaii. Ypsilanti?: Div. of Field Services, Eastern Michigan Univ., 1965. [Coverage through the Nineteenth Century of monographic and serial publications. Arranged by region, state, and topic. Lacks index.

U.S. Department of the Interior, U.S. Geological Survey. Bibliography of map projections. For sale by the Books and Open-File Reports Section, 1988. Contains map projections.

Current

Current Geographical Publications: Additions to the Research Catalogue of the American Geographical Society. Publisher varies, currently issued by the University of Wisconsin-Milwaukee Library, 1938- . (Monthly except July and August. Classed arrangement to current books, pamphlets, government publications and periodical articles. Subject, author, and regional indexes (except volume 1). Since 1964, selected maps are also listed. Publisher has varied.

Geobase. Elsevier Science. Records covering the worldwide literature on geology, geography, and ecology.

Geographical Abstracts: Human Geography. Norwich, UK: Elsevier Science Publishers, Annual Index, 1989. Contains unique bibliographic information sources providing comprehensive coverage of the human geography literature; 1000 leading geographic journals, plus books, conference proceedings, reports, and theses.

Geographical Abstracts: Physical Geography. Norwich, UK: Elsevier Science Publishers, Annual Index, 1989. Contains current coverage of physical geography literature; 900 leading geographic journals, plus books, conference proceedings, reports, Ph.D., M.Phil., and Masters theses.

The World Map Directory. 1988- . Santa Barbara, CA: Maplink. Maplink is a commercial map dealer. This is their catalog which is arranged according to L.C. classification so as to provide geographical access.

DICTIONARIES AND ENCYCLOPEDIAS

Sharma, Jagdish Saran.The National Geographical Dictionary of India. New Delhi, Sterling, 1972. This reference book provides details of the various places in India which have historical value. It show them according to the presently organized states. The entries are arranged alphabetically and it provides cross reference for ease in locating a particular place. It also provides an index at the end including names of places, persons and any other related information.

Bates, Robert L. Glossary of Geology. 3rd ed. Alexandria, VA: American Geological Institute, 1987. Dictionary of geological terms with an English language emphasis and reflecting North American usage.

Clark, Audrey N. Longman Dictionary of Geography: Human and Physical. London: Longman, 1985. Definitions are based on the Glossary of Geographical terms. Covers terms used over past 100 years. Intended for students and professionals. Does not include specific or specialized terms.

Day, Alan Edwin. Discovery and Exploration: A Reference Handbook. New York: K.G. Saur; London: Clive Bingley, 1980. Covers the old world with alphabetically arranged entries of people, institutions, and sources relevant to exploration; includes index. Also includes a regional index. (Listed in Sheehy, CL66, p. 941, 1986).

Delpar, Helen, ed. The Discoverers: An Encyclopedia of Explorers and Exploration. New York: McGraw-Hill, 1980. Includes biographical, geographical, and topically arranged material relating to the age of discovery. Cross references and index.

Dunbar, Gary S., ed. Modern Geography: An Encyclopedic Survey. New York: Garland Publishing, 1991. Presents an overview of developments in geography from about 1890 to present, emphasizing personalities, institutions, major concepts, subfields, and evolution of discipline. (Listed in Supplement by Balay, CL9, p. 361). Indexed by personal names.

Goodall, Brian. The Facts on File Dictionary of Human Geography. New York: Facts on File Publications, 1987. Contains dictionary of human geography and diagrams.

Goudie, Andrew, et al., eds. The Encyclopaedic Dictionary of Physical Geography. Oxford, UK; New York: Blackwell, 1994. Companion to R.J. Johnston's The Dictionary of Human Geography. Provides comprehensive range of short definitions of technical terms of physical geography. (Listed in Supplement by Balay, CL11, p. 361).

Huber, Thomas P, Robert P. Larkin, and Gary L. Peters, eds. Dictionary of Concepts in Physical Geography. Westport, CT: Greenwood Press, 1988. Companion to Dictionary of Concepts in Human Geography. Reference sources for the social sciences and humanities. Presents brief, substantive discussions of concepts in physical geography; with about 100 entries, reference bibliography, and index.

Johnston, R.J., ed. Dictionary of Human Geography. 3rd ed. Blackwell Reference, 1994. Includes about 500 definitions of basic concepts with references and bibliographies for the entries. Indexed.

Jones, Steve, ed. The Cambridge Encyclopedia of Human Evolution. Cambridge, England; New York: Cambridge University Press, 1992. Includes bibliographical references and index; covers aspects of human evolution. For browsing or cover-to-cover reading.

Kiple, Kenneth F., ed. The Cambridge World History of Human Disease. New York: Cambridge University Press, 1992. Cambridge History and Geography of Human Disease Project started this work in 1985; reflects widely varying differences in mortality rates from region-to-to-region and new maladies in more developed regions; indexed. Written by specialists, but intended to be comprehensible to people in other fields.

Kurian, George Thomas. Encyclopedia of the First World. New York: Facts on File, 1990. Profiles 26 advanced countries (and six European ministries), examining their potential and describing their growth and evolution; geography.

Mayhew, Susan and Anne Penny, eds. The Concise Oxford Dictionary of Geography. Oxford, UK; New York: Oxford University Press, 1992. Dictionary of geographic terms. Includes 5,000 definitions and cross references. Gives an initial brief definition and then a more in-depth explanation.

Maunder, W. John, comp. Dictionary of Global Climate Change. Contribution of the Stockholm Environmental Institute to the Second World Climate Conference. New York: Chapman & Hall, 1992. Contains global climate change terms.

McDonnell, Rachael. International GIS Dictionary. Cambrdige, Eng., New York: GeoInformation International; John Wiley & Sons, 1995.]

Small, R.J. and Michael Witherick. A Modern Dictionary of Geography, 2nd edition. London; New York: E. Arnold: Distributed in the USA by Routledge, Chapman and Hall, 1989. Reflects changes in geographic terms; good dictionary for secondary and undergraduates; a balance between physical and human definitions. Includes cross references and illustrations. (Listed in Supplement by Balay, CL12, p. 361).

U.S. Defense Mapping Agency. Topographic Center. Glossary of Mapping, Charting, and Geodetic Terms. 4th ed. Washington: The Agency, 1981. For the most part, only those terms considered germane to some specific aspect of mapping, charting, and geodesy were included.

Viney, Nigel. A Dictionary of Toponyms. Long: Library Association, 1986. Compiles list of most common English-language toponyms a reader may encounter, including fictional ones. (Dictionary and gazetteer.)

DIRECTORIES

Association of American Geographers. AAG Directory.

Washington, The Association, 1956- . (Irregular). Includes geographers and students, indicating areas of specialization.

Guide to Departments of Geography in the United States and Canada. Washington: Association of American Geographers, 1968- . (Annual). Program descriptions. Personal name index.

1995 International GIS Sourcebook: Fort Collins, CO: GIS World, 1991- . This is the 4th edition of what is now an annual reference work for the GIS industry. It contains various directories, state-of-the-industry essays, list of educational institutions and course offerings, descriptions of relevant professional associations, and several appendices, including a basic index.

Orbis Geographicus 1992/93 [serial]. World Directory of Geography. Stuttgart, Germany: Franz Steiner Verlag, 1992. The goal of this 7th edition is to be a comprehensive directory of international geography. Its lists by country (and under U.S. by state), all known committees, societies, associations, academies, departments, agencies, etc., of geography. Well designed, with a good index.

BIOGRAPHY

Freeman, T.W., M. Oughton, and P. Pinchemel, eds. Geographers: Biobibliographical Studies. London: Mansell, 1977- (Annual). Similar to the Dictionary of American Library Biography, this title includes essays with bibliographies on figures of importance to the field of geography. All biographees are deceased. International in scope. Indexed.

Tooley, Ronald V. Tooley's Dictionary of Mapmakers. New York: Alan R. Liss, 1979 (supplement 1985). Provides information such as name, address, and date of published work(s) on mapmakers from ancient times to 1900.

HANDBOOKS

Background Notes [http://www.state.gov/www/background_notes/]

Full-text and updated periodically, the U.S. State Department Background Notes on geographic entities and international organizations is now online. Organized by region and country or international organization, there's a lot more information here than the basic statistical and geographic information located in almanacs. History, government and political conditions are discussed, as well as the economy, foreign relations and basic travel information. Also listed are principal U.S. officials and consulate officers.

Boyer, Richard and David Savageau. Places Rated Almanac; Your Guide to Finding the Best Places to Live in America. All new ed. New York: Prentice Hall Travel, 1989. Ranks U.S. metropolitan areas according to climate, housing, health care and environment, crime, transportation, education, recreation, the arts, and economics. No index.

The World Factbook. Washington: Central Intelligence Agency, 1981- . (Annual). . http://www.odci.gov/cia/publications/factbook/] A product of the National Foreign Assessment Center. Includes information on each country of the world. Country and regional maps. The World Factbook is prepared by the Central Intelligence Agency for the use of US Government officials, and the style, format, coverage, and content are designed to meet their specific requirements.

GAZETTEERS

Chamber's World Gazetteer: An A-Z of Geographical Information. 5th ed. Cambridge, Eng.: Chambers, 1988. A general gazetteer with an emphasis on Great Britain. Indicates pronunciation. Geographical dictionary of world places and cross references.

Cohen, Saul B. The Columbia Gazetter of the World. New York: Columbia University Press, 1998.

Fisher, Morris. Provinces and Provincial Capitals of the World. 2d ed. Metuchen, N.J.: Scarecrow Pr., 1985. 224 countries included. Name index.

Kurian, George T. Geo-data; The World Almanac

Gazetteer. Detroit: Gale Research, 1989. All countries are included, but the main emphasis is on the United States. Descriptive encyclopedia of countries, continents, and oceans. Profiles of the physical environment of 204 nations and territories as well as maps.

Merriam-Webster's Geographical Dictionary 3rd ed. .Springfield, MA: Merriam-Webster, 1997. This completely new edition is "a comprehensive desk-sized guide to the places of the world. Its objective is to provide...essential information on spelling, pronunciation, type of feature, location...size, economy, history...."

The National Gazetteer of the United States of America. Prep. by the U.S. Geological Survey in cooperation with the U.S. Board on Geographic Names. Washington: Govt. Prt. Off., 1984. Information on approximately 2,000,000 place names in the U.S. Individual volumes for various U.S. states.

Omni Gazetteer of the United States of America. Detroit, MI: Omnigrahics, 1991. [

Paxton, John. The Stateman's Year-book World Gazetteer. 3rd ed. New York: St. Martin's Pr., 1986. A companion to the Stateman's Year-Book, this gives brief information for each location. Provides the essential data for each country but there is no attempt to duplicate the detailed Statesman's Year-Book descriptions.

Room, Adrian. Place-name Changes 1900-1991. Metuchen, N.J.: Scarecrow Press, 1993. Cross references to previous names. Each entry gives present name, identification, location, former name(s), and year or years of renaming. Contains an appendix of official country names.

Room, Adrian. Room, Adrian. Placenames of the World: Origins and Meanings of the Names for Over 5000 Natural Features, Countries, Capitals, Territories, Cities and Historic Sites. Jefferson, N.C.: McFarland, 1997. Title is self explanatory.

Times, London. Index-Gazetteer of the World. London: Times Pub. Co., 1965. Longitude and latitude coordinates to nearly 345,000 geographical features found in the Times Atlas. Also useful for other atlases.

U.S. Gazetteer [http://www.census.gov/cgi-bin/gazetteer]

This Census Bureau site provides names of state, type of place, longitude, latidtude, zip code, access to a TIGER map of the area, and access to census data.

USGS Geographic Names Information System [http://www-nmd.usgs.gov/www/gnis/gnisform.html]

Retrieves detailed information about a specific place or point of interest in the U.S. Includes: Elevation, Population, Description, History Notes, Variant Names, and USGS 7.5' Map Names. Can query by Feature Name, County, State or Feature Type. Can also combine Elevation or Population (up-to-date) with State, County, or Feature Type. Includes maps from the U.S. Census Bureau's Tiger Mapping Service. From the U.S. Geological Survey.

Webster's New Geographical Dictionary. Springfield, MA: Merriam-Webster, 1988. Dictionary arrangement with 47,000 entries. Emphasis is on the U.S. and Canada and other English language areas.

Wilcocks, Julie. Countries and Islands of the World: A Guide to Nomenclature. 2d ed. London: Clive Bingley, 1985. Name and government changes that have occurred since the 15th century in areas of importance to modern history. Intended for reference librarians.

Gazetteer of India: Indian Union. Gazetteer of India was first published in 1965 on behalf of the Gazetteers Unit, Ministry of Education and Social Welfare. It was published by Publications Division, Ministry of Information and Broadcasting. Apart from it District Gazetteers are also issued, They contain plenty of charts, tables, maps etc.

GEOGRAPHICAL NAMES AND TERMS

Kane, Joseph N. The American Counties. 4th ed.

Metuchen, N.J.: Scarecrow, 1983. Subtitle: Origins of county names, dates of creation and organization, area, population including 1980 census figures, historical data, and published sources.

Sealock, Richard B, Margaret M. Sealock, and Margaret S. Powell. Bibliography of Place-name Literature: United States and Canada. 3d ed. Chicago: American Library Association, 1982. More than 4,800 references to books and journal articles, many annotated. Arranged by form and geographic region. Indexed.

Sharp, Harold S. Handbook of Geographical Nicknames. Metuchen, N.J.: Scarecrow, 1980. Nicknames are cross-referenced with accepted names; locations and descriptions given. Does not cover U.S.; see Kane and Alexander.

U.S. Geographic Board. Sixth Report, 1890-1932. Washington: GPO, 1933. Reports geographic name changes and also the characteristics of place names.

ATLASES

A. Guides

Kister, Kenneth F. Kister's Atlas Buying Guide: General English-language World Atlases Available in North America. Phoenix: Oryx Pr., 1984. Provides detailed data and evaluation of 105 atlases. Discusses general evaluative principles for this format. Indexed.

B. World Atlases

1. Contemporary

Global Explorer: The Most Detailed World Atlas Ever. DeLorme Mapping, Lower Main Street, P.O. Box 298, Freeport, ME 04032. CD-ROM, Miscrosoft/Windows Compatible; full-color maps of the whole world; detail zoom in and out; indexed references more than 120,000 places; street maps of major world cities; detailed topographical maps of entire planet; country profiles with up-to-date economics, social, and cultural statistics; network of air routes; descriptions of 20,000 historical, cultural, and geographical features.

Goode, John Paul. Goode's World Atlas. 18th ed. Chicago: Rand McNally, 1990. A good atlas for student use including many physical and political maps. Index indicates pronunciation. First published in 1922 as Goode's School Atlas.

MapExpert: Version 2.0 for Windows. DeLorme Mapping, Lower Main Street, P.O. Box 298, Freeport, ME 04032 Map Printer; Map Marker; Map Note; Mural Maker. Offers latitude and longitude display and dozen of other features such as locating by phone number, zip code, street and place name; line, text, and symbol overlays calculating distances; pan and zoom; address ranges for major metro areas; etc.

Mapquest. [http://www.mapquest.com]

Includes interactive street guide to the U.S.

Maps on File. New York: Facts on File, 1981- . (Looseleaf. Convenient for photocopying. Indexed; annual supplements.

The National Atlas of the United States [http://www-atlas.usgs.gov/]

This Web site displays an interactive map of the United States allowing the user to "map more than 2 million geographic names" in a series of map layers. These map layers display airports, federal lands, urban areas, water features, parkways, rivers, railroads, roads, volcanoes and seismic events with a Zoom In/Zoom Out feature. All these map layers can be downloaded along with very detailed technical information.

National Geographic Society. Cartographic Division. National Geographic Atlas of the World. 6th ed. Washington, the Society, 1992. Based on maps from National Geographic. Indexed. See National Geographic's collection of online maps, Map Machine, at http://www.nationalgeographic.com/resources/ngo/maps/.

Prentice-Hall's Great International Atlas. Trade Ed. Englewood Cliffs, N.J.: Prentice-Hall, 1981. Current as well as historical and thematic maps. Includes economic statistical data for each country.

Rand McNally and Co. Rand McNally Cosmopolitan World Atlas. New ed. Chicago: Rand McNally, 1987. Regional breakdown of world; state-by-state maps of U.S.

New International Atlas. Chicago: Rand McNally, 1989. This atlas uses metric measurements and uses the local native language names for features when ever possible.

The Times Atlas of the World. 9th comp. ed. New York: Times Books, 1992. Includes various projections and scales. Index-Gazetteer includes over 200,000 names. Includes latitude and longitude coordinates. Uses British spelling of place names.

2. Historical and Thematic

Ahroni, Yohamn and Michael Avi-Yonah. The Macmillan Bible Atlas. 3rd ed. New York: Macmillan, 1993. "Shows, as far as possible through maps of each event, the changes and historical processes on the lands of Bible."

Chadwick, Henry and G.R. Evans, eds. Atlas of the Christian Church. New York: Facts on File, 1987. Portrait of Christian traditions and history through maps and illustrations. Includes an index and a bibliography.

De Lange, N.R.M. Atlas of the Jewish World. New York: Facts on File, 1984. Provides an historical background, essays on Jewish experiences, and a tour through today's Jewish communities.

The Economist Atlas. The Shape of the World Today. New York: Economist, 1989. World and regions cover of geographic (climate, resources), economic, demographic, finance, education and environmental aspects. World maps and world encyclopedia.

Femandez-Armesto, Felipe, ed. The Times Atlas of World Exploration: 3,000 Years of Exploring, Explorers, and Mapmaking. New York: Harper Collins, 1991. "Provides the most exhaustive coverage of world exploration."

Garwood, Alfred N., ed. Weather America: The Latest Detailed Climatological Data for over 4,000 Places with Rankings. Milpittas, CA: Toucan Valley Pubs., 1996.

Kirdon, Michael and Ronal dSegal. The State of the World Atlas. New rev. 5th ed. London; New York: Penguin, 1995. This atlas graphically portrays the world situation regarding a wide variety of social issues. Topics include the environmental crisis, population growth, international debt, income inequality, discrimination against women, the spread of AIDs, and world unemployment.

Kurian, George Thomas ed. Atlas of the Third World. 2nd ed. New York: Facts on File, 1992. This work contains "maps and statistical charts describing the economic, political, demographic, and geographic aspects of the world's developing countries."

Martin, Gilbert. Atlas of the Holocaust. Oxford, Eng.: Pergamon Press, 1993. [Contains 314 chronological maps of the Holocaust and explanatory texts of how it evolved.

Martin Greenwald Associates. Historical Maps on File. New York: Facts on File, 1984. Looseleaf as is Maps on File, but covering historical topics and time periods.

Seager, Joni. The State of Women in the World Atlas. New rev. 2nd ed. London; New York: Penguin, 1997. Contents include: women in the world; families; birthrights; body politics; work; to have and have not; power.

Shepherd, William R. Historical Atlas. New York, Holt, 1911- . This is consider the standard general historical atlas. The 1980 edition contains all the maps from earlier editions as well as a special supplement of historical maps covering 1929-1980.

The Times Atlas of the Second World War. New York: Harper and Row, 1989. Conveys to users the totality and complexity of World War II, including the economic and political factors as well as military ones. Covers the costs-both human and financial.

The Times Atlas of World History. 4th ed. Maplewood, NJ: Hammond, 1993 Attractive coverage of world history. Presents "world-wide" coverage of history. Economic and social history are covered as well as political history.

The Weather Almanac. Detroit, MI: Gale Research, 1974- Complements daily sources of weather information. Includes maps, charts, and safety rules.

C. Atlases of the United States.

1. National and State.

Atlas of North America: Space Age Portrait of a Continent. Washington, D.C.: Smithsonian Institution, 1985. Includes color Landsat photographs of the United States.

Martin Greenwald Associates. State Maps on File. New York: Facts on File, 1984—. Great variation in maps from one state to the next. Includes boundary and topographical data.

Mattson, Mark T. Atlas of 1990 Census. New York: Macmillan, 1992 Documents current American position. Provides a dynamic view by combining data of previous census, with the 1990 census.

North Carolina: County Maps. Lyndon Station, WI: County Maps, 1980. Contains interesting maps and interesting facts for each North Carolina county.

Rand McNally Road Atlas. Chicago: Rand McNally, 1926-

Rand McNally Standard Highway Mileage Guide. Chicago: Rand McNally, 1987. Contains 910,575 indexes mileage between 1,350 major U.S. and Canadian cities and 124,500 highway mileage segments for computing mileage between more than 110,000 places.

2. Historical and Thematic.

Allen, James P. and Eugene J. Turner. We The People: An Atlas of America's Ethnic Diversity. New York: Macmillan, 1988. Description of ethnic diversity in the U.S. as of 1980. Includes breakdowns for people originating from: early North

America, western Europe, northern Europe, eastern Europe, southern Europe, the Middle East, Africa, Middle and South America, and Asia and the Pacific.

Atlas of Demographics: U.S. by County. Boulder, CO: Infomap, 1982 Figures are based on the 1980 census. Provides "a graphical and tabular presentation at the county level of 16 statistics." Map of all U.S. counties.

Atlas of Early American History: The Revolutionary Era, 1760-1790. Princeton: Princeton Univ. Pr., 1976. Includes maps of cities, colonies; boundaries; Indian settlements; population and economic, cultural, political, and military activity.

Atlas of the United States: A Thematic and Comparative Approach. New York: Macmillan, 1986. This atlas provides geographic, demographic sociological, economic, and scientific data. Maps and corresponding tables and text appear on every two page spread.

Hammond Inc. Hammond Historical Atlas of the World. Maplewood, N.J.: Hammond, 1984.

United States History Atlas. Maplewood, N.J.: Hammond,

Hanson, Gerald T. Historical Atlas of Arkansas. Norman, OK: University of Oklahomas Press, 1989. Shows how geography of Arkansas has affected the lives of its residents and the state's history.

Historical Atlas of the United States. Centennial ed. Washington, D.C.: National Geographic Society, 1988.

Martis, Kenneth C. The Historical Atlas of Political Parties in the United States Congress, 1789-1989. New York: Macmillan, 1989. Published in celebration of bicentennial of the U.S. Congress in 1989. It is the second of a multivolume series "designed to elucidate the geographic aspects of the U.S. Congress and American political history." First work in series was The Historical Atlas of United States Congressional Districts. 1789-1983.

Martis, Kenneth C. The Historical Atlas of United States Congressional Districts, 1789-1983. New York: Free Pr., 1982First work to include maps of all U.S. congressional districts. "A complete congressional district and representative history of every city, county, and state in the U.S."

Rand McNally Commercial Atlas and Marketing Guide. 127th ed. Chicago: Rand McNally, 1996. Includes breakdowns for transportation, communication, economic, and population data. Brings economic and geographic data together.

D. Atlases of Europe.

1. Contemporary.

Bartholomew Road Atlas. Europe. Edinburgh: John Bartholomew, 1985. Written in English, French, German, and Italian. Includes country, regional, and city maps as well as a unique index.

The Economist Atlas of the New Europe. New York: Holt, 1992 Covers major European trends and issues based on data current to 1985-1990. Great sections on transportation, communications, political integration, finance, European trade, political and parliamentary systems, federalism, pollution, and environment.

Europa Auto-Atlas. Bern, Switz.: Hallway AG. [

Rand McNally Updated Road Atlas and City Guide of Europe. Chicago: Rand McNally, 1993. Includes road maps of all European countries and 18 cities; visa and tourist information, a route planner, mileage charts, a chart of international road signs, and tips for driving in Europe.

2. Historical and Thematic.

Ardagh, John and Colin Jones. Cultural Atlas of France. New York: Facts on File, 1991. As in the other books of this series (i.e. "Atlas of the Jewish World"), this books fills a gap between titles dealing with history and those focusing on travel. Focuses on events in the areas of French politics and government, religion, culture, society, and the economy.

Matthew, Donald. Atlas of Medieval Europe. Oxford, Eng.: Phaidon, 1983. Provides many illustrations and maps and text to put them in context. Includes a general survey of the period.

E. Atlases of Africa.

Historical Atlas of Africa. Cambridge, Eng.: Cambridge University Press, 1985.

TRAVEL GUIDES

Good articles concerning travel guides include:

Anthony, Carolyn. "The World in the '90s." Publishers Weekly 237 (Jan. 19, 1990: 20-30.

Crichton, Jean. "Travel USA." Publishers Weekly 237 (May 4, 1990): 17-28.

Haner, Barbara E. "Summertime Traveling with Geologic Maps." Information Bulletin of the Western Association of Map Libraries 21 (June 1990): 168-69.

Hooper, Brad. "Travel Guides." Booklist 89 (March 15, 1993): 1302-3 and Booklist 90 (Sept. 15, 1993): 134-5.

Langstaff, Peggy. "The digital traveler (electronic travel books: bibliographical essay)." Publisher's Weekly 240 (Sept. 13, 1993): 46-7.

Mroz, Marguerite. "Move your travel collection southeasterly (core collection)." Library Journal (March 1, 1992): 57-60.

Otness, Harold M. "Travel Guidebooks: a world of information for libraries." Wilson Library Bulletin 67 (Jan. 1993): 38-40+

Riipa, Karole. "A Round-up of 1990 Travel Books." Publishers Weekly 237 (Jan. 19, 1990): 38-56.

Riipa, Karole. "A Round-up of 1993 Travel Books." Publishers Weekly 240 (Jan. 25, 1993): 55-6+

American Automobile Association. Tour Book.

Washington, D.C.: AAA, various dates. Free to members. [Davis Ref. Desk]

Baedeker's Handbooks for Travelers. New York: Macmillian Travel.

City.Net [http://www.city.net/]

Comprehensive international guide to communities around the world. Provides information on travel, entertainment, and local business, plus government and community services for all regions of the world. Directory service of Excite.

The Complete Guide to America's National Parks. 1992-93 ed. Washington D.C.: The Foundation, 1990. Despite a rather confusing format, this book is full of valuable information to travelers, such as fees, accommodations, nearest medical facilities, average weather conditions, etc.

Durham, Michael S. Smithsonian Guide to Historic America. New York: Stewart, Tabori and Chang, 1989-. Series starts with 12 volumes such as The Mid-Atlantic States [U.L. F106 .D95 1989] Interesting to read even if you never travel.

Federal Writer's Program, comp. American Guide Series. Various publishers, 1937-49.

Fielding's Europe. New York: Fielding Pubs, 1979- . Continues: Fielding's Travel Guide to Europe. New York: Sloane, 1948-1978.

Fodor, Eugene, ed. Fodor's Travel Guides. New York: McKay, 1936- . For example:

Fodor's ... United States of America. New York: Fodor's Travel Pubs., 1988. Frommer's Travel Guides. New York: Frommer, various dates. For example:

Frommer's Guide to Dublin and Ireland. New York: Frommer/Pasmantier, 1981- . [Davis DA995 .D8F76]

Let's Go. The Budget Guide to....

Michelin Guides. New Hyde Park, N.Y.: Michelin Guides.

Microsoft Expedia [http://expedia.msn.com/]

Four major sections: Travel Agent, with flight, hotel and auto reservations; Maps; Resources, with a world guide, hotel directory, 10,000 links to Web sites around the world, currency converter, and weather info; and Communicate, where travelers exchange information.

Official Hotel Guide. Secaucus, N.J.: Reed Travel Group, 1991-

6. Yearbook, Almanacs and Directories

Yearbooks

Yearbook is an annual documentary, historical, or memorial compendium of facts, photographs, statistics, etc., about the events of the preceding year, often limited to a specific country, institution, discipline, or subject. Optional yearbooks are offered by some publishers of general encyclopedias. Most libraries place yearbooks on continuous order and shelve them in the reference collection. Yearbooks of historical significance may be stored in archive or special collections. Also spelled year book. The ALA Glossary defines yearbook as " an annual volume of current information in descriptive and/or statistical form, sometimes limited to a specified field".

Yearbooks provide recent and update information on subjects or personalities. Comparison with an encyclopedia reveals that the yearbook gives current information. There are yearbooks that are issued as supplements to encyclopedia like the Britannica Yearbook.

Almanacs

Originally, almanac is a book introduced by the Moors to Spain, listing the days, weeks, and months of the year and providing information about festivals, holidays, astronomical phenomena, etc. In modern usage, an annual compendium of practical dates, facts, and statistics, current and/or retrospective, often arranged in tables to facilitate comparison.

Almanacs can be traced all the way back to the ancient

Persians and Romans. Back then they mostly contained information on the movement of the heavens. Over the years they expanded to cover the calendar, weather forecasts, first aid, recipes and numerous random facts.

Directories

Directory is a list of people, companies, institutions, organizations, etc., in alphabetical or classified order, providing contact information (names, addresses, phone/FAX numbers, etc.) And other pertinent details (affiliations, conferences, publications, membership, etc.) In brief format, often published serially (example: American Library Directory). In most libraries, current directories are shelved in ready reference or in the reference records.

Some examples of yearbooks, almanacs and directories are given below:

The Statesman's Yearbook 2004: The Politics, Cultures and Economies of the World

For one hundred and forty years, The Statesman's Yearbook has been relied upon to provide accurate and comprehensive information on the current political, economic and social status of every country in the world. The appointment of the new editor - only the seventh in the book's history - brought enhancements to the 1998-99 edition and these have been continued since then. The 2004 edition is fully updated and contains more information than ever before. A foldout colour section provides a political world map and flags for the one hundred and ninety two countries of the world. - In an endlessly changing world, the annual publication of The Statesman's Yearbook gives all the information you need in one easily digestible single volume. It will save hours of research and cross-referencing between different sources, and it is an essential annual purchase.

Statesman's Yearbook was first published by Macmillan in 1864. The yearbooks presents statistical and historical facts about the states of the world. It is divided into the following main part:

- International Organizations
- The Commonwealth
- United States
- Other countries

It has listed all entries country wise in alphabetical order covering a brief account of its constitution, government, area, population, religion, education, finance, commerce, communication, defence etc. Bibliography is also provided at the end of information.

Europa Yearbook

Europa Yearbook was first published in in 1956 from London by Europa Publications in two volumes. The first volume covers international organizations and Europe whereas the second part is devoted to Africa, America, Asia and Australia. The first volume gives detailed information about the United Nations and its agencies and also other international organizations. The entries are arramged in alphabetical order. Each entry provides information on governments, constitution, population, religeon, press publishers, finance, trade and industry, transport, atomic energy, a brief list of universities etc.

Europa World is the online version of the Europa World Year Book, the indispensable source of information on world-wide affairs. First published in 1926, the year book is renowned as one of the world's leading reference works, covering political and economic information in over 250 countries and territories, from Afghanistan to Zimbabwe. For the first time, this invaluable resource is available in a dynamic new online format.

Europa World delivers

* Regular updates of authoritative content providing current data and impartial analysis

* The latest available statistics by country and the ability to directly compare multinational statistics
* Thousands of directory contact details with click-through web links to external sites
* Details of over 1,650 international organizations, such as the United Nations, the European Union and NATO
* Intuitive functionality allowing full accessibility to the data-rich content, including a full range of sophisticated search and browse functions
* A variety of interactive visual features, including downloadable graphs and maps

The World Almanac and Book of Facts

2004 Edition

World Almanac was first published in 1868 by Newspaper Enterprises Association, New York. It provides general information and statistical data on various subjects like industry, finance, labour, medicine, sports, literature, education, agriculture etc. It also provides data on census, major cities, population etc.

Now in its third century of publication, The World Almanac remains the one source people turn to when they need comprehensive and reliable information on just about any subject imaginable. Faster and easier to use than the Internet and other on-line sources, it's no wonder The World Almanac is a perennial bestseller on every national list and the one almanac found in homes, libraries, schools, businesses, and media outlets throughout the world. No other almanac comes close to matching The World Almanac's scope, breadth of information, authoritativeness, timeliness, and ease of use.

Completely updated from first page to last, and with more information than ever before, The World Almanac 2004 continues the 136-year tradition of providing the most information on the most topics, including:

* Get More Familiar with Your World: Authoritative, up-to-date information on population, nations, states, economy, environment, education, sports, health, computers, history, presidents, personalities, awards, religion, sciences, the sun, and everything under it
* Remember 2003: Color photo scrapbook, authoritative chronology, Top Ten news stories, obituaries, quotes, and offbeat news of the year.
* Compare Your Opinions with the Experts: Check out our Editors' Picks all-time rankings for films, music, history, and more; then send in your votes for next year's World Almanac
* Get Yourself or a Loved One into the Right College: A special essay by the editors of the Fiske Guides for college entrance
* Understand Baby Boomers: A statistical profile and memories timeline, with essays by Wendy Wasserstein and Joyce Maynard
* Use It All the Time: 2004 planning calendar; 2004 presidential election information; 2004 tax guide; business and associations directories; anti-terrorism preparation; crossword puzzle reference; mortgage-rate, mileage, and metric calculators; health and nutrition information; ZIP and area codes

Whitaker's Almanac

Published annually in Britain since 1868, Whitaker's Almanac is the ultimate single volume reference source. Such is its reputation that a copy of the 1878 edition was included in the time capsule beneath Cleopatra's Needle and Sherlock Holmes used it when deciphering a code in The Valley of Fear! During the Second World War, Winston Churchill wrote to the editor seeking reassurance that publication would not be interrupted by the Blitz.

Whitaker's Almanac covers a wide range of subject areas

and each page contains a wealth of essential facts and figures - perfect for keeping you up to date with who's who and what's what in today's ever-changing world.

Universities Handbook (30th Edition)

The 30th edition of 'Universities Handbook' is a compendium that contains latest information on 277 university-level institutions (AIU Members), including 60 'Deemed Universities' in India. Of these, 171 are conventional universities (including 32 institutions for specialized studies in various disciplines). 37 institutions provide education in agriculture, 38 engineering and technical institutions, 1 journalism, 4 law, 16 health sciences and 10 are open universities.

The Handbook, which is published every alternate year, gives information relating to Officers and Deans of Faculties; Library and Research Facilities; Scholarships and Fellowships; Academic year – last date for admission and the approximate dates of examinations; Courses of Studies; Minimum requirements for admission to each course; Duration and the subjects of study for each course; Names of Faculties; Names of Professors and Readers/Associate Professors with their specialisations (department-wise); Names of affiliated/ constituent Colleges together with names of Principals and Heads of Postgraduate Departments in the Colleges.

Commonwealth Universities Yearbook 2003-04

Commonwealth of Learning is a publication of the Commonwealth Countries. It was first published in 1914 from London by the Association of Commonwealth Universities. In the beginning the title of this publication was "Yearbook of the Universities of the Empire but from 1946 1948-57 it was published under the title "Yearbook of the Universities of the Commonwealth"

Compiled for academics, resource managers, students and others seeking comprehensive and reliable data at global level, the ACU Yearbook is a key resource on every aspect of higher education - senior staff, general facilities, degree programmes and research strengths - at over 700 universities throughout the Commonwealth. In total, 36 countries are covered in Africa, Asia, Australasia, Europe, Canada and the Caribbean.

The uniqueness of the Commonwealth Universities Yearbook lies in the huge range of institutions it covers and the depth of its data. With over 2,600 pages of fully verified facts, it retains its long-standing reputation for keeping the academic world up to date with the growth and changes taking place in higher education in much of the English-speaking world, and is an essential 'buy'.

Sourcing information about universities, whether old or new, at home or in distant lands, can often be a problem. The Yearbook will answer many queries. Its profiles provide a 'snapshot' of an institution's development, the people who work there and the courses taught.

A recent survey revealed these to be the institutional data and contact details. Nearly 60,000 telephone and fax numbers, e-mail and web addresses are listed. With these, it is easy to make contact with specific areas within an institution: campuses, faculties, schools, departments, research centres and, also, managers responsible for central services such as admissions, library, finance, international affairs, public relations, purchasing and quality assurance.

University heads and other senior institutional staff, academics and researchers including deans, heads of schools and faculty managers, continuing education professionals, university resource managers, international student recruiters, study abroad advisors, careers counselors, librarians and students regularly consult the book. Internationally it is seen as a kitemark of quality, the incentive for inclusion being to promote first and higher degrees and research standing in an increasingly competitive global marketplace.

The World of Learning

World of Learning is a brought out by Europa Publications. It is being published since 1971-72 in two volumes. The first volume covers a large number of international, educational scientific and cultural organizations and councils under various subjects arranging the names of the countries in alphabetical order.. It provides information about universities about year of foundation, addresses, addresses, languages of instruction, chief officers, affiliated or constituent colleges, university library and its collection, etc. The print edition of this internationally respected title has become widely acclaimed as the premier source of information on the academic sphere world-wide.

The online version of The World of Learning builds on this success by providing a full range of sophisticated search and browse functions, and regular updates of content. The result is a site that offers an unprecedented level of access to global institutions of higher education and learning, and to the people who work within them.

7. Bibliographies

The word bibliography has been originated from the Greek word 'bibliographia', meaning 'the writing of books'. The word has passed through various meanings but in the modern times, it is ordinarily associated with the activities of providing references to publications. Bibliography is now defined as a systematic list or enumeration of written works by a specific author or on a given subject, or which share one or more common characteristics (language, form, period, place of publication, etc.).

Representative Bibliographies

Universal Bibliographies

British Museum. Department of Printed Books. General Catalogue of Printed Books. London: Trustees of the British Museum, 1959-1966.

The catalog is a complete record of the printed books in the Library of the British Museum (now the British Library), which have appeared from the 15th century to the end of 1955, in all languages except those of Asia. The Library is particularly important because of the extent and richness of its collections in all fields and languages, and also because its possession of the copyright privilege helps make it the most comprehensive collection of British publications in existence. Its catalog, therefore, is an indispensable bibliographical source for the scholar and librarian. In the main, it is an author catalog only, with catchword title entries, cross-references for anonymous books, etc. Subject entries are included to a limited extent, principally for the following: (1) under personal names, biographical works are included; (2) under countries, e.g., England, France, etc., are entered official publications, some works about the country, and many titles in which the name of the country occurs; and (3) under names of sacred books, e.g., Bible, Kur'an, etc., are entered both texts and works about them. Two important reference features are: (1) the large amount of analytical material included (analysis of series, etc.), and (2) the many cross-references from names of editors, translators, or other personal names.

The amount of bibliographical information varies; titles taken from the 19th-century catalog usually include only author, title, editor, place, and date, whereas more recent cataloging adds publisher, paging, and size. Some cataloging for early printed books is fairly full.

Although the National Reference Library of Science and Invention (formerly the Patent Office Library) was amalgamated with the British Museum in 1966, its holdings are not recorded in the General catalogue nor in the 1966-70 supplement. Attention is called to some arrears in cataloging of United Kingdom materials published 1966-67, and the British national bibliography will have to be consulted for those years.

Bibliothèque nationale (France). Département des

imprimés. Catalogue général des livres imprimés de la Bibliothèque nationale. Auteurs... Paris: Imprimerie nationale, 1897-1981. 231v.

An important modern catalog, the value of which cannot be overestimated. An alphabetical author catalog, including only entries under names of personal authors, with the necessary cross-references; does not include title entries for anonymous books or entries for anonymous classics, periodicals or society transactions or government or corporate authors. The cataloging is excellent; the information given includes author's full name whenever possible, title, place, publisher, date, edition, paging or volumes, format, and occasional notes of contents, original publication in case of reprints from periodicals, etc. An important reference feature, in the case of authors whose works are voluminous, is the detailed alphabetical title index under the author's name, which indicates in what volumes or editions a given work may be found, and also indicates alternative and changed titles. In addition to its comprehensive coverage of French publications, the catalog is particularly strong in other Romance-language and classical materials.

Originally each volume included titles acquired up to the date of publication of that particular volume, so that there is a wide spread in coverage between the first volumes published in 1900 and those issued half a century later. Beginning with v. 189, however, no imprints after 1959 have been included, and this policy continues through the end of the alphabet. There have been published supplements from time to time

National Bibliographies

British National Bibliography

Books and new serials have been recorded since 1950 in the British National Bibliography (BNB). The BNB is the single most comprehensive body for listing of books and serials published in the U.K and obliged by law to send a copy of all new publications, including serial titles, to the Legal Deposit Office of the British Library. This material is catalogued by experienced staff using the Anglo-American Cataloguing Rules (AACR2) and subject indexed using Library of Congress Subject Headings (LCSH) and the Dewey Decimal Classification system (21st edition). This work is done in partnership with the five other British and Irish libraries allowed by law the privilege of legal deposit, under the Copyright Libraries Shared Cataloguing Programme (CLSCP).

BNB also contains details of forthcoming books. Under the Cataloguing-in-Publication Programme (CIP) information on new titles appears up to 16 weeks ahead of the announced publication date. Advance information on well over 50,000 titles each year is provided in this way.

The coverage of BNB has always been selective (see exclusions policy) with the emphasis being on mainstream monographs available through normal book buying channels.

BNB is published monthly on CD-ROM and weekly in print.

American National Bibliographies:

Although many of the bibliographies listed below are incomplete and contain inaccuracies, they still provide some of the most comprehensive listings of titles published in the United States. Microform collections may reproduce the some of the works described. For additional information on bibliographies, see James Harner's Literary Research Guide shelved behind the Reference Desk) or volume one of The Reader's Advisor

Databases 1473-1800

LOCATION: Library Databases (Univ. of Delaware users only)

The ESTC contains descriptions of English or English-language letterpress materials published before 1801. The database includes records for items of all types published in

Great Britain or its colonies or in English anywhere in the world from 1473 to 1800. The records provide extensive descriptions and holdings information. Use the Early English Books Online database to obtain digitized images of books published in England from 1475 to 1700. (It is important to note that ESTC was for many years the abbreviation for the Eighteenth Century Short Title Catalogue. ESTC numbers belong to this printed bibliography.)

Databases 1800-1900

The Nineteenth Century Short Title Catalogue database may be used for 19th-century bibliographic research due to the lack of a national or trade bibliography for this period. Series I. and II. are available at Workstation #33 in the Reference Room. A portion of Series III. is also available and will be completed in a series of fourteen discs published until 2002.

The NSTC is a catalog of nineteenth-century imprints in English, wherever published, held by the the Bodleian Library, Oxford University; the University Library, Cambridge University; Trinity College Library, Dublin; National Library of Scotland, Edinburgh; Harvard University Library; the British Library, London; the University Library, Newcastle; and the Library of Congress, Washington, D.C. A guide to searching the NSTC electronic database is available on the Web at http://www2.lib.udel.edu/ref/howto/nstc.htm.

Check DELCAT by title or author for University of Delaware holdings of items listed in the NSTC. A small number of the items may be found in a microfiche collection called The Nineteenth Century (Microforms Area - Microfiche S 306). The Library owns only a portion of the entire collection available. Some, but not all, of these microfiche items are cataloged in DELCAT. An index to microfiche units 1-70 of The Nineteenth Century collection is available on CD-ROM

Printed Bibliographies 1492-1639

Sabin's Dictionary provides bibliographic information on publications related to the political, governmental, economic, social, intellectual, and religious history of the Western Hemisphere from 1492-1876. There is an author-title index: John Edgar Molnar, comp. Author-Title Index to Joseph Sabin's Dictionary of Books Relating to America. There is no subject index to Sabin's work. The Dictionary was begun by Sabin in the mid-nineteenth century and was continued by Eames and Vail after his death

Printed Bibliographies 1639-1800

Evans, Charles. The American Bibliography: A Chronological Dictionary of All Books, Pamphlets and Periodical Publications Printed in the United States of America from the Genesis of Printing in 1639 Down to and Including the Year 1800; with Bibliographical and Biographical Notes. New York: P. Smith, 1941-59.

The American Bibliography attempts to list bibliographic information for all works published in America from 1639 through 1800. Entries are arranged chronologically and within each year, alphabetically by author. Each entry contains the book's full title, author's name, author's birth and death dates, date and place of publication, number of pages, size, and often the library holding a copy of the book. Clifford Shipton completed volume 13 for 1799-1800 and Roger Pattrell Bristol provided volume 14, the index, in The American Bibliography of Charles Evans (Microforms Area—Microfiche S 269.2). Bristol's two-volume Supplement to Charles Evans' American Bibliography (Microforms Area—Microfiche S 269.3) and its index identified about 11,000 additional items. Each item in the Evans and Bristol volumes has been assigned a unique "Evans" number.

Printed Bibliographies 1801-1819

Sabin's A Dictionary of Books Relating to America, from Its Discovery to the Present Time (see entry above).

Shaw, Ralph R. and Richard H. Shoemaker. American Bibliography: A Preliminary Checklist. New York: Scarecrow Press, 1958.

Shaw and Shoemaker continue the American national bibliography begun by Evans into the nineteenth century, identifying and listing chronologically by year over 50,000 works printed in America from 1801 through 1819. Each item is assigned a unique "Shaw-Shoemaker" number that identifies it in the microfiche collection based on the catalog (Early American Imprints, 1801-1819, Microforms Area—Microfiche S269.5). Many of the items are cataloged in DELCAT

Printed Bibliographies 1820-1861

Sabin's A Dictionary of Books Relating to America, from Its Discovery to the Present Time

Roorbach, Orville Augustus. Bibliotheca Americana: A Catalogue of American Publications, Including Reprints and Original Works, from 1820 [to Jan. 1861]. Together with a List of Periodicals Published in the United States. New York: P. Smith, 1939.

Roorbach's bibliography is an author and title list of books published in the United States from 1820 to January 1861. Biographies are listed under subject, rather than author. Legal publications and periodicals occupy separate lists in the 1820-1852 volumes

Printed Bibliographies 1861-1876

Sabin's A Dictionary of Books Relating to America, from Its Discovery to the Present Time

The Checklist is a continuation of Shaw's American Bibliography for 1820-1886, supplying more detailed information than Roorbach. Like Shaw, it devotes a volume to each year and lists entries alphabetically by author, corporate author, or title of an anonymous work; unlike Evans, its predecessor, it excludes serial publications. Author and title indexes have been compiled for entries from 1820-1829.

Printed Bibliographies 1876-1910

Leypoldt, Frederick. American Catalogue: Author and Title Entries of Books in Print and for Sale (Including Reprints and Importations), July 1, 1876 [-Dec. 31, 1910]. New York:

Leypoldt's American Catalogue records books in print and for sale. Its entries are arranged by author, title, and subject.

The Checklist is a continuation of Shaw's American Bibliography for 1820-1886, supplying more detailed information than Roorbach. Like Shaw, it devotes a volume to each year and lists entries alphabetically by author, corporate author, or title of an anonymous work; unlike Evans, its predecessor, it excludes serial publications. Author and title indexes have been compiled for entries from 1820-1829.

Entitled The United States Catalog: Books in Print from 1898-1928, the CBI lists the books (in print) of many U.S. publishers. The University of Delaware Library holds the volumes from 1912-1991.

Printed Bibliographies and Databases 1910 to present

Cumulative Book Index. Minneapolis: H.W. Wilson.

Entitled The United States Catalog: Books in Print from 1898-1928, the CBI lists the books (in print) of many U.S. publishers. The University of Delaware Library holds the volumes from 1912-1991.

The BIP database provides bibliographic descriptions and ordering information for over a million books currently in print, declared out of print (from July 1979 to date), and soon-to-be-published titles from many publishers. The University of Delaware Library does not hold the printed volumes of Books in Print, published by Bowker. The printed volumes were issued from 1948-72 as an author-title-series index to Publishers' Trade List Annual. Ask at the Reference Desk for assistance in obtaining retrospective cumulations of the printed Books in Print from the Center for Research Libraries.

Indian National Bibliography

The Indian National Bibliography is brought out by the National Library of India from Kolkatta. Its accumulation issue of 1977 was published during the year 1980. In order to bring the Bibliography upto-date within the shortest possible time, it has been decided to publish the Indian National Bibliography 1978 and onwards as Annual Volumes only. The periodicity will again be changed to monthly as soon as the Government of India Presses will be able to print Bibliography upto-date and bring out regularly in time. Sanskrit fascicule 1971-80 (Ten year Cumulation) has been published. Malayalam Bibliography 1971-80 is expected to be published by March, 1983.

Trade Bibliographies

British Books in Print

British Books in Print provides comprehensive indexing of books published in the United Kingdom, plus those books published throughout the world that are printed in the English language and that are available within the U.K. from an exclusive stockholding agent. Information on titles not yet in print is provided up to 24 months in advance of publication.

All data are supplied directly from publishers. New title information is subjected to rigorous editorial control before it is entered into the database.

Books, audio tapes, and CDs are eligible for inclusion in the database if they are published in the U.K., carry a minimum retail price of L0.15, and are generally available for purchase by the public. Books published outside the U.K. are also eligible, provided they fulfill the same conditions, are printed in the English language, and are available within the U.K. from an exclusive stockholding agent. Only those government publications that are considered to be of wide general interest are included. Maps published by, or available through book publishers, are also included. The following items are excluded:

* periodicals
* serial publications
* limited circulation publications
* subscription-only publications

Indian Books in Print 2003

Indian Books in Print 2003, containing nearly 3,75,000 entries spanning through three volumes, reports on Indian books in print in English language published till June 2003—Volume 1-Authors: Volume 2-Titles: and Volume 3-Subject Guide. The subject guide is classified according to the Dewey decimal classification with feature headings and the Directory of Indian Publishers with complete addresses also appears in this volume.

Authentic and reliable source of bibliographical information about Indian Books in English language. Built over four decades of experience and expertise in bibliographical control, Indian Books in Print constitutes an authentic and reliable source of bibliographical information about Indian Books published in English language. It comes handy to individuals and institutions engaged in research in areas and in subjects relating to the vast subcontinent of India.

"Teachers, librarians, documentalists, information officers, research scholars, professors, editors and the book trade will find it a mine of valuable bibliographical information.

National Union Catalog (United States of America)

Catalogue, with locations, of the principal portions of the collections of the Library of Congress and 1000 major research libraries in the United States and Canada. Includes books, periodicals, pamphlets, maps, atlases, music and manuscripts.

1953-1994 (in microfiche cabinets): until 1982 arranged by author or title; then full records in numerical order in register, indexed by author, title, series, and subject.

R.R. Bowker's New BooksInPrint.com Professional

For more than fifty years, Books In Print has served the library and book trade communities as the definitive bibliographic resource, and currently features more than 1,879,000 active titles and over 2,226,000 active ISBNs, providing unparalleled coverage of the full range of books currently published or distributed in the United States.

Children's Books In Print

Produced from Books In Print, it is a vital resource for any librarian with patrons who are young readers — a two-volume index of more than 250,000 books, 13,000 United States publishers, 243,000 contributors, and nearly 75,000 contributor cross-references.

Ulrich's Periodical Directory

An essential reference tool for any serials librarian, Ulrich's Periodical Directory is overflowing with the latest international bibliographic information on journals, magazines and newspapers. With over 178,600 regularly and irregularly issued serials classified under 897 subject headings, Ulrich's is the most comprehensive directory available worldwide.

Subject Bibliographies

The International Bibliography of the Social Sciences (IBSS)

The International Bibliography of the Social Sciences was established in 1951. It was set up by the International Committee for Social Science Information and Documentation, a non-governmental organisation recognised by Unesco. The aim of the Committee was to promote the free flow of scholarly social science information around the world, inspired in part by the need to overcome the political barriers thrown up at that time by the Cold War and the Iron Curtain.

Until 1989 the International Bibliography of the Social Sciences was compiled at the Fondation Nationale des Science Politiques in Paris by Professor Jean Meyriat and Professor Jean Viet, supported by an international network of contributors. The bibliography was produced in four printed volumes, Economics, Political Science, Anthropology and

Sociology. In the beginning it was treated as an experiment and each volume had a different editorial board responsible for compilation. It is worth noting that the first volume of the International Bibliography of Economics was sent to the Library of The London School of Economics and Political Science for comments and criticism.

IBSS moved to the British Library of Political and Economic Science at The London School of Economics and Political Science. The editorial team consisted initially of three people. By 1993 the new IBSS office had indexed some 600,000 new records, bringing the total in the database to about 1.4 million records dating back to 1951. It was at this stage that the first steps were taken towards making the data available in electronic formats. A CD-Rom was produced by SilverPlatter Information.

In 1995 IBSS was made available online free of charge to members of UK higher and further education institutions. The service was funded by the Economic and Social Research Council and the Joint Information Systems Committee and was made available via BIDS. Today IBSS includes approximately 2 million records dating back to 1951 and each year some 100,000 new records are added. Over 100 languages and countries are covered by IBSS. The database is available online, in print and on CD Rom.

It is the essential online resource for social science and interdisciplinary research. It includes over 2 million bibliographic references to journal articles and to books, reviews and selected chapters dating back to 1951. It is unique in its broad coverage of international data and incorporates over 100 languages and countries. Over 2,700 journals are regularly indexed and some 7,000 books included each year. Abstracts are provided for up to half of all current journal articles and full text availability is increasing steadily.

IBSS key facts

* The mission of the International Bibliography of the

Social Sciences (IBSS) is to provide easy access to international social science and interdisciplinary research by compiling current and historic bibliographic data from journal articles and books, reviews and selected chapters and making this available in a range of appropriate media, including online, print and CD versions.

* IBSS has been compiling social science bibliographies since 1951.
* IBSS has been produced at The London School of Economics and Political Science (LSE) since 1989.
* IBSS is funded by the Economic and Social Research Council (ESRC), the Joint Information Systems Committee (JISC) and The London School of Economics and Political Science (LSE).
* IBSS focuses mainly on the social sciences, but it also covers a wide range of related and interdisciplinary fields, such as agriculture, social policy, archaeology, business studies, criminology, education, environmental issues, history, law and social work.
* The IBSS database holds over 2 million references to journal articles and books, reviews and selected chapters.
* Approximately 100,000 new references are added each year.
* Over 2,700 journals are regularly indexed.
* Approximately 2,000 new records are added each week and the database is updated weekly.
* Approximately 7,000 books are covered each year.
* IBSS is unique in its broad coverage of international data from over 100 countries. Approximately one quarter of records are in languages other than English.
* Searchable are available for half of all current journals covered.

* Access to fulltext versions of journal articles continues to grow.
* The high standards of IBSS are maintained by an international Editorial Advisory Board consisting of key academics in the field of social sciences.
* The IBSS database is available online, on CD-ROM and in printed volumes (see Access to IBSS).
* All members of UK higher and further education institutions are eligible to use IBSS online free of charge.
* Subscriptions are charged for UK commercial and not-for-profit organisations and for non-UK organisations.

Bibliography of Southeast Asia: A Decade of Selected Social Science Publications in the English Language, 1990-2000

This bibliography lists nearly 6,500 English-language books by Southeast Asian authors covering a vast array of social science topics from agriculture to urbanization. Ch'ng Kim See (head of the Institute of Southeast Asian Studies) provides an informative preface and entries covering Brunei, Cambodia, Singapore, Thailand, and Vietnam, as well as the region as a whole. Her list focuses on longer works, excluding dissertations, most government publications, works of popular culture, and works by Westerners among many others exclusions. Annotation (c) Book News, Inc., Portland, OR (booknews.com).

8. Statistical Sources

Statistical data form a very important category of reference materials in all types of libraries. They represent numerical facts which are hard to find in normal circumstances. Statistical data are of various kinds which are produces, collected and processed by official and non-official organizations.

Statistics are among the hardest kinds of information to find. The expectations of our clients and patrons compound the problem. In order for statistics to exist, someone has to gather them. This implies a reason to do so, as well as manpower. Statistics are often buried within articles, reports, books, and transcripts, with no indexing or guide that points to them. Even if you find figures on your subject, much of the time they're not "cut" the way you want to see them (what you want counted isn't counted). And there are so many sources from which to choose that only researchers who deal with statistics on a regular basis can know who generates them and where to look.

Some sources as given below will be helpful in answering a large proportion of statistical questions. Most are available free or at low cost on the Web. These statistical sources are heavy on government publishers. They are collected to support public policy decision-making, planning, and resource allocation. The decennial census, mandated by the Constitution, is also a major source of statistics.

Statistical Yearbook

Statistical yearbook is compiled by the United Nation's Statistical Office in New York. It gives a summary of international data pertaining to the various countries of the world. It covers the basic data from over 150 areas in the field of agriculture, finance, manufacturing, mining, transportation, trade, population, education etc. The data is provided in tabular form usually covering a number of years. The data in the tables in arranged by subject. The statistics relating to the different countries is given side by side in order to allow comparison of statistics for various countries over a given period of time. The data is considered authentic since it is collected from the official and reliable sources. The Yearbook gives statistical details of the conditions prevailing in various countries of the world. It is updated annually.

Statistical Abstract of the U.S.

The annual *Statistical Abstract* consists wholly of statistics and includes data from private as well as government sources. It covers a wide range of topics, such as: People and Society, Money, Government, Health, Industry, The Land, State Rankings, and Other Countries.

The *Abstract* answers questions such as: How much is spent on health care? How many trucks were sold last year? What is Australia's tax revenue? Best of all, it includes inter-census population estimates, which are critical when you're well into the decade following the decennial census.

The online *Abstract* is divided into general sections, each of which comprises a PDF file, so you need to have Adobe Acrobat configured to work with your browser

The index, also in PDF format, is the printed index *verbatim* and refers to printed page numbers only, not table numbers or sections. However, from the index, you can tell if your subject is covered and approximately where in the *Abstract* it falls. The best way to get to the table you want is to choose the most likely section, display its PDF file, and use Acrobat's Find icon (the binoculars) to search for your term.

U.S. Bureau of the Census

The Census Bureau covers, among other topics: Population, Housing, Retail and Wholesale Sales, Income, State and Local Area Profiles, and Service Industries and Manufacturing.

The Bureau does not limit itself to data from the decennial census, but constantly conducts specialized surveys, sometimes for other agencies. It can help you answer questions like: What are the most common names? How much is Raleigh expected to grow? How many people live alone?

If you're going to use the Bureau's Web site, know that:

* There are handy links to foreign statistical agencies.
* The search engine isn't very helpful; use the Subject A to Z list instead.

U.S. Bureau of Labor Statistics

Many government sources provide better online

interfaces than the Bureau of Labor Statistics, but few offer more critical data. The Bureau covers Labor, Employment, Earnings, Prices, Foreign Labor Statistics, and the Consumer Price Index.

You can find out how many workers keep flexible schedules, which states feature the highest pay rates, and how the consumer price index for auto insurance rates has fluctuated over time.

If you're going to use the Bureau's Web site, don't search by keyword. Instead, use links to Data, News Releases (current and backfiles), Most Requested Series, and Economy at a Glance (see Search Tip 2). The custom query facility called Selective Access is difficult to use. It's a successive series of forms to fill in-you alternate between searching on text or a code to represent the variable you want, and hitting the Next Form button.

Fedstats

If you think the government might have collected statistics on your topic, this Web site is for you. You don't have to guess which agency you need-Fedstats will locate it for you. Currently, the site points to data from 14 federal agencies, but eventually, 70 will be represented.

As with the other government Web sites in the Top Ten, don't use the search engine. Browse by subject instead. If you must use the search engine, try including the word table to help limit the search to statistical material (see Search Tip 4), though you won't succeed completely. Do use links to Press Releases and Regional Statistics (see Search Tip 2).

A Matter of Fact

The A Matter of Fact database consists of statistical material and facts. Sources include mainstream and alternative publications and government hearings. The focus is public policy issues, such as economics, health, government, and the environment, but you'll also find miscellanea, such as how many people are using the Internet and how many versions of "Beethoven's Fifth" have been recorded. A Matter of Fact is a gem because it is primarily statistics (see Search Tip 1), but in full-text form, so you get explanation and context with the numbers.

You don't really need to practice Search Tips 3 and 5 here because the information is all statistics and facts. Using keywords intelligently is sufficient.

The major drawback to this excellent source is its limited availability. Vended primarily by library automation systems (check your local library), it can also be found on SilverPlatter's Search by Search, but that system requires a hefty deposit ($500). I urge you to lobby your favorite pay-as-you-go vendor to pick up this excellent resource.

World Almanac, Information Please Almanac

The mission of these statistics-rich sources is to answer questions posed by the general reader. The beauty of the almanacs is that they gather frequently-consulted material in one place, and almost everything is a statistic. The almanacs answer questions, such as: Which plays have had the longest Broadway runs? How many Americans died in the War of 1812? How long is the space shuttle?

If you have a paper copy, great, but you can also use these sources online at low Electric Library and Encarta Online prices. There isn't much to searching them, other than to be sure that you limit your search to the almanac alone. Once you've found a page of text, save your eyes by using your browser's Find feature to zero in on your terms.

American Demographics

Dow Jones Interactive; Electric Library; LEXIS-NEXIS (BUSFIN, MARKET, and NEWS Libraries); ProQuest Direct; Wall Street Journal Interactive Edition; and hardcopy

Like A Matter of Fact, American Demographics presents rich statistical content in full-text form (see Search Tip 1).

Strong on consumer demographics, the magazine reveals what people are thinking, doing, and purchasing. You can find out how much candy Americans eat, how many of us listen to public radio, and how many hours people spend reading.

The Web site is shareware, meaning that the company would like you to subscribe if you find the information useful. If you do much consumer-oriented market research, or answer one important question, the subscription price of $59 will pay for itself many times over.

The Excite search facility at the Web site isn't very sophisticated. However, because the magazine is so rich in statistics, the lack of power isn't a major drawback, and the false drops aren't overwhelming. For example, museum and attendance works well. So does skin care products. You don't have to indicate anything further, such as statistics or market share or sales or preferences.

Census of India

Census of India was first conducted in the year 1872. It has now become a regular exercise after every 10 years. The census was started mainly to obtain census figures. Now, it does not only provide census figures but also gives other useful data regarding demographic studies and information on social and ethnological, religious and other aspects of Indian population. Descriptive statistical reports given by the central and state governments are highly useful. District handbooks, village monographs and special papers provide tremendous information. Maps and tables are given in plenty.

Apart from the population statistics the census of India provides housing details, survey reports on towns and villages, survey of industries, language survey reports and various types of tables. It is made up of a number of series. The first of the series covers the central government whereas the others covers states and union territories separately. Each of the series is further divided into parts and sub-parts containing different types of information.

Statistical Abstract of the Indian Union

Statistical Abstract of the Indian Union is the publication of the Central Statistical Organization of India. It contains vital statistical data grouped under important heads of social and economic matters. The publication provides information about individual states and union territories. It also includes maps and charts.

The CIA's World Factbook

The *World Factbook* is another easily searchable statistical compendium (see Search Tip 1). It includes country profiles as well as world summary figures. The Factbook is especially helpful for data on small and obscure countries. The *Factbook* covers the following categories: Flag and Map, Geography, People, Government, Economy, Transportation, Communication, and Defense. Navigation at the Web site is easy. You can get from anywhere to anywhere with one click. Browse by country, region, or subject. A word of warning: data currency varies.

Other Sources by Country

Europe

CISSTAT *www.cisstat.com*

Interstate Statistical Committee of the Commonwealth of Independent States. Gives macroeconomic data on an annual basis back to 1995. Countries covered are Armenia, Azerbaijan, Belarus, Georgia, Kazakhstan, Kyrgyzstan, Moldova, Russia, Tajikistan, Turkmenistan. Ukraine, and Uzbekistan. Available in Russian and English.

European Central Bank www.ecb.int

The statistics section includes statistics on the Euro zone from the Monthly Bulletin. Data is available in CSV and PDF format and includes market interest rates, stock market indices and retail bank interest rates.

Eurostat Key Indicators europa.eu.int/comm/eurostat/

Key indicators covering a range of topics such as transport, external trade, environment and energy.

UK Trade Information On-line www.uktradeinfo.com

This site uses HM Customs and Excise data on UK imports and exports. Information is taken directly from returns and reports required with every export and import consignment.

The free services include a section on EU enlargement with country profiles and the top 10 UK imports and exports by value in GBP. Similar data on the existing EU countries is also available. The free quarterly UK Trade Trends focuses on trade-in-goods statistics between the UK and the rest of the World. Content includes time series data tables and articles on trade related subjects such as bi-lateral trade and statistical policy. UK Trade Trends is published in hard copy and as downloadable PDFs.

The Intrastat database is a subscription service and provides UK overseas trade data at 8 digit commodity code level showing UK imports and exports worldwide from 1997 to date. Data is available by trading partner country and is updated monthly.

UK

National Statistics - the official UK statistics site *www.statistics.gov.uk*

2003 Official Yearbook of the United Kingdom of Great Britain and Northern Ireland

www.statistics.gov.uk/statbase

The yearbook has a mass of information in the form of text, maps and graphs on all aspects of life in Great Britain and Northern Ireland. Free to download from National Statistics Online in PDF fromat.

Social Trends *www.statistics.gov.uk/statbase/Product.asp?vlnk=5748&More=N*

Published by the UK National Statistics Office, Social Trends "draws together social and economic data from a wide range of government departments and other organisations to paint a broad picture of British society today, and how it has been changing. 13 chapters each focusing on a different social policy area, described in tables, charts and text. Population, Households and Families, Education, Labour Market, Income and Wealth, Expenditure, Health, Social Protection, Crime and Justice, Housing, Environment, Transport, Lifestyles and Social Participation". Available in hardcopy or you can download it together with the related StatBase datasets free of charge.

Bank of England *www.bankofengland.co.uk*

The Statistics section includes current and historical base rates (interest rates), exchange rates, domestic and international banking statistics, monetary statistics (includes MO and M4), balance of payments and a database of successive sets of data for series that make up the GDP (total imports, total exports, investment, private consumption, government consumption).

HBOS - Economic View *www.hbosplc.com/economy/EconomicFactbook.asp*

The Halifax/Bank of Scotland Economic View includes an 'Outlook' that provides a five year view on the prospects for the global and UK economies, a House Price Index and The Factbook (XLS format), which contains historical data covering the key UK economic indicators, housing and mortgage markets and personal savings. Also included is information on income tax rates, the housing and savings tax regimes and a league table of the top 20 UK residential estate agents by number of offices.

HM Treasury *www.hm-treasury.gov.uk*

Details of the latest economic indicators, forecasts for the UK economy, GDP deflators and government economic strategy.

Jobstats - the current state of the UK computer job market www.jobstats.co.uk

Provides a detailed picture of the computing job market in the UK. Graphs and figures show trends in hourly rates and annual salaries. There are also links to job listings pages and a monthly newsletter.

Nomis *www.nomisweb.co.uk*

Nomis is the Web site for the official UK labour market statistics. It gives access to the most up-to-date and detailed labour market data produced from official sources. Nomis is a free service provided by National Statistics but you have to register for an ID and password in order to access it.

Workthing.com *www.workthing.com*

Run by the Guardian Media Group with AC Nielsen as a partner, the Salary Checker option allows you to search by job, title, industry and location. The data is collected from jobs advertised over the last twelve months in newspapers, trade magazines and the regional press. The salaries given are the highest recorded for that job/title.

UK Online *www.ukonline.gov.uk*

The official gateway to UK government departments and sources of information on the Web. The Search facility searches across all the central government Web sites.

Bank of England Monetary and Financial Statistics Division *www.bankofengland.co.uk/mfsd/index.htm*

Links to detailed information on reserves, consumer credit, exchange and interest rates. The Base Rates link is a spreadsheet that gives details of UK interest rates, and when they became effective, going back to 1970.

Austria

STATISTICS AUSTRIA *www.statistik.at*

Austrian Federal Financing Agency www.oebfa.co.at

Provides information on the economy, federal budget (going back to 1998) and debt statistics. Available in German, French and English.

Austrian Institute of Economic Research ***www.wifo.ac.at***

IFO analyzes national and international economic trends and supplies short- to medium-term economic forecasts. Some of the data sets are compiled by WIFO, but most of the data are obtained from domestic data producers (such as the Austrian National Bank, the Austrian Central Statistical Office, the Main Association of Austrian Social Security Institutions). The Economic Data Bases contain comprehensive statistical data on the Austrian economy, for example national income, production, foreign trade, the labour market and the financial sector. A selection of tables containing current national and international statistics are freely available. Available in German and English.

Institute of Advanced Studies ***www.ihs.ac.at***

IHS is a private non-profit organization. The IHS Economic Forecasts are freely available (in German only) as are their various report series and newsletters, many of which are in English.

Oesterreichische Nationalbank ***www.oenb.co.at***

Data on the Austrian economy including interest rates, capital market, public finances and economic indicators. Some information is available in English but some of the more detailed data is in German only.

Belarus

CISSTAT: Belarus ***www.cisstat.com/eng/bel.htm***

Interstate Statistical Committee of the Commonwealth of Independent States. Gives macro-economic data on an annual basis back to 1995.

Belgium

Statistics Belgium ***www.statbel.fgov.be***

A division of the Ministry of Economic Affairs. Statistics inlcude short term inidicators, demographics, industrial production figures, energy, construction and agriculture. A limited amount of information is available in German and English. More detailed information and the publications are available only in Dutch and French.

Federal Planning Bureau ***www.plan.fgov.be***

Economic analyses and forecasts. The FPB. is responsible for carrying out macro-economic forecasting, for evaluating the consequences of economic and social policy decisions and for performing structural analyses mainly on economic, social and environmental issues. Available in Dutch, French and English but some of the data is only available in Dutch and French.

Ministère fédéral de l'Emploi et du Travail (Federal Ministry of Employment and Labour) meta.fgov.be

The Statistics section is available in French and Dutch. Other areas are also available in English and German.

National Bank of Belgium ***www.bnb.be***

Data available includes economic indicators, business survey barometer, consumer survey, foreign trade, National Accounts (Dutch and French only) and a monthly Statistical Bulletin. In French, Dutch, German and English.

Estonia

Bank of Estonia ***www.ee/epbe/***

An abundance of useful economic and financial data, and news on the economy.

Finland

Statistics Finland *www.stat.fi/* In English, Finnish and Swedish.

Georgia

CISSTAT: Georgia ***www.cisstat.com/eng/georg.htm***

Interstate Statistical Committee of the Commonwealth of Independent States. Gives macroeconomic data on an annual basis back to 1995.

Germany

Federal Statistical Office *www.destatis.de/e_home.htm*

In German and English.

Hungary

Hungarian Statistical Office *www.ksh.hu/*

Selected statistics on Hungary - "Hungary in Figures" - e.g. population, earnings, GDP, Prices, External Trade Turnover covering a range of years.

Ministry of Economic Affairs *www.ikm.iif.hu/english/economy/*

Facts and data on the economy, privatisation, and legal forms of companies.

Ireland

Central Statistics Office *www.cso.ie*

Italy

Statistics Italy *www.italyemb.org/Statistics.htm*

Main Economic Indicators produced by the Bank of Italy plus excerpts from Italian National Institute of Statistics.

Moldova

CISSTAT: Moldova *www.cisstat.com/eng/mol.htm*

Interstate Statistical Committee of the Commonwealth of Independent States. Gives macroeconomic data on an annual basis back to 1995.

Netherlands

Statistics Netherlands *www.cbs.nl*

Norway

Statistics Norway *www.ssb.no*

Poland

Polish Market Review *www.polishmarket.com*

News and newsletters aimed at anyone interested in investing, managing an investment, or marketing a product on the Polish market. Regular columns include demographics of Polish society, information about Polish households, data on the volume of different markets and the amount of foreign investment, analysis of trends and issues that affect the market.

Russia

State Committee of the Russian Federation on Statistics *www.gks.ru*

Available in Russian and English.

CISSTAT: Russia *www.cisstat.com/eng/rus.htm*

Interstate Statistical Committee of the Commonwealth of Independent States. Gives macroeconomic data on an annual basis back to 1995.

Bank of Russia *www.cbr.ru*

Slovenia

Statistical Office of the Republic of Slovenia *www.sigov.si/zrs/*

Details of their Statistical Yearbook and other publications. Also tables of short term economic indicators giving 4- 5 years broken down monthly and quarterly. There are figures for retail sales, earnings, energy, consumer prices, industrial production, producer and retail price indices, employment , foreign trade and finance.

SKB Banka DD *www.skb.si*

A financial services group which, in addition to information about the group itself, has put up several pages of summary statistics and economic indicators under the section "About Slovenia".

Sweden

Statistics Sweden *www.scb.se*

Ukraine

CISSTAT: Ukraine *www.cisstat.com/eng/ukr.htm*

Interstate Statistical Committee of the Commonwealth of Independent States. Gives macroeconomic data on an annual basis back to 1995.

Asia

Asia and the Pacific in Figures www.unescap.org/stat/statdata/apinfig.htm

Maintained by the United Nations Economic and Social Commission for Asia and the Pacific, this site has data for 57 countries in HTML and Excel format. Data includes summary statistics on topics such as population, land use, price indices and transport. The data is gleaned from a number of sources; details are available on the Web site.

CISSTAT *www.cisstat.com*

Interstate Statistical Committee of the Commonwealth of Independent States. Gives macroeconomic data on an annual basis back to 1995. Countries covered are Armenia, Azerbaijan, Belarus, Georgia, Kazakhstan, Kyrgyzstan, Moldova, Russia, Tajikistan, Turkmenistan. Ukraine, and Uzbekistan. Available in Russian and English.

Armenia

Central Bank of Armenia *www.cba.am*

Economic indicators can be found under Publications & Statistics.

Ministry of Statistics *www.armstat.am*

Statistical overviews can be found under publications. The information is available in a variety of formats depending on the year in which you are interested.

CISSTAT: Armenia *www.cisstat.com/eng/arm.htm*

Interstate Statistical Committee of the Commonwealth of Independent States. Gives macroeconomic data on an annual basis back to 1995.

Azerbaijan

CISSTAT: Azerbaijan *www.cisstat.com/eng/azer.htm*

Interstate Statistical Committee of the Commonwealth of Independent States. Gives macroeconomic data on an annual basis back to 1995.

Bangladesh

Bangladesh Bureau of Statistics *www.bbsgov.org*

Cambodia

National Institute of Statistics *www.nis.gov.kh*

China

National Bureau of Statistics *www.stats.gov.cn*

The official government statistical office. In Chinese and English.

China Statistical Data *www.china.org.cn/e-company/*

This service repackages some of the data from the National Bureau of Statistics. Available in Chinese, English, French, German, Russian, Spanish, Arabic, Japanese and Esperanto.

Hong Kong

Hong Kong Census & Statistics Department *www.info.gov.hk/censtatd/*

Click on the Site Map link to get to the English version. In Chinese and English.

India

Ministry of Statistics *mospi.nic.in*

Japan

Bank of Japan *www.boj.or.jp*

Information on the Bank of Japan and its publications. Various reports on the economy are available here and can be downloaded free of charge but do check the format first: several are available in PDF, MS Word, MS Excel or text files.

Japan Information Network *www.jinjapan.org*

Events, regional information, statistics from the Census, economics and labour, education and culture, social security, medical care, crime, prices and household expenses, lifestyle, leisure activities.

Statistics Bureau and Statistics Centre *www.stat.go.jp*

Japan in Figures and Economic and Financial Data from the Japan Management and Co-ordination Agency.

Kazakhstan

CISSTAT: Kazakhstan *www.cisstat.com/eng/kaz.htm*

Interstate Statistical Committee of the Commonwealth of Independent States. Gives macroeconomic data on an annual basis back to 1995.

Kyrgyzstan

National Statistical Committee of the Kyrgyzstan Republic

stat-gvc.bishkek.su

Available in Russian and English.

CISSTAT: Kyrgyzstan *www.cisstat.com/eng/kir.htm*

Interstate Statistical Committee of the Commonwealth of Independent States. Gives macroeconomic data on an annual basis back to 1995.

Malaysia

Department of Statistics Malaysia *www.statistics.gov.my*

Mongolia

National Statistics Office *www.nso.mn*

Ministry of Infrasructure, Mongolia *gate1.pmis.gov.mn/mid/statistic_e.htm*

Philippines

Philippines National Statistical Co-ordination Board www.nscb.gov.ph

National Statistics Office *www.census.gov.ph*

Republic of Korea

National Statistical Office, Republic of Korea *www.nso.go.kr*

Singapore

Statistics Singapore *www.singstat.gov.sg*

Sri Lanka

Department of Census and Statistics *www.statistics.gov.lk*

Tajikistan

CISSTAT: Tajikistan *www.cisstat.com/eng/tad.htm*

Interstate Statistical Committee of the Commonwealth of Independent States. Gives macroeconomic data on an annual basis back to 1995.

Thailand

National Statistical Office Thailand *www.nso.go.th*

Turkey

State Institute of Statistics *www.die.gov.tr*

Turkmenistan

CISSTAT: Turkmenistan *www.cisstat.com/eng/tur.htm*

Interstate Statistical Committee of the Commonwealth of Independent States. Gives macroeconomic data on an annual basis back to 1995.

Uzbekistan

CISSTAT: Uzbekistan *www.cisstat.com/eng/uzb.htm*

Interstate Statistical Committee of the Commonwealth of Independent States. Gives macroeconomic data on an annual basis back to 1995.

Oceania

Asia and the Pacific in Figures *www.unescap.org/stat/statdata/apinfig.htm*

Maintained by the United Nations Economic and Social Commission for Asia and the Pacific, this site has data for 57 countries in HTML and Excel format. Data includes summary statistics on topics such as population, land use, price indices and transport. The data is gleaned from a number of sources; details are available on the Web site.

Australia

Australian Bureau Of Statistics *www.abs.gov.au*

Key national indicators, Statistics by state and searchable by keyword.

Fiji

Fiji Islands Statistics Bureau *www.statsfiji.gov.fj*

New Zealand

Statistics New Zealand *www.stats.govt.nz*

Information on publications and services, press releases and New Zealand in Profile statistics (Main trading partners, land use, retail trade, Consumer Price Index, Household Spending per week, Average weekly earnings, Geography, Principle exports and imports, national economy, population, transport), plus some census data.

Papua New Guinea

National Statistical Office of Papua New Guinea *www.nso.gov.pg*

The Americas

Canada

Statistics Canada *www.statcan.ca*

Agri-Food Trade Service - Trade Statistics *atn-riae.agr.ca/stats/stats-e.htm*

Trade statistics on the Canadian agricultural products and food industry. Includes import and export data.

Back to List of Countries

US

FedWorld *www.fedworld.gov*

Bureau of Labour Statistics *www.bls.gov*

US Department of Commerce (STAT-USA) *www.stat-usa.gov*

US Census Bureau www.census.gov

US Bureau of Economic Analysis *www.bea.doc.gov*

US Bureau of Justice Statistics *www.ojp.usdoj.gov/bjs/*

US National Center for Health Statistics *www.cdc.gov/nchs/*

US National Center for Education Statistics *www.ed.gov/NCES/*

To find the statistical data one needs to search either paper or online. There are many sources as well as the services of library reference staff members. After determining the subject of the numbers it is needed to consider time frame i. e. current, recent, historical and then considering the search strategy, including the terminology to be employed for the search.

Bibliography

A. Gupta, V. Harinarayan, and A. Rajaraman. Virtual Database Technology. In *Proceedings of the Fourteenth International Conference on Data Engineering*, pp. 23-27, February, 1998.

Ahmad Rafee Che Kassim and Thomas R. Kochtanek. *Interactive Digital Library Resource Information System: A Web Portal for Digital Library Education.* In *Proceedings of the Second ACM/IEEE-CS Joint Conference on Digital Libraries*, 2002.

Alex Hauptmann and Norman Papernick. *Video-Cuebik: Adapting Image Search to Video Shots.* In *Proceedings of the Second ACM/IEEE-CS Joint Conference on Digital Libraries*, 2002.

Alex Hauptmann, Rong Jin, and Tobun Dorbin Ng. *Multimodal Information Retrieval from Broadcast Video using OCR and Speech Recognition.* In *Proceedings of the Second ACM/IEEE-CS Joint Conference on Digital Libraries*, 2002

Alexander G. Hauptmann, Michael J. Witbrock, and Michael G. Christel. *News-on-Demand: An Application of Informedia Technology. D-Lib Magazine*, Sep, 1995. Format:

Allan Heydon and Marc Najork. Mercator: A Scalable, Extensible Web Crawler. *World Wide Web*, 2(4):219-229, December, 1999.

Allen Brewer, Wei Ding, Karla Hahn, and Anita Komlodi. The Role of Intermediary Services in Emerging Digital Libraries. In *Proceedings of DL'96*, 1996.

Allison Druin, Benjamin B. Bederson, Juan Pablo Hourcade, Lisa Sherman, Glenda Revelle, Michele Platner, and Stacy Weng. Designing a Digital Library for Young Children: An Intergenerational Partnership. In *Proceedings of the First ACM/IEEE-CS Joint Conference on Digital Libraries*, 2001.

Altavista Incorporated. *http://www.altavista.com.*

Alvin T.S. Chan. Web-enabled Smart Card for Ubiquitous Access of Patient's Medical Record. In *Proceedings of the Eighth International World-Wide Web Conference*, 1999.

Amarnath Gupta, Bertram Ludaescher, and Reagan W. Moore. *Ontology Services for Curriculum Development in NSDL.* In *Proceedings of the Second ACM/IEEE-CS Joint Conference on Digital Libraries*, 2002.

Amazon Inc. *http://www.amazon.com.*

An Annotated Bibliography of Interoperability Literature. *Stanford University. http://www-diglib.stanford.edu/diglib/pub/interopbib.html.*

An Feng and Toshiro Wakayama. SIMON: a grammar-based transformation system for structured documents. *Electronic Publishing: Origination, Dissemination and Design*, 6(4):361-372, December, 1993.

Andy Dong and Alice M. Agogino. Design Principles for the Information Architecture of a SMET Education Digital Library. In *Proceedings of the First ACM/IEEE-CS Joint Conference on Digital Libraries*, 2001.

Ann Blandford, Hanna Stelmaszewska, and Nick Bryan-Kinns. Use of Multiple Digital Libraries: A Case Study. In *Proceedings of the First ACM/IEEE-CS Joint Conference on Digital Libraries*, 2001.

Ann Blandford, Suzette Keith, Iain Connell, and Helen

Edwards. Analytical usability evaluation for Digital Libraries: a case study. In *Proceedings of the Fourth ACM/IEEE-CS Joint Conference on Digital Libraries*, 2004.

Ann Peterson Bishop. Making Digital Libraries Go: Comparing Use Across Genres. In *Proceedings of the Fourth ACM International Conference on Digital Libraries*, 1999.

Ann Peterson Bishop. *Working Towards an Understanding of Digital Library Use: A Report on the User Research Efforts of the NSF/ARPA/NASA DLI Projects. D-Lib Magazine*, October, 1995.

Anna Keller Gold, Karen Baker, Kim Baldridge, and Jean-Yves Le Meur. *Building FLOW: Federating Libraries on the Web*. In *Proceedings of the Second ACM/IEEE-CS Joint Conference on Digital Libraries*, 2002.

Antony Corfield, Matthew Dovey, Richard Mawby, and Colin Tatham. *JAFER ToolKit Project - Interfacing Z39.50 and XML*. In *Proceedings of the Second ACM/IEEE-CS Joint Conference on Digital Libraries*, 2002.

Aparna Gurijala and J.R. Deller, Jr. A quantified fidelity criterion for parameter-embedded watermarking of audio archives [short paper]. In *Proceedings of the Third ACM/IEEE-CS Joint Conference on Digital Libraries*, 2003.

Armando Fox, Steven D. Gribble, Eric A. Brewer, and Elan Amir. Adapting to network and client variability via on-demand dynamic distillation. *SIGPLAN Not. (USA), SIGPLAN Notices*, 31(9):160-70, Sep, 1996.

Arts and Humanities Data Service. A Strategic Policy Framework for Creating and Preserving Digital Collections. October 23, 1995. URL: http://ahds.ac.uk/manage/framework.htm

Arturo Crespo and Eric A. Bier. *WebWriter: A Browser-Based Editor for Constructing Web Applications*. In *Proceedings of the Fifth International World-Wide Web Conference*, 1996.

Arturo Crespo and Hector Garcia-Molina. *Archival Storage for Digital Libraries.* In *Proceedings of the Third ACM International Conference on Digital Libraries,* 1998. Accessible at http://dbpubs.stanford.edu/pub/1998-49.

Arturo Crespo and Hector Garcia-Molina. Awareness Services for Digital Libraries. In *Lecture Notes in Computer Science.* Vol. 1324. 1997.

Arturo Crespo and Hector Garcia-Molina. Cost-Driven Design for Archival Repositories. In *Proceedings of the First ACM/IEEE-CS Joint Conference on Digital Libraries,* 2001.

Arturo Crespo and Hector Garcia-Molina. *Modeling Archival Repositories for Digital Libraries.* In *Submitted for publication,* 2000. Available at http://dbpubs.stanford.edu/pub/1999-23.

Arturo Crespo and Hector Garcia-Molina. *Routing Indices For Peer-to-Peer Systems.* Number 2001-48. Stanford University, 2001.

Arturo Crespo, Bay-Wei Chang, and Eric A. Bier. *Responsive Interaction for a Large Web Application: The Meteor Shower Architecture in the WebWriter II Editor.* In *Proceedings of the Sixth International World-Wide Web Conference,* 1997.

Arturo Crespo, Orkut Buyukkokten, and Hector Garcia-Molina. *Efficient Query Subscription Processing in a Multicast Environment* . In *Proceedings of the 16th International Conference on Data Engineering,* 2000. Available at http://dbpubs.stanford.edu/pub/2000-54.

Arvind Arasu, Junghoo Cho, Hector Garcia-Molina, Andreas Paepcke, and Sriram Raghavan. *Searching the Web. ACM Transactions on Internet Technology,* 2001.

Association of Research Libraries. Definition and Purposes of a Digital Library. October 23, 1995. URL: http://www.ifla.org/documents/libraries/net/arl-dlib.txt

Augusto Celentano and others. Knowledge-Based Document Retrieval in Office Environments: The Kabiria System. *ACM Transactions on Information Systems*, 13(3):237-268, July, 1995.

B. Amento, L. Terveen, and W. Hill. Does authority mean quality? Predicting expert quality ratings of web documents. In *Proceedings of the Twenty-Third Annual International ACM SIGIR Conference on Research and Development in Information Retrieval*. ACM, 2000.

Bernardo A. Huberman and Lada A. Adamic. Growth dynamics of the World-Wide Web. *Nature*, 401(6749), September, 1999.

Boris Chidlovskii, Claudia Roncancio, and Marie-Luise Schneider. Semantic Cache Mechanism for Heterogeneous Web Querying. In *Proceedings of the Eighth International World-Wide Web Conference*, 1999.

Branko Gerovac and Richard J. Solomon. *Protect Revenues, Not Bits: Identify Your Intellectual Property*. In *IP Workshop Proceedings*, 1994.

Brett Kessler, Geoffrey Nunberg, and Hinrich Schuetze. *Automatic Detection of Text Genre*. In *Proceedings ACL/EACL*, 1997.

Brian Cooper and Hector Garcia-Molina. *Bidding for storage space in a peer-to-peer data preservation system*. Number 2001-52. Stanford University, 2001.

Brian Cooper and Hector Garcia-Molina. *Bidding for storage space in a peer-to-peer data preservation system (Extended version)*. Number 2002-22. Stanford University, 2002.

Brian Cooper and Hector Garcia-Molina. Creating Trading Networks of Digital Archives. In *Proceedings of the First ACM/IEEE-CS Joint Conference on Digital Libraries*, 2001.

Brian Cooper and Hector Garcia-Molina. *Creating trading networks of digital archives*. Number 2001-23. Stanford University, 2001.

Brian Cooper and Hector Garcia-Molina. *Creating trading networks of digital archives.* Number 2001-04. Stanford University, 2001.

Brian Cooper and Hector Garcia-Molina. *InfoMonitor: Unobtrusively Archiving a World Wide Web Server.* In *Submitted for publication,* 2000. Available at http://dbpubs.stanford.edu/pub/2000-15.

Brian Cooper and Hector Garcia-Molina. *Peer to peer data trading to preserve information (Extended version).* Number 2000-38. Stanford University, 2000.

Brian Cooper and Hector Garcia-Molina. *Peer to peer data trading to preserve information.* Number 2001-7. Stanford University, 2001.

Brian Cooper and Hector Garcia-Molina. *Peer to peer data trading to preserve information.* Number 2000-33. Stanford University, 2000.

Brian Cooper and Hector Garcia-Molina. *Peer to peer data trading to preserve information (Extended version).* Number 2001-6. Stanford University, 2001.

Brian Cooper, Arturo Crespo, and Hector Garcia-Molina. *Implementing a Reliable Digital Object Archive.* In *Submitted for publication,* 2000. Available at http://dbpubs.stanford.edu/pub/2000-27.

Brian Cooper, Mayank Bawa, Neil Daswani, and Hector Garcia-Molina. *Protecting the PIPE from malicious peers.* Number 2002-97. Stanford University, 2002.

Brian Cooper, Mayank Bawa, Neil Daswani, and Hector Garcia-Molina. *Protecting the PIPE from malicious peers.* Number 2002-03. Stanford University, 2002..

Brian F. Cooper and Hector Garcia-Molina. *Modeling and measuring scalable peer-to-peer search networks.* Number 2002-44. Stanford University, 2002.

Brian F. Cooper and Hector Garcia-Molina. *Modeling and measuring scalable peer-to-peer search networks*

(Extended version). Number 2002-43. Stanford University, 2002.

Brian Kahin. *Institutional and Policy Issues in the Development of the Digital Library*. In *JEP*, 1994.

Brian Kahin. *The Strategic Environment for Protecting Multimedia*. In *IP Workshop Proceedings*, 1994.

BrightPlanet.com. *http://www.brightplanet.com.*

British Library. The British Library Information Systems Strategy. November 1995.

B-S. Jeong and E. Omiecinski. Inverted File Partitioning Schemes in Multiple Disk Systems. *IEEE Transactions on Parallel and Distributed Systems*, 6(2):142-153, February, 1995.

ByungHoon Kang and Robert Wilensky. Toward a Model of Self-administering Data. In *Proceedings of the First ACM/IEEE-CS Joint Conference on Digital Libraries*, 2001.

C. Batini, M. Lenzerini, and S. Navathe. A Comparative Analysis of Methodologies for Database Schema Integration. *ACM Computing Surveys*, 18(4), 1986.

C. Faloutsos and D. Oard. *A Survey of Information Retrieval and Filtering Methods*. Dept. of Computer Science, University of Maryland, 1995.

C. Faloutsos and S. Christodoulakis. Signature Files: An Access Method for Documents and its Analytical Performance Evaluation. *ACM Transactions on Office Information Systems*, 2(4):267-288, October, 1984.

C. K. Kantarjiev, A. Demers, R. Frederick, R. T. Krivacic, and M. Weiser. Experiences with X in a wireless environment. In *Proceedings of the USENIX Mobile and Location-Independent Computing Symposium*, pp. 117-28, Aug, 1993.

C. Mic Bowman, Peter B. Danzig, Darren R. Hardy, Udi Manber, Michael F. Schwartz, and Duane P. Wessels. *Harvest: A Scalable, Customizable Discovery and Access System.*

Number CU-CS-732-94. Dept. of Computer Science, Univ. of Colorado, Boulder, Colo. August, 1994. Accessible at http://harvest.transarc.com/.

C.W. Bailey, Scholarly electronic publishing bibliography. URL: http://info.lib.uh.edu/sepb/sepb.html

C.M. Bowman, Peter B. Danzig, Darren R. Hardy, Udi Manber, and Michael F. Schwartz. The Harvest information discovery and access system. *Computer Networks and ISDN Systems*, 28(1-2):119-125, December, 1995.

Chad Carson, Megan Thomas, Serge Belongie, Joseph M. Hellerstein, and Jitendra Malik. Blobworld: A system for Region-Based Image Indexing and Retrieval. In *Proceedings of the Third International Conference on Visual Information Systems*, June, 1999.

Charles F. Goldfarb. *The SGML Handbook*. Oxford University Press, New York, 1990.

Charles Kacmar, Dean Jue, David Stage, and Christie Koontz. *Automatic Creation and Maintenance of an Organizational Spatial Metadata and Document Digital Library*. In *Proceedings of the Second Annual Conference on the Theory and Practice of Digital Libraries*, 1995.

Charles Kacmar, Susan Hruska, Chris Lacher, Dean Jue, Christie Koontz, Myke Gluck, and Stuart Weibel. *An Architecture and Operation Model for a Spatial Digital Library*. In *Proceedings of the First Annual Conference on the Theory and Practice of Digital Libraries*, 1994.

Charlotte Jenkins, Mike Jackson, Peter Burden, and Jon Wallis. Automatic RDF Metadata Generation for Resource Discovery. In *Proceedings of the Eighth International World-Wide Web Conference*, 1999.

Chen-Chuan K. Chang and Hector Garcia-Molina. *Conjunctive Constraint Mapping for Data Translation*. Number SIDL-WP-1998-0083; 1998-47. Stanford University, January, 1998. Accessible at http://dbpubs.stanford.edu/pub/1998-47.

Chen-Chuan K. Chang and Hector Garcia-Molina. *Evaluating the Cost of Boolean Query Mapping*. In *Proceedings of the Second ACM International Conference on Digital Libraries*, 1997. At http://dbpubs.stanford.edu/pub/1997-25.

Chen-Chuan K. Chang and Héctor García-Molina. Mind Your Vocabulary: Query Mapping Across Heterogeneous Information Sources. In *Proceedings of the International Conference on Management of Data*, pp. 335-346. ACM Press, New York, Philadelphia, Pa. June, 1999.

Chen-Chuan K. Chang, Héctor García-Molina, and Andreas Paepcke. *Boolean Query Mapping Across Heterogeneous Information Sources. IEEE Transactions on Knowledge and Data Engineering*, 8(4):515-521, Aug, 1996.

Chen-Chuan K. Chang, Héctor García-Molina, and Andreas Paepcke. *Boolean Query Mapping Across Heterogeneous Information Sources (Extended Version)*. Number SIDL-WP-1996-0044; 1996-1. Dept. of Computer Science, Stanford Univ. Stanford, California, Sep, 1996. Accessible at http://dbpubs.stanford.edu/pub/1996-1.

Chen-Chuan K. Chang, Héctor García-Molina, and Andreas Paepcke. *Predicate Rewriting for Translating Boolean Queries in a Heterogeneous Information System. ACM Transactions on Information Systems*, 17(1):1-39, January, 1999. Available at http://dbpubs.stanford.edu/pub/1999-34.

Chetan Gopal and Roger Price. Multimedia Information Delivery and the MHEG Standard. In *DAGS '95*, 1995.

Chia-Hui Chang and Ching-Chi Hsu. Customizable Multi-engine Search Tool with Clustering. In *Proceedings of the Sixth International World-Wide Web Conference*, 1997.

Christine L. Borgman, Gregory Leazer, Anne Gilliland-Swetland, Kelli Millwood, Leslie Champeny, Jason Finley, and Laura J. Smart. How Geography Professors Select

Materials for Classroom Lectures: Implications for the Design of Digital Libraries. In *Proceedings of the Fourth ACM/IEEE-CS Joint Conference on Digital Libraries*, 2004.

Christoph Bussler, Stefan Jablonski, Thomas Kirsche, Hans Schuster, and Hartmut Wedekind. Architectural Issues of Distributed Workflow Management Systems. In V. Malyshkin, editor, *Parallel Computing Technologies. Third International Conference, PACT-95, Proceedings.* Springer-Verlag, Berlin, Germany, 1995.

Christopher B. Jones, R. Purves, A. Ruas, M. Sanderson, M. Sester, M. van Kreveld, and R. Weibel. Spatial information retrieval and geographical ontologies an overview of the SPIRIT project. In *Proceedings of the 25th annual international ACM SIGIR conference on Research and development in information retrieval*, pp. 387-388. ACM Press, 2002.

Christos Faloutsos. Access Methods for Text. *ACM Computing Surveys*, 17(1):49-74, March, 1985.

Claus Brabrand, Anders Moller, Anders Sandholm, and Michael I. Schwartzbach. A Runtime System for Interactive Web Services. In *Proceedings of the Eighth International World-Wide Web Conference*, 1999.

Colin Day. *Economics of Electronic Publishing*. In *JEP*, 1994

Colin Day. *Pricing Electronic Products*. In *JEP*, 1994.

Common Gateway Interface (CGI). *http://hoohoo.ncsa.uiuc.edu/cgi/overview.html.*

Copyright and Fair Use. Stanford University Libraries, 2000. Available at http://fairuse.stanford.edu/.

CyberCash. CyberCash Home Page. CyberCash website: http://www.cybercash.com/.

Cyrus Azarbod and William Perrizo. Building Concept Hierarchies for Schema Integration in HDDBS Using Incremental Concept Formation. In B. and Finin, T. and Yesha, Y. Bhargava, editors, *CIKM 93. Proceedings of the*

Second International Conference on Information and Knowledge Management, pp. 732-734. ACM, Washington, D.C., November, 1993.

D. A. Gorssman and J. R. Driscoll. Structuring Text within a Relation System. In *Proç. of the 3rd Intl. Conf. on Database and Expert System Applications*, pp. 72-77, September, 1992.

D. Bachiochi, M. Berstene, E. Chouinard, N. Conlan, M. Danchak, T. Furey, C. Neligon, and D. Way. Usability Studies And Designing Navigational Aids for The World Wide Web. In *Proceedings of the Sixth International World-Wide Web Conference*, 1997.

D. Dubois and H. Prade. *Fuzzy Sets and Systems: Theory and Applications*. Academic Press, New York, 1980.

D. Eastlake. Universal Payment Preamble Specification. W3C website: http://www.w3.org/ECommerce/specs/upp.txt.

D. Faensen, L. Faulstich, H. Schweppe, A. Hinze, and A. Steidinger. Hermes - A Notification Service for Digital Libraries. In *Proceedings of the First ACM/IEEE-CS Joint Conference on Digital Libraries*, 2001.

D. Georgakopoulos, M. Hornick, and A. Sheth. An Overview of Workflow Management: From Process Modeling to Infrastructure for Automation. *Journal on Distributed and Parallel Database Systems*, 3(2), 1995.

D. Goldberg, D. Nichols, B.M. Oki, and D. Terry. Using collaborative filtering to weave an information tapestry. *Communications of the ACM*, 35(12):61-70, 1992.

D. Goldberg, D. Nichols, B.M. Oki, and D. Terry. Using Collaborative Filtering to Weave an Information Tapestry. *Communications of the ACM*, 35(12):61-70, December, 1992.

D. Hawking and N. Craswell. *Overview of TREC-7 Very Large Collection Track*. In *Proc. of the Seventh Text Retrieval*

Conf. pp. 91-104, November, 1998. lhttp://trec.nist.gov/pubs/trec7/papers/vlc_overview.pdf.gz.

D. T. Hawkins and L. R. Levy. Front End Software for Online Database Searching Part 1: Definitions, System Features, and Evaluation. *Online*, 9(6):30-37, November, 1985.

D.Choy, R. Dievendorff, C. Dwork, J. B. Lotspiech, R. T. Morris, L. C. Anderson, A. E. Bell, S. K. Boyer, T. D. Griffin, B. A. Hoenig, J. M. McCrossin, A. M. Miller, N. J. Pass, F. P estoni, and D. S. Picciano. The Almaden Distributed Digital Library System. In *Advances in Digital Libraries '95*, 1995.

D.W. Embley. NFQL: The Natural Forms Query Language. *ACM Transactions on Database Systems*, 14(2):168-211, June, 1989.

Dan Ancona, Jim Frew, Greg Janâe, and Dave Valentine. Accessing the Alexandria Digital Library from Geographic Information Systems. In *Proceedings of the Fourth ACM/IEEE-CS Joint Conference on Digital Libraries*, 2004.

Daniel V Pitti. The Berkeley Finding Aid Project: Standards in Navigation. University of California, Berkeley. URL: http://www.ifla.org/documents/libraries/net/pitd1.txt

Daniela Florescu, Alon Y. Levy, and Alberto O. Mendelzon. Database Techniques for the World-Wide Web: A Survey. *SIGMOD Record*, 27(3):59-74, 1998.

Daniela Florescu, Daphne Koller, and Alon Levy. Awareness Services for Digital Libraries. In *Proceedings of the Twenty-third International Conference on Very Large Databases*, 1997.

Darren R. Hardy, Michael F. Schwartz, and Duane Wessels. *Harvest User's Manual.* January, 1996. Accessible at http://harvest.transarc.com/afs/transarc.com/public/trg/Harvest/ user-manual.

Dataware Search and Retrieval. *2000. http://www.dataware.com/technology/.*

David A. Hull and Gregory Grefenstette. Querying Across Languages: A Dictionary-Based Approach to Multilingual Information Retrieval. In *Proceedings of the Nineteenth Annual International ACM SIGIR Conference on Research and Development in Information Retrieval*, 1996.

David B. Johnson and Willy E. Zwaenepoel. Recovery in distributed systems using optimistic message logging and checkpointing. *Journal of Algorithms*, 11(3):462-491, September, 1990.

David Bainbridge, Craig G. Nevill-Manning, Ian H. Witten, Lloyd A. Smith, and Rodger J. McNab. Towards a Digital Library of Popular Music. In *Proceedings of the Fourth ACM International Conference on Digital Libraries*, 1999.

David Bainbridge, John Thompson, and Ian H. Witten. Assembling and enriching digital library collections. In *Proceedings of the Third ACM/IEEE-CS Joint Conference on Digital Libraries*, 2003.

David Chesnutt. *The Model Editions Partnership: Historical Editions in the Digital Age. D-Lib Magazine*, Nov, 1995.

David Frohlich, Allan Kuchinsky, Celine Pering, Abbe Don, and Steven Ariss. Requirements for Photoware. In *Proceedings of the 2002 ACM conference on Computer supported cooperative work*, 2002.

David Gibson, Jon M. Kleinberg, and Prabhakar Raghavan. Inferring Web Communities from Link Topology. In *HyperText*, 1998.

David Hawking, Nick Craswell, Paul Thistlewaite, and Donna Harman. Results and Challenges in Web Search Evaluation. In *Proceedings of the Eighth International World-Wide Web Conference*, 1999.

David J Harper, Sara Coluthard, Raja Kalpana, and Sun Yixing. *A Language Modelling Approach to Relevance Profiling for Document Browsing*. In *Proceedings of the Second ACM/IEEE-CS Joint Conference on Digital Libraries*, 2002.

David Karger, Alex Sherman, Andy Berkheimer, Bill Bogstad, Rizwan Dhanidina, Ken Iwamoto, Brian Kim, Luke Matkins, and Yoav Yerushalmi. Web Caching with Consistent Hashing. In *Proceedings of the Eighth International World-Wide Web Conference*, 1999.

David, Bearman. Virtual Archives. ICA Meeting, September 1996, Beijing. Draft paper. URL: http://www.ifla.org/documents/libraries/net/bearman.txt

Dennis E. Egan, Joel R. Remde, and Thomas K. Landauer. Behavioral Evaluation and Analysis of a Hypertext Browser. In *Proceedings of the Conference on Human Factors in Computing Systems CHI'89*, 1989.

Dennis S. Arnon. Scrimshaw: a language for document queries and transformations. *Electronic Publishing: Origination, Dissemination and Design*, 6(4):361-372, December, 1993.

Diane Kelly and Colleen Cool. *The Effects of Topic Familiarity on Information Search Behavior*. In *Proceedings of the Second ACM/IEEE-CS Joint Conference on Digital Libraries*, 2002.

Digest of Papers. First International Symposium on Wearable Computers (Cat. No.97TB100199). Oct, 1997.

DigiCash. DigiCash: Solutions for Security and Privacy. DigiCash website: http://www.digicash.com/.

Digital Equipment Corporation. MilliCent. MilliCent website: http://www.millicent.digital.com/.

Digital Preservation Consortium. Mission and Goals. March 1994. URL: http://www.ifla.org/documents/libraries/net/dpc1.txt

Dion Goh and John Leggett. Patron-augmented Digital Libraries. In *Proceedings of the Fifth ACM International Conference on Digital Libraries*, 2000.

Document Object Model Level 1 Specification. *http://www.w3.org/TR/REC-DOM-Level-1/*.

Don Gentner, Frank Ludolph, and Chris Ryan. Simplified Applications for Network Computers. In *Proceedings of the Conference on Human Factors in Computing Systems CHI'97*, 1997.

Don Waters. Electronic Technologies and Preservation. Based on a Presentation to the Annual Meeting of the Research Libraries Group, June 25, 1992. URL: http://www.ifla.org/documents/libraries/net/waters1.txt

Don Waters. Some Considerations on the Archiving of Digital Information. January, 1995. URL: http://www.ifla.org/documents/libraries/net/waters1.htm

Don Waters. The Social Organization of Archiving Digital Information. URL: http://www.ifla.org/documents/libraries/net/waters2.htm

Donald Byrd and Eric Isaacson. Music Representation in a Digital Music Library [short paper]. In *Proceedings of the Third ACM/IEEE-CS Joint Conference on Digital Libraries*, 2003.

Donald Byrd. A Scrollbar-based Visualization for Document Navigation. In *Proceedings of the Fourth ACM International Conference on Digital Libraries*, 1999.

Donald Byrd. Music-Notation Searching and Digital Libraries. In *Proceedings of the First ACM/IEEE-CS Joint Conference on Digital Libraries*, 2001.

Donatella Castelli and Pasquale Pagano. A System for Building Expandable Digital Libraries. In *Proceedings of the Third ACM/IEEE-CS Joint Conference on Digital Libraries*, 2003.

Donna Bergmark. *Collection Synthesis*. In *Proceedings of the Second ACM/IEEE-CS Joint Conference on Digital Libraries*, 2002.

Donna Harman. Document Detection Overview. In *Proceedings TIPSTER Text Program (Phase I)*. Morgan Kaufmann, San Francisco, Calif. Fredricksburg, Va. September, 1993.

Dorothy E. Denning and Peter J. Denning. Data Security. *ACM Computing Surveys*, 11(3):227-249, September, 1979.

Doug Beeferman, Adam Berger, and John D. Lafferty. Statistical Models for Text Segmentation. *Machine Learning*, 34(1-3):177-210, 1999.

Doug Cutting, Bill Janssen, Mike Spreitzer, and Farrell Wymore. *ILU Reference Manual*. Xerox Palo Alto Research Center, December, 1993. Accessible at ftp://ftp.parc.xerox.com/pub/ilu/ ilu.html.

Douglass R. Cutting, David Karger, and Jan Pedersen. Constant interaction-time Scatter/Gather browsing of very large document collections. In *Proceedings of the Sixteenth Annual International ACM SIGIR Conference on Research and Development in Information Retrieval*, pp. 126-135, 1993.

Douglass R. Cutting, Jan O. Pedersen, David Karger, and John W. Tukey. Scatter/Gather: A Cluster-based Approach to Browsing Large Document Collections. In *Proceedings of the Fifteenth Annual International ACM SIGIR Conference on Research and Development in Information Retrieval*, pp. 318-329, 1992.

Duncan Cavens, Stephen Sheppard, and Michael Meitner. Image Database Extension to ArcView: How to Find the Photograph You Want. In *Proceedings of ESRI Users Conference*, 2001.

E. Amoroso. *Fundamentals of Computer Security Technology*. Prentice Hall, Englewood Cliffs, NJ., 1994.

E. Bauer, D. Koller, and Y. Singer. Update Rules for parameter estimation in Bayesian networks. In *Proceedings of the 13th Annual Conference on Uncertainty in AI (UAI)*, 1997.

E. Fernandez, R. Summers, and C. Wood. *Database Security and Integrity*. Addison-Wesley, 1981.

E. Garfield. Citation Analysis as a tool in journal evaluation. *Science*, 178:471-479, 1972.

E.G. Coffman, Jr., Zhen Liu, and Richard R. Weber. *Optimal Robot Scheduling for Web Search Engines*. INRIA, 1997.

Eamonn J. Keogh, Selina Chu, David Hart, and Michael J. Pazzani. An Online Algorithm for Segmenting Time Series. In *IEEE International Conference on Data Mining*, pp. 364-373, 2001.

Ed H. Chi, James Pitkow, Jock Mackinlay, Peter Pirolli, Rich Gossweiler, and Stuart K. Card. Visualizing the Evolution of Web Ecologies. In *Proceedings of the Conference on Human Factors in Computing Systems CHI'98*, 1998.

Edward Chang and Hector Garcia-Molina. *Cost-Based Media Server Design*. In *To appear in the proceedings of the 8th Research Issues in Data Engineering*, Feb, 1998.

Edward Chang and Hector Garcia-Molina. Effective Memory Use in a Media Server. In *Proceedings of the 23rd Very Large Data Base (VLDB) Conference*, 1997.

Edward Chang and Hector Garcia-Molina. *MEDIC: A Memory & Disk Cache for Multimedia Clients*. Number SIDL-WP-1997-0076; 1997-9. Stanford University, October, 1997.

Edward Chang and Hector Garcia-Molina. *Minimizing Memory Requirements In Media Servers*. Number SIDL-WP-1996-0045; 1996-4. Stanford University, December, 1996.

Edward Chang and Hector Garcia-Molina. Reducing Initial Latency in Media Servers. In *IEEE Multimedia*. Vol. 4. 1997.

Edward Chang and Héctor García-Molina. *Reducing Initial Latency in a Multimedia Storage System*. In *Third International Workshop of Multimedia Database Systems*, 1996.

Edward Chang. *An Image Coding and Reconstruction Scheme for Mobile Computing*. In *Proceedings of the 5th IDMS (Springer-Verlag LNCS 1483), p.137- 148, Oslo, Norway, September 1998*. 1998. Accessible at http://dbpubs.stanford.edu/pub/1997-10

Edward Fox, ed. Digital Library Source Book. 1993. URL: http://fox.cs.vt.edu/DLSB.html

Edward Fox, ed. Rethinking Libraries in the Information Age: Lessons Learned with Five Digital Library Projects URL: http://fox.cs.vt.edu:80/talks/UNC96/

Edward Galloway A. and V. Michalek Gabrielle. The Heinz Electronic Library Interactive Online System (HELIOS): Building a Digital Archive Using Imaging, OCR, and Natural Language Processing Technologies. The Public-Access Computer Systems Review 6, no. 4 (1995). URL: http://www.ifla.org/documents/libraries/net/gale1.txt

Eija Kaasinen, Matti Aaltonen, Juha Kolari, Suvi Melakoski, and Timo Laakko. Two Approaches to Bringing Internet Services to WAP Devices. In *Proceedings of the Ninth International World-Wide Web Conference*, 2000.

Elizabeth Anderson, et. al. Digitizing Legacy Documents: A Knowledge-Based Preservation Project. Fermi National Accelerator Laboratory, September 1998. PDF: http://www.ifla.org/documents/libraries/net/tm-2056.pdf

Elke Dunker. *Cross-cultural Usability of the Library Metaphor*. In *Proceedings of the Second ACM/IEEE-CS Joint Conference on Digital Libraries*, 2002.

Eric Bier, Lance Good, Kris Popat, and Alan Newberger. A Document Corpus Browser for In-Depth Reading. In *Proceedings of the Fourth ACM/IEEE-CS Joint Conference on Digital Libraries*, 2004.

Eric H. Johnson and Pauline A. Cochrane. *A Hypertextual Interface for a Searcher's Thesaurus*. In *Proceedings of the Second Annual Conference on the Theory and Practice of Digital Libraries*, 1995.

Eric W. Brown, James P. Callan, and W. Bruce Croft. Fast Incremental Indexing for Full-Text Information Retrieval. In *Proceedings of the Twentieth Internationl Conference on Very Large Databases*, pp. 192-202, September, 1994.

Eric W. Brown, James P. Callan, W. Bruce Croft, and J. Eliot B. Moss. Supporting Full-Text Information Retrieval with a Persistent Object Store. In *Proceedings of the Fourth Internationl Conference on Extending Database Technology-EDBT'94*, pp. 365-378, March, 1994.

ESI 1.0. *http://www.w3.org/TR/esi-lang.*

Eugene Agichtein and Luis Gravano. Snowball: Extracting Relations from Large Plain-Text Collections. In *Proceedings of the Fifth ACM International Conference on Digital Libraries*, 2000.

Eytan Adar and Jeremy Hylton. *On-the-fly Hyperlink Creation for Page Images.* In *Proceedings of the Second Annual Conference on the Theory and Practice of Digital Libraries*, 1995.

Fabio Crestani. Vocal Access to a Newspaper Archive: Design Issues and Preliminary Investigations. In *Proceedings of the Fourth ACM International Conference on Digital Libraries*, 1999.

FineGround Networks. Breaking New Ground in Content Acceleration. *http://www.fineground.com/pdf/FGCWhitepaper.pdf.*

First Virtual Home Page. First Virtual website: http://www.fv.com/.

Forms in HTML Documents - W3C HTML 4.01 Recommendation. *http://www.w3.org/TR/html401/interact/forms.html.*

Francine Chen, Marti Hearst, Julian Kupiec, Jan Pedersen, and Lynn Wilcox. *Mixed-Media Access.* In *Proceedings of the First Annual Conference on the Theory and Practice of Digital Libraries*, 1994.

Frank M. Shipman III, Haowei Hsieh, J. Michael Moore, and Anna Zacchi. Supporting Personal Collections across Digital Libraries in Spatial Hypertext. In *Proceedings of the Fourth ACM/IEEE-CS Joint Conference on Digital Libraries*, 2004.

Frankie James. AHA: Audio HTML Access. In Michael R. Genesereth and Anna Patterson, editors, *Proceedings of the Sixth International World Wide Web Conference. Published in Computer Networks and ISDN Systems, vol.29, no.8-13, p.1395-404, 0169-7552 Elsevier Sept. 1997*, pp. 129-140. IW3C, Santa Clara, CA, April, 1997.

Frankie James. *Distinguishability vs. Distraction in Audio HTML Interfaces.* In *Submitted to International Journal on Digital Libraries*, 1997.

Frankie James. *Lessons from Developing Audio HTML Interfaces. ACM SIGCAPH Conference on Assistive Technologies Proceedings of the third international ACM conference on Assistive technologies. April 15-17, 1998, Marina del Rey, CA USA, pages 27-34.* 1998.

Frankie James. *Lessons from Developing Audio HTML Interfaces.* In *ASSETS 98*, pp. 27-34. ACM SIGCAPH, Marina del Rey, CA, April, 1998.

Frankie James. Presenting HTML Structure in Audio: User Satisfaction with Audio Hypertext. In *ICAD '96 Proceedings*, pp. 97-103. Xerox PARC, November, 1996. Also appeared in Web Techniques entitled Experimenting with Audio Interfaces, February 1998, vol 3 no 2, pages 55-58.

Frankie James. *Presenting HTML Structure in Audio: User Satisfaction with Audio Hypertext.* Number 97-201. Stanford University, 1997. Available at http://dbpubs.stanford.edu/pub/1996-83.

Franz J. Hauck. Supporting hierarchical guided tours in the World Wide Web. In *Proceedings of the Fifth International World-Wide Web Conference*, 1996.

Fred Douglis, Anja Feldmann, and Balachander Krishnamurthy. Rate of Change and other metrics: a Live Study of the World Wide Web. In *USENIX Symposium on Internetworking Technologies and Systems*, 1999.

Fred Douglis, Antonio Haro, and Michael Rabinovich. HPP: HTML Macro-Preprocessing to Support Dynamic Document Caching. In *Proceedings of the USENIX Symposium on Internet Technologies and Systems, Monterey, California*, 1997.

Fred Douglis, Thomas Ball, Yih-Farn Chen, and Eleftherios Koutsofios. WebGUIDE: Querying and Navigating Changes in Web Repositories. In *Proceedings of the Fifth International World-Wide Web Conference*, May, 1996.

Fred Douglis, Thomas Ball, Yih-Farn Chen, and Eleftherios Koutsofios. The AT&T Internet Difference Engine: Tracking and Viewing Changes on the Web. *World Wide Web*, 1(1):27-44, January, 1998.

Fred Friedman, Arthur M. Keller, Gio Wiederhold, Mike R. Berkowitz, John Salasin, and David L. Spooner. Reference Model for ADA Interfaces to Database Management Systems. In *Proceedings Second IEEE Computer Society Data Engineering Conference*, 1986.

G. Golub and C. Van Loan. *Matrix Computations*. John Hopkins Press, 1989.

G. W. Fitzmaurice. Situated information spaces and spatially aware palmtop computers. *Communications of the ACM*, 36(7):38-49, Jul, 1993.

Gary Geisler, Sarah Giersch, David McArthur, and Marty McClelland. *Creating Virtual Collections in Digital Libraries: Benefits and Implementation Issues*. In *Proceedings of the Second ACM/IEEE-CS Joint Conference on Digital Libraries*, 2002.

Gary King, H. T. Kung, Barbara Grosz, Sidney Verba, Dale Flecker, and Brian Kahin. *The Harvard Self-Enriching Library Facilities (SELF) Project*. In *Proceedings of the First Annual Conference on the Theory and Practice of Digital Libraries*, 1994.

Gary N. Griswold. *A Method for Protecting Copyright on Networks*. In *IP Workshop Proceedings*, 1994.

Gaurav Banga, Fred Douglis, and Michael Rabinovich. Optimistic Deltas for WWW Latency Reduction. In *Proceedings of USENIX Technical Conference*, pp. 289-303, 1997.

Gene Golovchinsky. Queries? Links? Is there a difference? In *Proceedings of the Conference on Human Factors in Computing Systems CHI'97*, 1997.

George W. Furnas. Generalized Fisheye Views. In *Proceedings of the Conference on Human Factors in Computing Systems CHI'86*, 1986.

Geri Gay and June P. Mead. The Common Ground Surrounding Access: Theoretical and Practical Perspectives. In *Proceedings of DL'96*, 1996.

Government Information Locator Service (GILS). *1998. Accessible at http://www.gils.net/index.html.*

Greg Janée and James Frew. *The ADEPT Digital Library Architecture.* In *Proceedings of the Second ACM/IEEE-CS Joint Conference on Digital Libraries*, 2002.

Greg Janee, James Frew, and David Valentine. Content Access Characterization in Digital Libraries [short paper]. In *Proceedings of the Third ACM/IEEE-CS Joint Conference on Digital Libraries*, 2003.

Gregor Kiczales and Andreas Paepcke. *Open Implementations and Metaobject Protocols.* 1994. Expanded tutorial notes. At http://db.stanford.edu/ paepcke/shared-documents/Tutorial.ps.

Gregor Kiczales, Jim des Rivières, and Daniel G. Bobrow. *The Art of the Metaobject Protocol.* MIT Press, 1991.

Gregory B Newby. The Digital Electronic Library. January 29, 1991. URL: http://www.ifla.org/documents/libraries/net/newby.txt

Gregory Crane, Clifford E. Wulfman, Lisa M. Cerrato, Anne Mahoney, Thomas L. Milbank, David Mimno, Jeffrey A. Rydberg-Cox, David A. Smith, and Christopher York.

Towards a Cultural Heritage Digital Library. In *Proceedings of the Third ACM/IEEE-CS Joint Conference on Digital Libraries*, 2003.

Gregory Crane, David A. Smith, and Clifford E. Wulfman. Building a Hypertextual Digital Library in the Humanities: A Case Study on London. In *Proceedings of the First ACM/IEEE-CS Joint Conference on Digital Libraries*, 2001.

Gregory Crane. Building a Digital Library: The Perseus Project as a Case Study in the Humanities. In *Proceedings of DL'96*, 1996.

H. Anan, X. Liu, K. Maly, M. Nelson, M. Zubair, J. C. French, E. Fox, and P. Shivakumar. *Preservation and Transition of NCSTRL Using an OAI-Based Architecture.* In *Proceedings of the Second ACM/IEEE-CS Joint Conference on Digital Libraries*, 2002.

H. Garcia-Molina, J. Hammer, J. Widom, W. Labio, and Y. Zhuge. The Stanford Data Warehousing Project. *IEEE Data Engineering Bulletin*, 18(2):41-48, June, 1995.

H. Garcia-Molina, J. Ullman, and J. Widom. *Database System Implementation*. Prentice-Hall, 2000.

H. Kautz, B. Selman, and and M. Shah. Referral Web: Combining Social Networks and collaborative Filtering. *Communications of the ACM*, 40(3):63-65, March, 1997.

H. Ulrich Hoppe and Jian Zhao. C-TORI: An Interface for Cooperative Database Retrieval. In Dimitris Karagiannis, editor, *5th International Conference, DEXA '94, Database and Expert Systems Applications*. Springer-Verlag, Berlin, Germany, 1994.

Handango, Inc. *http://www.handango.com.*

Hayley Dunlop, Matt Jones, and Sally Jo Cunningham. *A Digital Library of Conversational Expressions: A Communication Aid for People with Profound Physical Disabilities.* In *Proceedings of the Second ACM/IEEE-CS Joint Conference on Digital Libraries*, 2002.

Héctor García-Molina, Joachim Hammer, Kelly Ireland, Yannis Papakonstantinou, Jeffrey Ullman, and Jennifer Widom. *Integrating and Accessing Heterogeneous Information Sources in TSIMMIS.* In *AAAI Spring Symposium on Information Gathering,* 1995.

Hector Garcia-Molina, Luis Gravano, and Narayanan Shivakumar. *dSCAM: Finding Document Copies Across Multiple Databases. Proceedings of 4th International Conference on Parallel and Distributed Information Systems,* 1996.

Hector Garcia-Molina, Steven Ketchpel, and Narayanan Shivakumar. *Safeguarding and Charging for Information on the Internet.* In *Proceedings of the Fourteenth International Conference on Data Engineering,* 1998. Available at http://dbpubs.stanford.edu/pub/1998-26.

Héctor García-Molina, Wilburt Labio, and Ramana Yerneni. *Capability Sensitive Query Processing on Internet Sources.* In *Proceedings of the 15th International Conference on Data Engineering,* Sydney, Australia, March, 1999. Accessible at http://dbpubs.stanford.edu/pub/1998-40.

Heidi Johnson. Graded Access to Sensitive Materials at the Archive of the Indigenous Languages of Latin America [short paper]. In *Proceedings of the Third ACM/IEEE-CS Joint Conference on Digital Libraries,* 2003.

Henry Kautz, Al Milewski, and Bart Selman. *Agent Amplified Communication.* In *AAAI Spring Symposium on Information Gathering,* 1995.

Henry M. Gladney, Edward A. Fox, Zahid Ahmed, Ron Ashany, Nicholas J. Belkin, Michael Lesk, Richard Tong, and Maria Zemankova. *Digital Library: Gross Structure and Requirements (Report from a March 1994 Workshop).* In *Proceedings of the First Annual Conference on the Theory and Practice of Digital Libraries,* 1994.

Henry M. Gladney, et. al. Digital Library: Gross Structure and

Requirements (Report from a Workshop.) IBM Research Report RJ 9840, May 1994. PDF: http://www.ifla.org/documents/libraries/net/rj9840.pdf

Henry N. Jerez, Xiaoming Liu, Patrick Hochstenbach, and Herbert Van de Sompel. The multi-faceted use of the OAI-PMH in the LANL Repository. In *Proceedings of the Fourth ACM/IEEE-CS Joint Conference on Digital Libraries*, 2004.

Herb Becker. The Role of the Library of Congress in the National Digital Library. In *Proceedings of DL'96*, 1996.

Hong Cui, P. Bryan Heidorn, and Hong Zhang. *An Approach to Automatic Classification of Text for Information Retrieval.* In *Proceedings of the Second ACM/IEEE-CS Joint Conference on Digital Libraries*, 2002.

Howard Besser. MESL Project Description. In *Proceedings of DL'96*, 1996.

Hrishikesh Deshpande, Mayank Bawa, and Hector Garcia-Molina. *Streaming Live Media over Peers.* Number 2002-21. Stanford University, 2002.

Hrishikesh Deshpande, Mayank Bawa, and Hector Garcia-Molina. *Streaming Live Media over a Peer-to-Peer Network.* Number 2001-30. Stanford University, 2001.

Hrishikesh Deshpande, Mayank Bawa, and Hector Garcia-Molina. *Streaming Live Media over a Peer-to-Peer Network.* Number 2001-31. Stanford University, 2001.

HTTP - Hypertext Transfer Protocol. *2000. http://www.w3.org/Protocols/.*

Hugh Davis and Jessie Hey. *Automatic Extraction of Hypermedia Bundles from the Digital Library.* In *Proceedings of the Second Annual Conference on the Theory and Practice of Digital Libraries*, 1995.

Hugh Davis. *Using Microcosm to Access Digital Libraries.* In *Proceedings of the First Annual Conference on the Theory and Practice of Digital Libraries*, 1994.

Hui Han, C. Lee Giles, Eren Manavoglu, Hongyuan Zha, Zhenyue Zhang, and Edward A. Fox. Automatic Document Metadata Extraction using Support Vector Machines. In *Proceedings of the Third ACM/IEEE-CS Joint Conference on Digital Libraries*, 2003.

Hui Han, C. Lee Giles, Hongyuan Zha, Cheng Li, and Kostas Tsioutsiouliklis. Two Supervised Learning Approaches for Name Disambiguation in Author Citations. In *Proceedings of the Fourth ACM/IEEE-CS Joint Conference on Digital Libraries*, 2004.

Hypertext Transfer Protocol - HTTP/1.1. *ftp://ftp.isi.edu/in-notes/rfc2616.txt.*

Hyunki Kim, Hakgene Shin, and Jaewoo Chang. An Object-Oriented Hypermedia System for Structured Documents. In *Proceedings of DL'96*, 1996.

Hyunmo Kang and Ben Shneiderman. *Submitted to International Journal on Digital Libraries*. 2004.

Hyunmo Kang and Ben Shneiderman. Visualization Methods for Personal Photo Collections: Browsing and Searching in the PhotoFinder. In *IEEE International Conference on Multimedia and Expo*, 2000.

Information Retrieval: Application Service Definition and Protocol Specification. ANSI/NISO, April, 1995. Available at http://lcweb.loc.gov/z3950/agency/document.html.

InvisibleWeb.com. *http://www.invisibleweb.com.*

Isabel Cruz. . Effective Abstractions in Multimedia. *In DAGS '95, 1995.*

ISO. *ISO 8777:1993 Information and Documentation - Commands for Interactive Text Searching.* Int'l Organization for Standardization, First, Geneva, Switzerland, 1993.

Israel Ben-Shaul, Michael Herscovici, Michal Jacovi, Yoelle S. Maarek, Dan Pelleg, Menachem Shtalhaim, Vladimir Soroka, and Sigalit Ur. Adding Support for Dynamic and

Focused Search with Fetuccino. In *Proceedings of the Eighth International World-Wide Web Conference*, 1999.

Israel Ben-Shaul, Michael Herscovici, Michal Jacovi, Yoelle S. Maarek, Dan Pelleg, Menachem Shtalhaim, Vladimir Soroka, and Sigalit Ur. Adding support for dynamic and focused search with Fetuccino. In *Proceedings of the Eighth International World-Wide Web Conference*, 1999.

ITU/ISO ODP Trading Function. ISO/IEC, 1997. ISO/IEC IS 13235-1, ITU/T Draft Rec X950-1.

J. Bonigk and A. Lubinski. A basic architecture for mobile information access. *Computers & Graphics*, 20(5):683-91, 1996.

J. Bumiller and S. Rather. Electronic meeting assistance. In *Human Computer Interaction. Vienna Conference, VCHCI'93 Fin de Siecle Proceedings*, pp. 425-6, Sep, 1993.

J. Davis, D. Krafft, and C. Lagoze. Dienst: Building a Production Technical Report Server. In *Advances in Digital Libraries '95*, 1995.

J. Frew, M. Aurand, B. Buttenfield, L. Carver, P. Chang, R. Ellis, C. Fischer, M. Gardner, M. Goodchild, G. Hajic, M. Larsgaard, K. Park, M. Probert, T. Smith, and Q. Zheng. The Alexandria Rapid Prototype: Building A Digital Library for Spatial Information. In *Advances in Digital Libraries '95*, 1995.

J. P. Deschrevel. *The ANSA Model for Trading and Federation*. Number APM.1005.01. APM, Cambridge, 1989.

J.A. Blakeley, W.J. McKenna, and G. Graefe. Experiences building the Open OODB query optimizer. In *Proceedings of the International Conference on Management of Data*, 1993.

J.D. Day and H. Zimmermann. The OSI Reference Model. *Proc. of the IEEE*, 71:1334-1340, December, 1983.

Jack B. Dennis and Earl C. Van Horn. Programming Semantics for Multiprogrammed Computations. In *Communications of the ACM*, 1966.

Jack Brassil. SEPTEMBER - Secure Electronic Publishing Trial. In *Proceedings of DL'96*, 1996.

Jack Kessler. *The French Minitel: Is There Digital Life Outside of the US ASCII Internet? A Challenge or Convergence? D-Lib Magazine*, Dec, 1995.

James C. French, A. C. Chapin, and Worthy N. Martin. An Application of Multiple Viewpoints to Content-Based Image Retrieval [short paper]. In *Proceedings of the Third ACM/IEEE-CS Joint Conference on Digital Libraries*, 2003.

James C. French. *Modeling Web Data*. In *Proceedings of the Second ACM/IEEE-CS Joint Conference on Digital Libraries*, 2002.

James Davis, and Carl Lagoze. Dienst, A Protocol for a Distributed Digital Document Library. URL: http://www.broadcatch.com/dienst.html

James J. Hunt, Kiem-Phong Vo, and Walter F. Tichy. Delta Algorithms: An Empirical Analysis. *ACM Transactions on Software Engineering and Methodology*, 7:192-214, 1998.

James R. Davis. Creating a Networked Computer Science Technical Report Library. In *Proceedings of DL'96*, 1996.

James R. Davis. *Creating a Networked Computer Science Technical Report Library. D-Lib Magazine*, Sep, 1995.

James W. Cooper, Mahesh Viswanathan, Donna Byron, and Margaret Chan. Building Searchable Collections of Enterprise Speech Data. In *Proceedings of the First ACM/IEEE-CS Joint Conference on Digital Libraries*, 2001.

Jane Hunter and Sharmin Choudhury. A Semi-Automated Digital Preservation System based on Semantic Web Services. In *Proceedings of the Fourth ACM/IEEE-CS Joint Conference on Digital Libraries*, 2004.

Janet Fisher. *Copyright: The Glue of the System*. In *JEP*, 1994.

Jason J. Hyon and Rosana Bisciotti Borgen. Data Archival and Retrieval Enhancement (DARE) Metadata Modeling and its User Interface. In *Proceedings of the First IEEE Metadata Conference.* IEEE, Silver Spring, Md. April, 1996.

Java Commerce Messages White Paper. Sun Microsystems website: http://java.sun.com/products/commerce/docs/whitepapers/jcm_whitepaper/jcm_whitepaper.html.

Java Servletxttrademark Technology. *http://java.sun.com/products/servlet/.*

JavaServer Pages (JSPxttrademark) Technology. *http://java.sun.com/products/jsp/.*

Jean-Daniel Fekete and Micole Dufournaud. Compus: Visualization and Analysis of Structured Documents for Understanding Social Life in the 16th Century. In *Proceedings of the Fifth ACM International Conference on Digital Libraries*, 2000.

Jeff Conklin and Michael L. Begeman. gIBIS: A Hypertext Tool for Exploratory Policy Discussion. In *Proceedings of the Conference on Computer-Supported Cooperative Work*, 1988.

Jeffrey Dean and Monika R. Henzinger. Finding Related Pages in the World Wide Web. In *Proceedings of the Eighth International World-Wide Web Conference*, 1999.

Jeromy Carriere and Rick Kazman. WebQuery: Searching and Visualizing the Web through Connectivity. In *Proceedings of the Sixth International World-Wide Web Conference*, 1997.

Jesper Juhne, Anders T. Jensen, and Kaj Gronbaek. Ariadne: a Java-based guided tour system for the World Wide Web. In *Proceedings of the Seventh International World-Wide Web Conference*, 1998.

Jezekiel Ben-Arie, Purvin Pandit, and ShyamSundar Rajaram. Design of A Digital Library for Human Movement. In *Proceedings of the First ACM/IEEE-CS Joint Conference on Digital Libraries*, 2001.

Jianping Fan, Hangzai Luo, and Lide Wu. Semantic Video Classification and Feature Subset Selection under Context and Concept Uncertainty. In *Proceedings of the Fourth ACM/IEEE-CS Joint Conference on Digital Libraries*, 2004.

Jim Challenger, Arun Iyengar, Karen Witting, Cameron Ferstat, and Paul Reed. A publishing system for Efficiently Creating Dynamic Web Content. In *Proceedings of IEEE INFOCOM 2000, Tel Aviv, Israel*, 2000.

Jim Challenger, Paul Dantzig, and Arun Iyengar. A Scalable System for Consistently Caching Dynamic Web Data. In *Proceedings of the 18th Annual Joint Conference of the IEEE Computer and Communications Societies*, New York, New York, 1999".

Jim Dorward, Derek Reinke, and Mimi Recker. *An Evaluation Model for a Digital Library Services Tool.* In *Proceedings of the Second ACM/IEEE-CS Joint Conference on Digital Libraries*, 2002.

Jim French, Ed Fox, Kurt Maly, and Alan Selman. Wide Area Technical Report Service: Technical Reports Online. *Communications of the ACM*, 38(4):45, April, 1995.

Jim Gray and Andreas Reuter. *Transaction Processing: concepts and techniques*. Morgan Kaufmann Publishers, Inc. 1993.

Jim Gray, Pat Helland, Patrick E. O'Neil, and Dennis Shasha. Dangers of Replication and a Solution. *SIGMOD*:173-82, June, 1996.

Jinwei Cao and Jay F. Nunamaker, Jr. Question Answering On Lecture Videos: A Multifaceted Approach. In *Proceedings of the Fourth ACM/IEEE-CS Joint Conference on Digital Libraries*, 2004.

Joachim Hammer, Hector Garcia-Molina, Junghoo Cho, Arturo Crespo, and Rohan Aranha. Extracting Semistructured Information from the Web. In *Proceedings of the Workshop on Management of Semistructured Data*, 1997.

John Buford. Evaluation of a Query Language for Structured HyperMedia Documents. In *DAGS '95*. 1995.

John Garrett. Digital Libraries: The Grand Challenges. EDUCOM Review, July/August 1993, Volume 28, Number 4. URL: http://www.ifla.org/documents/libraries/net/garrett.txt

John R. Garrett. *Task Force on Archiving of Digital Information. D-Lib Magazine*, Sep, 1995.

John S. Erickson. *A Copyright Management System for Networked Interactive Multimedia*. In *DAGS '95*, 1995..

Jon W. Dunn and Costance A. Mayer. VARIATIONS: A Digital Music Library System at Indiana University. In *Proceedings of the Fourth ACM International Conference on Digital Libraries*, 1999.

Jonathan T. Hujsak. *Digital Libraries and Corporate Technology Reuse. D-Lib Magazine*, Jan, 1996.

Josâ Borbinha, Nuno Freire, and JoÉo Neves. BND: A National Digital Library as a jigsaw. In *Proceedings of the Fourth ACM/IEEE-CS Joint Conference on Digital Libraries*, 2004.

Jose Kahan. WDAI: A Simple World Wide Web Distributed Authorization Infrastructure. In *Proceedings of the Eighth International World-Wide Web Conference*, 1999..

Jose-Luis Ambite and Craig A. Knoblock. Reconciling Distributed Information Sources. *In AAAI Spring Symposium on Information Gathering, 1995.*

José-Marie Griffiths and Kimberly K. Kertis. *Access to Large Digital Libraries of Scientific Information Across Networks*. In *Proceedings of the First Annual Conference on the Theory and Practice of Digital Libraries*, 1994.

Joseph L. Ebersole. *Response to Dr. Linn's Paper*. In *IP Workshop Proccedings*, 1994.

Joseph Y. Halpern and Carl Lagoze. The Computing Research Repository: Promoting the Rapid Dissemination and Archiving of Computer Science Research. In *Proceedings of the Fourth ACM International Conference on Digital Libraries*, 1999.

Judith Edwards. *The Electronic World and Central Queensland University*. In *Proceedings of the First Annual Conference on the Theory and Practice of Digital Libraries*, 1994.

Jun Hirai, Sriram Raghavan, Hector Garcia-Molina, and Andreas Paepcke. *WebBase: A repository of web pages*. In *Proceedings of the Ninth International World-Wide Web Conference*, pp. 277-293, May, 2000. Available at http://dbpubs.stanford.edu/pub/2000-51.

Junghoo Cho and Hector Garcia-Molina. *Estimating Frequency of Change*. In *submitted for publication*, 2000. Available at http://dbpubs.stanford.edu/pub/2000-4.

Junghoo Cho and Hector Garcia-Molina. *Synchronizing a Database to Improve Freshness*. In *Proceedings of the International Conference on Management of Data*, 2000. Available at http://dbpubs.stanford.edu/pub/1999-40.

Junghoo Cho and Hector Garcia-Molina. *The Evolution of the Web and Implications for an Incremental Crawler*. In *Proceedings of the Twenty-sixth International Conference on Very Large Databases*, 2000. Available at http://dbpubs.stanford.edu/pub/1999-22.

Junghoo Cho, Hector Garcia-Molina, and Lawrence Page. *Efficient Crawling Through URL Ordering*. In *Proceedings of the Seventh International World-Wide Web Conference*, 1998.

Junghoo Cho, Narayanan Shivakumar, and Hector Garcia-Molina. Computing Document Clusters on the Web. In *Proceedings of the International Conference on Management of Data*, 1998.

Junghoo Cho, Narayanan Shivakumar, and Hector Garcia-Molina. *Finding Replicated Web Collections*. In *Proceedings of the International Conference on Management of Data*, 2000. Available at http://dbpubs.stanford.edu/pub/1999-64.

Kaj Gronbaek, Lennert Sloth, and Peter Orbaek. Webvise: Browser and Proxy Support for Open Hypermedia Structuring Mechanisms on the World Wide Web. In *Proceedings of the Eighth International World-Wide Web Conference*, 1999.

Kaj Gronbaek, Lennert Sloth, and Peter Orbaek. Webvise: browser and proxy support for open hypermedia structuring mechanisms on the World Wide Web. In *Proceedings of the Eighth International World-Wide Web Conference*, 1999.

Karen D. Grant, Adrian Graham, Tom Nguyen, Andreas Paepcke, and Terry Winograd. *Beyond the Shoe Box: Foundations for Flexibly Organizing Photographs on a Computer*. Number 2002-45. Stanford University, 2002.

Kate Ehrlich and Debra Cash. *Turning Information into Knowledge: Information Finding as a Collaborative Activity*. In *Proceedings of the First Annual Conference on the Theory and Practice of Digital Libraries*, 1994.

Kathleen M. Flynn. *The Knowledge Manager as a Digital Librarian: An Overview of the Knowledge Management Pilot Program at the MITRE Corporation*. In *Proceedings of the Second Annual Conference on the Theory and Practice of Digital Libraries*, 1995.

Katy Borner, Ying Feng, and Tamara McMahon. *Collaborative Visual Interfaces to Digital Libraries*. In *Proceedings of the Second ACM/IEEE-CS Joint Conference on Digital Libraries*, 2002.

Kenichi Kamiya, Martin Röscheisen, and Terry Winograd. *Grassroots: A System Providing a Uniform Framework for Communicating, Structuring, Sharing Information, and Organizing People*. In *Proceedings of the Fifth International World-Wide Web Conference*, 1996.

Kenneth Arnold. *The Electronic Librarian Is a Verb/The Electronic Library Is Not a Sentence*. In *JEP*, 1994.

Kenneth Furuta. *Librarianship in the Digital Library.* In *Proceedings of the First Annual Conference on the Theory and Practice of Digital Libraries*, 1994.

Kenneth M. Anderson, Aaron Andersen, Neet Wadhwani, and Laura M. Bartolo. Metis: Lightweight, Flexible, and Web-based Workflow Services for Digital Libraries. In *Proceedings of the Third ACM/IEEE-CS Joint Conference on Digital Libraries*, 2003.

Kenneth R. Abbott and Sunil K. Sarin. Experiences with Workflow Management: Issues for the Next Generation. In Richard Furuta and Christine Neuwirth, editors, *CSCW '94*. ACM, New York, 1994.

Kiyokuni Kawachiya and Hiroshi Ishikawa. NaviPoint: An Input Device for Mobile Information Browsing. In *Proceedings of the Conference on Human Factors in Computing Systems CHI'98*, 1998.

Kobus Barnard and David .A. Forsyth. Learning the Semantics of Words and Pictures. In *Proceedings of the IEEE International Conference on Computer Vision*, July, 2001.

Krishna Bharat and Andrei Broder. Mirror, Mirror on the Web: A Study of Host Pairs with Replicated Content. In *Proceedings of the Eighth International World-Wide Web Conference*, 1999.

Krishna Bharat, Andrei Broder, Monika Henzinger, Puneet Kumar, and Suresh Venkatasubramanian. The Connectivity Server: Fast Access to Linkage Information on the Web. In *Proceedings of the Seventh International World-Wide Web Conference*, April, 1998.

Kristian Hammond, Robin Burke, Charles Martin, and Steven Lytinen. *FAQ Finder: A Case-Based Approach to Knowledge Navigation.* In *AAAI Spring Symposium on Information Gathering*, 1995.

Kurt D. Bollacker, Steve Lawrence, and C. Lee Giles. A System For Automatic Personalized Tracking of Scientific Literature on the Web. In *Proceedings of the Fourth ACM*

International Conference on Digital Libraries, 1999.

Kyoichi Arai, Teruo Yokoyama, and Yutaka Matsushita. A window sytems with leafing through mode: Bookwindow. In *Proceedings of the Conference on Human Factors in Computing Systems CHI'92*, 1992.

L. Egghe and R. Rousseau. *Introduction to Informetrics*. Elsevier, 1990.

L. Francis. Mobile computing-a fact in your future. In *15th Annual International Conference on Computer Documentation Conference Proceedings. SIGDOC '97. Crossroads in Communication*, pp. 63-7, 1997.

Laura Fillmore. *Internet Publishing in a Borderless Environment: Bookworms into Butterflies*. In *JEP*, 1994.

Laura Fillmore. *Online Publishing: Threat or Menace?* In *JEP*, 1994.

Laura M. Bartolo, Cathy S. Lowe, Adam C. Powell IV, Donald R. Sadoway, Jorges Vieyra, and Kyle Stemen. Use of MatML with Software Applications for E-learning. In *Proceedings of the Fourth ACM/IEEE-CS Joint Conference on Digital Libraries*, 2004.

Laura M. Haas, Donald Kossmann, Edward L. Wimmers, and Jun Yang. Optimizing Queries Across Diverse Data Sources. In *Proceedings of the Twenty-third International Conference on Very Large Databases*, pp. 276-285. VLDB Endowment, Athens, Greece, August, 1997.

Lee Breslau, Pei Cao, Li Fan, Graham Phillips, and Scott Shenker. Web Caching and Zipf-like Distributions: Evidence and Implications. In *Proceedings of Infocom*, 1999.

Leonard N. Foner. Clustering and Information Sharing in an Ecology of Cooperating Agents. *In AAAI Spring Symposium on Information Gathering, 1995.*

Leslie Bondaryk. *Calculus Modules OnLine: An Internet Multimedia Application*. In *DAGS'95*, 1995.

Leslie Champeny, Christine L. Borgman, Patricia Mautone, Richard E. Mayer, Richard A. Johnson, Gregory H. Leazer, Anne J. Gilliland-Swetland, Kelli A. Millwood, Leonard D'Avolio, Jason Finley, and Laura J. Smart. Developing a Digital Learning Environment: an evaluation of design and implementation processes. In *Proceedings of the Fourth ACM/IEEE-CS Joint Conference on Digital Libraries*, 2004.

Lian-Heong Chua, Dion Hoe-Lian Goh, Ee-Peng Lim, Zehua Liu, and Rebecca Pei-Hui Ang. *A Digital Library For Geography Examination Resources*. In *Proceedings of the Second ACM/IEEE-CS Joint Conference on Digital Libraries*, 2002.

Librarians Association of the University of California. New Horizons in Scholarly Communications. URL: http://libweb-01.ucsc.edu/scomm/

Linda L. Hill, James Frew, and Qi Zheng. *Geographic Names - The Implementation of a Gazetteer in a Georeferenced Digital Library*. *CNRI D-Lib Magazine*, January, 1999.

Lisa Freeman. *Testimony prepared on behalf of the Association of American University Presses for the National Information Infrastructure Task Force Working Group on Intellectual Property*. In *JEP*, 1994.

Lorcan Dempsey. Network resource discovery: a European library perspective. British Library. Research and Development Department, 1994. URL: http://www.lub.lu.se/UB2proj/LIS_collection/lorcan.html

Luis Francisco-Revilla, Frank Shipman, Richard Furuta, Unmil Karadkar, and Avital Arora. Managing Change on the Web. In *Proceedings of the First ACM/IEEE-CS Joint Conference on Digital Libraries*, 2001.

Luis Gravano and Héctor García-Molina. *Generalizing GlOSS to Vector-Space Databases and Broker Hierarchies*. In *Proceedings of the Twenty-first International Conference on Very Large Databases*, pp. 78-89, September, 1995.

Luis Gravano and Hector Garcia-Molina. *Merging Ranks from Heterogeneous Internet Sources.* In *Proceedings of the Twenty-third International Conference on Very Large Databases,* 1997.

Luis Gravano, Chen-Chuan K. Chang, Hector Garcia-Molina, and Andreas Paepcke. STARTS: Stanford Proposal for Internet Meta-Searching. In *Proc. of the 1997 ACM SIGMOD International Conference On Management of Data,* 1997.

Luis Gravano, Chen-Chuan K. Chang, Héctor García-Molina, and Andreas Paepcke. *STARTS: Stanford protocol proposal for Internet retrieval and search.* Number SIDL-WP-1996-0043; 1997-68. Stanford University, August, 1996. Accessible at http://dbpubs.stanford.edu/pub/1997-68.

Luis Gravano, Chen-Chuan K. Chang, Héctor García-Molina, and Andreas Paepcke. *STARTS: Stanford Proposal for Internet Meta-Searching.* In *Proceedings of the International Conference on Management of Data,* 1997.

Luis Gravano, Héctor García-Molina, and Anthony Tomasic. *The effectiveness of GlOSS for the text-database discovery problem.* In *Proceedings of the International Conference on Management of Data,* May, 1994.

Lynn, M. Stuart. The Relationship Between Digital and Other Media Conversion Processes: A Structured Glossary of Technical Terms. Commission for Preservation and Access. Technology Assessment Advisory Committee. August 1990. (160 K)

M. Baker, X. Zhao, S. Cheshire, and J. Stone. Supporting Mobility in MosquitoNet. In *Proceedings of the 1996 USENIX Conference,* Jan, 1996.

M. Baker. Changing Communication Environments in MosquitoNet. In *Proceedings of the IEEE Workshop on Mobile Computing Systems and Applications,* Dec, 1994.

M. Balabanovic and Y. Shoham. Fab: content-based collaborative recommendation. *Communications of the ACM*, 40(3):66-72, March, 1997.

M. Balabanovic and Y. Shoham. Learning information retrieval agents: Experiments with automated web browsing. In *AAAI spring symposium on Information Gathering*, 1995.

M. Balabanovic, Y. Shoham, and Y. Yun. An Adaptive Agent for Automated Web Browsing. *Journal of Visual Communication and Image Representation*, 6(4), December, 1995.

M. Bearman. ODP-Trader. *Open Distributed Processing*, 2:19 - 33, 1994.

M. Beigl and R. Rudisch. System support for mobile computing. *Computers & Graphics*, 20(5):619-625, 1996.

M. Bellare, J.A. Garay, R. Hauser, A. Herzberg, H. Krawczyk, M. Steiner, G. Tsudik, and M. Waidner. iKP-a family of secure electronic payment protocols. In *Proceedings of the First USENIX Workshop of Electronic Commerce*. USENIX Assoc, Berkeley, CA, USA, 1995.

M. Chalmers, K. Rodden, and D. Brodbeck. The order of things: activity-centered information access. In *Proceedings of the 7th World Wide Web Conference*, 1998.

M. Chen, M. Hearst, J. Hong, and J. Lin. Cha-Cha: A System for Organizing Intranet Search Results. In *Proceedings of the second USENIX Symposium on Internet Technologies and SYSTEMS (USITS)*, 1999.

M. Diligenti, F. M. Coetzee, S. Lawrence, C. L. Giles, and M. Gori. Focused Crawling Using Context Graphs. In *Proceedings of the Twenty-sixth International Conference on Very Large Databases*, 2000.

M. Fuchs. The User Interface as Document: SGML and Distributed Applications. *Computer Standards & Interfaces*, 18(1):79-92, January, 1996.

M. H. Dunham and A. Helal. A mobile transaction model that

captures both the data and movement behavior. *Mobile Networks and Applications*, 2(2):149-62, 1997.

M. Hersovici, M. Jacovi, Y. Maarek, D. Pelleg, M. Shtalhaim, and S. Ur. The shark-search algorithm - An application: tailored Web site mapping. In *Proceedings of the 7th World Wide Web Conference*, 1998.

M. I. Crystal and G. E. Jakobson. FRED, A Front End for Databases. *Online*, 6(5):27-30, September, 1982.

M.N. Huhns and M.P. Singh. Automating Workflows for Service Provisioning: Integrating AI and Database Technologies. In *Proceedings of the Tenth Conference on Artificial Intelligence for Applications*. IEEE Computer Society Press, Los Alamitos, CA, 1994.

M.R. Genesereth, A.M. Keller, and O.M. Duschka. Infomaster: an information integration system. In *SIGMOD Record*. ACM Press, New York, 1997.

M.W. Bright, A.R. Hurson, and S. Pakzad. Automated Resolution of Sematic Heterogeneity in Multidatabases. *ACM Transaction on Database Systems*, 19(2):212-253, June, 1994.

M.W. Bright, A.R. Hurson, and Simin H. Pakzad. A Taxonomy and Current Issues in Multidatabase Systems. *IEEE Computer*, 25(3):51-60, March, 1992.

M.W. DayPreservation of electronic information: a bibliography. URL: http://homes.ukoln.ac.uk/~lismd/preservation.html

Maayan Geffet and Dror G. Feitelson. Hierarchical Indexing and Document Matching in BoW. In *Proceedings of the First ACM/IEEE-CS Joint Conference on Digital Libraries*, 2001

Mao Lin Huang, Peter Eades, and Robert F. Cohen. WebOFDAV - navigating and visualizing the Web on-line with animated context swapping. In *Proceedings of the Seventh International World-Wide Web Conference*, 1998.

Marc Abrams, Constantinos Phanouriou, Alan L. Batongbacal, Stephen M. Williams, and Jonathan E. Shuster. UIML: An Appliance-independent XML User Interface Language. In *Proceedings of the Eighth International World-Wide Web Conference*, 1999.

Marc Gyssens, Jan Paredaens, and Dirk Van Gucht. A Grammar-Based Approach Towards Unifying Hierarchical Data Models. In *Proceedings of the International Conference on Management of Data.* ACM Press, Portland, Oreg. June, 1989.

Marcos Andrâ Gonáalves, Ganesh Panchanathan, Unnikrishnan Ravindranathan, Aaron Krowne, Edward A. Fox, Filip Jagodzinski, and Lillian Cassel. The XML Log Standard for Digital Libraries: Analysis, Evolution, and Deployment [short paper]. In *Proceedings of the Third ACM/IEEE-CS Joint Conference on Digital Libraries*, 2003.

Marcos Andre Goncalves and Edward A. Fox. *5SL - A Language for Declarative Specification and Generation of Digital Libraries.* In *Proceedings of the Second ACM/IEEE-CS Joint Conference on Digital Libraries*, 2002.

Marcos Andre Goncalves, Edward A. Fox, Aaron Krowne, Pavel Calado, Alberto H.F. Laender, Altigran S. da Silva, and Berthier Ribeiro-Neto. The Effectiveness of Automatically Structured Queries in Digital Libraries. In *Proceedings of the Fourth ACM/IEEE-CS Joint Conference on Digital Libraries*, 2004.

Mark Derthick. *Interfaces for Palmtop Image Search.* In *Proceedings of the Second ACM/IEEE-CS Joint Conference on Digital Libraries*, 2002.

Mark G.K.M. van Doorn and Arjen P. de Vries. The Psychology of Multimedia Databases. In *Proceedings of the Fifth ACM International Conference on Digital Libraries*, 2000.

Mark S. Ackerman and Roy T. Fielding. *Collection Maintenance in the Digital Library.* In *Proceedings of the Second Annual*

Conference on the Theory and Practice of Digital Libraries, 1995.

Mark S. Ackerman. *Providing Social Interaction in the Digital Library.* In *Proceedings of the First Annual Conference on the Theory and Practice of Digital Libraries*, 1994.

Marko Balabanovic and Yoav Shoham. Combining Content-Based and Collaborative Recommendation. *Communications of the ACM*, 40(3), March, 1997.

Marko Balabanovic and Yoav Shoham. *Learning Inforamtion Retrieval Agents: Experiments with Automated Web Browsing.* In *Proceedings of the AAAI Spring Symposium on Information Gathering from Heterogenous, Distributed Resources*, 1995. Format: Compressed PostScript.

Marko Balabanovic, Yoav Shoham, and Yeogirl Yun. An Adaptive Agent for Automated Web Browsing. *Journal of Visual Communication and Image Representation*, 6(4), December, 1995.

Marko Balabanovic. *An Adaptive Web Page Recommendation Service.* In *Proceedings of the First International Conference on Autonomous Agents p. 378-385*, February, 1997.

Marko Balabanovic. *An Interface for Learning Multi-topic User Profiles from Implicit Feedback.* Number SIDL-WP-1998-0089. Stanford University, 1998.

Marko Balabanovic. *Exploring versus Exploiting when Learning User Models for Text Recommendation. User Modeling and User-Adapted Interaction (to appear)*, 8(1), 1998.

Marko Balabanovic. The "Slider" Interface. *IBM interVisions*, 11, February, 1998.

Markus Jakobsson, Philip D. MacKenzie, and Julien P. Stern. Secure and Lightweight Advertising on the Web. In *Proceedings of the Eighth International World-Wide Web Conference*, 1999.

Marti A. Hearst. TileBars: Visualization of Term Distribution Information in Full Text Information Access. In *Proceedings of the Conference on Human Factors in Computing Systems CHI'95*, 1995.

Mary F. Fernandez, Daniela Florescu, Jaewoo Kang, Alon Y. Levy, and Dan Suciu. STRUDEL: A Web-site Management System. In *Proceedings of the International Conference on Management of Data*, pp. 549-552, 1997.

Masanori Harada, Shin-ya Sato, and Kazuhiro Kazama. Finding Authoritative People from the Web. In *Proceedings of the Fourth ACM/IEEE-CS Joint Conference on Digital Libraries*, 2004.

Matt Jones, Gary Marsden, Norliza Mohd-Nasir, Kevin Boone, and George Buchanan. Improving Web Interaction on Small Displays. In *Proceedings of the Eighth International World-Wide Web Conference*, 1999.

Matthew Cooper, Jonathan Foote, Andreas Girgensohn, and Lynn Wilcox. Temporal event clustering for digital photo collections. In *Proceedings of the eleventh ACM international conference on Multimedia*, pp. 364-373. ACM Press, 2003.

Mayur Datar. *Butterflies and Peer-to-Peer Networks*. In *Proceedings of the 10th European Symposium on Algorithms*, 2002.

Mayur Datar. *Butterflies and Peer-to-Peer Networks*. Number 2002-5. Stanford University, 2002.

Melinda Finch, Michelle Ferebee, Bruce R. Barkstrom and Calvin Mackey. *Adapting Digital Libraries to Continual Evolution*. In *Proceedings of the Second ACM/IEEE-CS Joint Conference on Digital Libraries*, 2002.

Michael Chau, Hsinchun Chen, Jialun Qin, Yilu Zhou, Yi Qin, Wai-Ki Sung, and Daniel McDonald. *Comparison of Two Approaches to Building a Vertical Search Tool: A Case in the Nanotechology Domain*. In *Proceedings of the Second ACM/IEEE-CS Joint Conference on Digital Libraries*, 2002.

Michael Chau. Personalized Spiders for Web Search and Analysis. In *Proceedings of the First ACM/IEEE-CS Joint Conference on Digital Libraries*, 2001.

Michael Droettboom, Karl MacMillan, Iciro Fujinaga, G. Sayeed Choudhury, Tim DiLauro, Mark Patton, and Teal Anderson. *Using the Gamera Framework for the Recognition of Cultural Heritage Materials.* In *Proceedings of the Second ACM/IEEE-CS Joint Conference on Digital Libraries*, 2002.

Michael Droettboom. Correcting broken characters in the recognition of historical printed documents [short paper]. In *Proceedings of the Third ACM/IEEE-CS Joint Conference on Digital Libraries*, 2003.

Michael G. Christel, Bryan Maher, and Andrew Begun. XSLT for Tailored Access to a Digital Video Library. In *Proceedings of the First ACM/IEEE-CS Joint Conference on Digital Libraries*, 2001.

Michael J. Ackerman. *Accessing the Visible Human Project. D-Lib Magazine*, October, 1995.

Michael J. Carey and Donald Kossmann. On Saying "Enough Already!" in SQL. In *Proceedings of the International Conference on Management of Data*, pp. 219-230. ACM Press, Tucson, Arizona, 1997.

Michael J. Carey and Donald Kossmann. Reducing the Braking Distance of an SQL Query Engine. In *Proceedings of the Twenty-fourth International Conference on Very Large Databases*, pp. 158-169. VLDB Endowment, New York City, USA, 1998.

Michael J. Hu and Ye Jian. Multimedia Description Framework (MDF) for Content Description of Audio/Video Documents. In *Proceedings of the Fourth ACM International Conference on Digital Libraries*, 1999.

Michael Jensen. *Need-Based Intellectual Property Protection and Networked University Press Publishing.* In *IP Workshop Proceedings*, 1994.

Michael Khoo. Community Design of DLESE's Collections Review Policy: A Technological Frames Analysis. In *Proceedings of the First ACM/IEEE-CS Joint Conference on Digital Libraries*, 2001.

Michael L.W. Jones, Robert H. Rieger, Paul Treadwell, and Geri K. Gay. Live from the Stacks: User Feedback on Mobile Computers and Wireless Tools for Library Patrons. In *Proceedings of the Fifth ACM International Conference on Digital Libraries*, 2000.

Michael Lesk. Image Formats for Preservation and Access. Commission for Preservation and Access. Technology Assessment Advisory Committee. July 1990. URL: http://www.ifla.org/documents/libraries/net/lesk.txt

Michael Lesk. The Seven Ages of Information Retrieval. URL: http://www.ifla.org/VI/5/op/udtop5/udtop5.htm

Michael R. Genesereth and Steven P. Ketchpel. Software Agent. *Communications of the ACM*, 37(7), July, 1994.

Michael R. Genesereth, Arthur M. Keller, and Oliver M. Duschka. Infomaster: An Information Integration System. In *Proceedings of the International Conference on Management of Data*. ACM Press, Tucson, Ariz. 1997.

Michael S. Brown and Desmond Tsoi. Correcting Common Image Distortions in Library Materials Acquired by a Camera [short paper]. In *Proceedings of the Third ACM/IEEE-CS Joint Conference on Digital Libraries*, 2003.

Michael S. Brown and W. Brent Seales. Beyond 2D Images: Effective 3D Imaging for Library Materials. In *Proceedings of the Fifth ACM International Conference on Digital Libraries*, 2000.

Michael S. Brown and W. Brent Seales. The Digital Atheneum: New Approaches for Preserving, Restoring and Analyzing Damaged Manuscripts. In *Proceedings of the First ACM/IEEE-CS Joint Conference on Digital Libraries*, 2001.

Michael Schwartz, ed. Report of the Distributed Indexing/ Searching Workshop. May 28-19, 1996. Cambridge, Massachusetts. Sponsored by the World Wide Web Consortium. URL: http://www.w3.org/Search/9605-Indexing-Workshop/

Michelangelo Diligenti, Frans Coetzee, Steve Lawrence, C. Lee Giles, and Marco Gori. Focused Crawling Using Context Graphs. In *Proceedings of the Twenty-sixth International Conference on Very Large Databases*, pp. 527-534, September, 2000.

Michelle Baldonado, Chen-Chuan K. Chang, Luis Gravano, and Andreas Paepcke. *Metadata for Digital Libraries: Architecture and Design Rationale.* Number SIDL-WP-1997-0055; 1997-26. Stanford University, 1997. Accessible at http://dbpubs.stanford.edu/pub/1997-26.

Michelle Baldonado, Chen-Chuan K. Chang, Luis Gravano, and Andreas Paepcke. *Metadata for Digital Libraries: Architecture and Design Rationale.* In *Proceedings of the Second ACM International Conference on Digital Libraries*, pp. 47-56, 1997. At http://dbpubs.stanford.edu/pub/1997-26.

Michelle Baldonado, Chen-Chuan K. Chang, Luis Gravano, and Andreas Paepcke. *The Stanford Digital Library Metadata Architecture. International Journal of Digital Libraries*, 1(2), February, 1997. See also http://dbpubs.stanford.edu/pub/1997-56.

Michelle Baldonado, Seth Katz, Andreas Paepcke, Chen-Chuan K. Chang, Hector Garcia-Molina, and Terry Winograd. *An Extensible Constructor Tool for the Rapid, Interactive Design of Query Synthesizers.* In *Proceedings of the Third ACM International Conference on Digital Libraries*, 1998. Accessible at http://dbpubs.stanford.edu/pub/1998-48.

Michelle Baldonado, Steve Cousins, B. Lee, and Andreas

Paepcke. Notable: An Annotation System for Networked Handheld Devices. In *Proceedings of the Conference on Human Factors in Computing Systems CHI'99*, pp. 210-211, 1999.

Michelle Baldonado. Searching, Browsing, and Metasearching with SenseMaker. *Web Techniques Magazine*, May, 1997.

Michelle Chang, John J. Leggett, Richard Furuta, Andruid Kerne, J. Patrick Williams, Samuel A. Burns, and Randolph G. Bias. Collection Understanding. In *Proceedings of the Fourth ACM/IEEE-CS Joint Conference on Digital Libraries*, 2004.

Michelle Ferebee, Greg Boeshaar, Kathryn Bush, and Judy Hertz. A Scientific Digital Library in Context: An Earth Radiation Budget Experiment Collection in the Atmospheric Sciences Data Center Digital Library [short paper] . In *Proceedings of the Third ACM/IEEE-CS Joint Conference on Digital Libraries*, 2003.

Michelle Q Wang Baldonado and Steve B. Cousins. *Addressing heterogeneity in the networked information environment. New Review of Information Networking*, 2:83-102, 1996.

Michelle Q Wang Baldonado and Terry Winograd. *A User Interaction Model for Browsing Based on Category-Level Operations*. Number SIDL-WP-1996-0029; 1996-75. Stanford University, 1996.

Michelle Q Wang Baldonado and Terry Winograd. *SenseMaker: An Information-Exploration Interface Supporting the Contextual Evolution of a User's Interests*. In *Proceedings of the Conference on Human Factors in Computing Systems CHI'97*, pp. 11-18. ACM Press, New York, Atlanta, Ga. March, 1997.

Michelle Q Wang Baldonado and Terry Winograd. *Techniques and Tools for Making Sense out of Heterogeneous Search Service Results*. Number SIDL-WP-1995-0019; 1995-59. Stanford University, 1995.

Microsoft Corporation. Microsoft Wallet. Microsoft wallet website: http://www.microsoft.com/wallet/.

Miles Efron and Donald Sizemore. Link Attachment (Preferential and Otherwise) in Contributor-Run Digital Libraries [short paper]. In *Proceedings of the Third ACM/IEEE-CS Joint Conference on Digital Libraries*, 2003.

Miles Efron, Jonathan Elsas, Gary Marchionini, and Junliang Zhang. Machine Learning for Information Architecture in a Large Governmental Website. In *Proceedings of the Fourth ACM/IEEE-CS Joint Conference on Digital Libraries*, 2004.

Min-Yen Kan and Judith L. Klavans. *Using Librarian Techniques in Automatic Text Summarization for Information Retrieval.* In *Proceedings of the Second ACM/IEEE-CS Joint Conference on Digital Libraries*, 2002.

Mitchell N. Charity. *Multiple Standards? No problem.* In *Proceedings of the First Annual Conference on the Theory and Practice of Digital Libraries*, 1994.

Mohamed Kholief, Kurt Maly, and Stewart Shen. Event-Based Retrieval from a Digital Library containing Medical Streams [short paper]. In *Proceedings of the Third ACM/IEEE-CS Joint Conference on Digital Libraries*, 2003.

Moises Goldszmidt and Mehran Sahami. *A Probabilistic Approach to Full-Text Document Clustering.* SRI International, 1998.

Monika R. Henzinger, Allan Heydon, Michael Mitzenmacher, and Marc Najork. Measuring Index Quality Using Random Wals on the Web. In *Proceedings of the Eighth International World-Wide Web Conference*, 1999.

N. Adam, Y. Yesha, B. Awerbuch, K. Bennet, B. Blaustein, A. Brodsky, R. Chen, O. Dogramaci, B. Grossman, R. Holowczak, J. Johnson K. Kalpakis, C. McCollum, A.-L. Neches, B. Neches, A. Rosenthal, J. Slonim, H. Wactlar, and O. Wolfson. Strategic directions in electronic commerce and digital libraries: towards a digital Agora. *ACM Computing Surveys*, 28(4):818-35, December, 1996.

N. Asokan, P.A. Janson, M. Steiner, and M. Waidner. The state of the art in electronic payment systems. *Computer*, 30(9):28-35, September, 1997.

N. Beagrie, and D. Greenstein. A strategic policy framework for creating and preserving digital collections: a report to the Digital Archiving Working Group. British Library Research and Innovation report, 107 London: British Library Research and Innovation Centre, July 1998.

N. Borenstein and N. Freed. *MIME (Multipurpose Internet Mail Extensions) Part One: Mechanisms for Specifying and Describing the Format of Internet Message Bodies.* September, 1993.

N. Gershon, W. Ruh, J. LeVasseur, J. Winstead, and A. Kleiboemer. Searching and Discovery of Resources in Digital Libraries. In *Advances in Digital Libraries '95*, 1995.

N.J. Belkin and W. Bruce Croft. Information filtering and information retrieval: two sides of same coin? *Communications of the ACM*, 35(12):29-38, December, 1992.

Nancy A. Van House, Mark H. Butler, Virginia Ogle, and Lisa Schiff. *User-Centered Iterative Design for Digital Libraries: The Cypress Experience. D-Lib Magazine*, Feb, 1996.

Nancy A. Van House. *User Needs Assessment and Evaluation for the UC Berkeley Electronic Environmental Library Project.* In *Proceedings of the Second Annual Conference on the Theory and Practice of Digital Libraries*, 1995.

Nancy Van House. *Trust and Epistemic Communities in Biodiversity Data Sharing.* In *Proceedings of the Second ACM/IEEE-CS Joint Conference on Digital Libraries*, 2002.

Naomi Dushay, James C. French, and Carl Lagoze. Using Query

Mediators for Distributed Searching in Federated Digital Libraries. In *Proceedings of the Fourth ACM International Conference on Digital Libraries*, 1999.

Naomi Dushay. Localizing Experience of Digital Content via Structural Metadata. In *Proceedings of the Second ACM/IEEE-CS Joint Conference on Digital Libraries*, 2002.

Nathaniel Borenstein. Cooperative Work in the Andrew Message System. In *Proceedings of the Conference on Computer-Supported Cooperative Work*, 1988.

National Digital Library Federation (NDLF). America's Heritage: Mission and Goals for a National Digital Library Federation. URL: http://www.ifla.org/documents/libraries/net/digfed2.htm

National Digital Library Federation (NDLF). National Digital Library Federation Agreement Signed. May 1, 1995. URL: http://www.ifla.org/documents/libraries/net/digfed1.htm URL: http://lcweb.loc.gov/loc/ndlf/agree.html

National Digital Library Federation (NDLF). NDLF Planning Task Force. Final Report. June 1996. URL: http://www.ifla.org/documents/libraries/net/plntfrep.htm

Neil Daswani, Dan Boneh, Hector Garcia-Molina, Steven Ketchpel, and Andreas Paepcke. *A Generalized Digital Wallet Architecture.* In *Proceedings of the 3rd USENIX Workshop on Electronic Commerce, p. 121-39* , 1998.

Neil Daswani, Hector Garcia-Molina, and Beverly Yang. *Open Problems in Data-sharing Peer-to-peer Systems.* In *Proceedings of the 9th International Conference on Database Theory*, 2003.

Nick Craswell and Peter Bailey. Server Selection on the World Wide Web. In *Proceedings of the Fifth ACM International Conference on Digital Libraries*, 2000.

Ning Hu and Roger B. Dannenberg. *A Comparison of Melodic Database Retrieval Techniques Using Sung Queries.* In

Proceedings of the Second ACM/IEEE-CS Joint Conference on Digital Libraries, 2002.

Noah Green, Panagiotis G. Ipeirotis, and Luis Gravano. SDLIP + STARTS = SDARTS: A Protocol and Toolkit for Metasearching. In *Proceedings of the First ACM/IEEE-CS Joint Conference on Digital Libraries*, 2001.

Nohema Castellanos and Alfredo Sßnchez. PoPS: Mobile Access to Digital Library Resources [short paper]. In *Proceedings of the Third ACM/IEEE-CS Joint Conference on Digital Libraries*, 2003.

Object Management Group. *The Common Object Request Broker: Architecture and Specification*. Dec, 1993. Accessible at ftp://omg.org/pub/CORBA.

OCLC. Tomorrow's Access, Today's Decisions: Ensuring Access to Today's Electronic Resources Tomorrow. Proceedings of the Fourteenth Annual Conference of Research Library Directors. Sponsored by OCLC and the OCLC Research Libraries Advisory Committee. URL: http://www.oclc.org/oclc/man/9680rldc/toc.htm

Olga Kapitskaia, Anthony Tomasic, and Patrick Valduriez. *Dealing with Discrepancies in Wrapper Functionality*. Number RR-3138. INRIA, 1997.

Oliver Gunther, Rudolf Muller, and Andreas S. Wiegand. *The Design of MMM: A Model ManageMent System for Time Series Analysis*. In *DAGS '95*, 1995.

Oliver Kaljuvee, Orkut Buyukkokten, Hector Garcia-Molina, and Andreas Paepcke. *Efficient Web Form Entry on PDAs*. In *To appear in the Proceedings of the 10th Intl. WWW conference*, 2000. Available at http://dbpubs.stanford.edu/pub/2001-44.

Oliver Kaljuvee, Orkut Buyukkokten, Hector Garcia-Molina, and Andreas Paepcke. *Efficient Web Form Entry on PDAs*. In *Proceedings of the Tenth International World-Wide Web Conference*, 2001. Available at http://dbpubs.stanford.edu/pub/2001-44.

Oliver M. Duschka. *Query Planning and Optimization in Information Integration.* PhD thesis, Stanford University, December, 1997.

Onn Brandman, Hector Garcia-Molina, and Andreas Paepcke. *Where Have You Been? A Comparison of Three Web Tracking Technologies.* In *Submitted for publication,* 1999. Available at http://dbpubs.stanford.edu/pub/1999-61.

Onn Brandman, Junghoo Cho, Hector Garcia-Molina, and Narayanan Shivakumar. *Crawler-Friendly Web Servers.* In *Proceedings of the Workshop on Performance and Architecture of Web Servers (PAWS),* Santa Clara, California, June, 2000.

Orkut Buyukkokten, Hector Garcia Molina, Andreas Paepcke, and Terry Winograd. *Power Browser: Efficient Web Browsing for PDAs.* In *Proceedings of the Conference on Human Factors in Computing Systems CHI'00,* 2000.

Orkut Buyukkokten, Hector Garcia-Molina, and Andreas Paepcke. *Accordion Summarization for End-Game Browsing on PDAs and Cellular Phones.* In *Proceedings of the Conference on Human Factors in Computing Systems CHI'01,* 2000.

Orkut Buyukkokten, Hector Garcia-Molina, and Andreas Paepcke. *Focused Web Searching with PDAs.* In *Proceedings of the Ninth International World-Wide Web Conference,* 2000.

Orkut Buyukkokten, Hector Garcia-Molina, and Andreas Paepcke. *Seeing the Whole in Parts: Text Summarization for Web Browsing on Handheld Devices.* In *10th International WWW Conference,* 2000.

Orkut Buyukkokten, Hector Garcia-Molina, and Andreas Paepcke. *Seeing the Whole in Parts: Text Summarization for Web Browsing on Handheld Devices.* In *Proceedings of the Tenth International World-Wide Web Conference,* 2001.

Orkut Buyukokkten, Junghoo Cho, Hector Garcia-Molina, Luis Gravano, and Narayanan Shivakumar. *Exploiting Geographical Location Information of Web Pages.* In *Proceedings of Workshop on Web Databases (WebDB'99)*, June, 1999.

P. Buneman, S.B. Davidson, K. Hart, C. Overton, and L. Wong. A Data Transformation System for Biological Data Sources. In *Proceedings of the Twenty-first International Conference on Very Large Databases.* VLDB Endowment, Zurich, Switzerland, 1995.

P.W. Foltz and S.T. Dumais. Personalized information delivery: an analysis of information methods. *Communications of the ACM*, 35(12):51-60, December, 1992.

Palm Inc. Palm OS Emulator. Palm website: http://www.palm.com/dev/tech/tools/emulator/.

Palm Inc. Web Clipping Development. Palm website: http://www.palm.com/dev/tech/webclipping/.

Panagiotis G. Ipeirotis, Tom Barry, and Luis Gravano. *Extending SDARTS: Extracting Metadata from Web Databases and Interfacing with the Open Archives Initiative.* In *Proceedings of the Second ACM/IEEE-CS Joint Conference on Digital Libraries*, 2002.

Paolo Frasconi, Giovanni Soda, and Alessandro Vullo. Text Categorization for Multi-page Documents: A Hybrid Naive Bayes HMM Approach. In *Proceedings of the First ACM/IEEE-CS Joint Conference on Digital Libraries*, 2001.

Patrick Baudisch and Ruth Rosenholtz. Halo: a technique for visualizing off-screen objects. In *Proceedings of the conference on Human factors in computing systems*, pp. 481-488. ACM Press, 2003.

Patrick Hochstenbach, Henry Jerez, and Herbert Van de Sompel. The OAI-PMH Static Repository and Static Repository Gateway. In *Proceedings of the Third ACM/IEEE-CS Joint Conference on Digital Libraries*, 2003.

Paul Conway. *Yale University Library's Project Open Book: Preliminary Research Findings. D-Lib Magazine*, Feb, 1996.

Paul Gherman. *IMAGE VISION: Forging A National Image Alliance.* In *JEP*, 1994.

Pei Cao, Jin Zhang, and Kevin Beach. Active Cache: Caching Dynamic Contents on the Web. In *Proceedings of IFIP International Conference on Distributed Systems Platforms and Open Distributed Processing (Middleware '98)*, pp. 373-388, 1998.

Peter Domel. WebMap: a graphical hypertext navigation tool. In *Proceedings of the Second International World-Wide Web Conference*, 1994.

Peter Graham. Intellectual Preservation in the Electronic Environment. (1992) Arnold Hirshon, ed., After the Electronic Revolution, Will You Be the First to Go? Proceedings of the 1992 Association for Library Collections and Technical Services President's Program (Chicago: ALA, 1993). URL: http://www.ifla.org/documents/libraries/net/intpres_.htm

Peter Graham. Intellectual Preservation: Electronic Preservation of the Third Kind. Washington, DC: Commission on Preservation and Access, March, 1994. URL: http://www.ifla.org/documents/libraries/net/cpaintpr.htm

Peter Graham. Long-Term Intellectual Preservation. RLG Symposium on Digital Imaging Technology at Cornell University, March, 1994. URL: http://www.ifla.org/documents/libraries/net/dps.htm

Peter Graham. Requirements for the Digital Research Library. College and Research Libraries, July, 1995, p. 331-339. URL: http://www.ifla.org/documents/libraries/net/drc.htm

Peter S. Graham. *Intellectual Preservation and Electronic Intellectual Property.* In *IP Workshop Proceedings*, 1994.

Peter S. Graham. *The Digital Research Library: Tasks and Commitments.* In *Proceedings of the Second Annual Conference on the Theory and Practice of Digital Libraries*, 1995.

Peter Schäuble and Alan F Smeaton, eds. An International Research Agenda for Digital Libraries: Summary Report of the Series of Joint NSF-EU Working Groups on Future Directions for Digital Libraries Research. October 12, 1998. URL: http://www.iei.pi.cnr.it/DELOS//NSF/Brussrep.htm PDF: http://www.ifla.org/documents/diglib/98eunsf.pdf

Peter T. Davis, David K. Elson, and Judith L. Klavans. Methods for Precise Named Entity Matching in Digital Collections [short paper]. In *Proceedings of the Third ACM/IEEE-CS Joint Conference on Digital Libraries*, 2003.

Peter W. Foltz. Using Latent Semantic Indexing for Information Filtering. In *Proceedings of the Conference on Office Information Systems*, 1990.

Philip Greenspun. *We Have Chosen Shame and Will Get War*. In *JEP*, 1994.

Pierre Cubaud, Pascal Stokowski, and Alexandre Topol. *Binding Browsing and Reading Activities in a 3D Digital Library.* In *Proceedings of the Second ACM/IEEE-CS Joint Conference on Digital Libraries*, 2002.

Prasanne Ganesan, Qixiang Sun, and Hector Garcia-Molina. *YAPPERS: A Peer-to-Peer Lookup Service Over Arbitrary Topology*. Number 2002-24. Stanford University, 2002.

Prasun Dewan, Kevin Jeffay, John Smith, David Stotts, and William Oliver. *Early Prototypes of the Repository for Patterned Injury Data.* In *Proceedings of the Second Annual Conference on the Theory and Practice of Digital Libraries*, 1995.

R. Acuff, L. Fagan, T. Rindfleisch, B. Levitt, and P. Ford. .Lightweight, Mobile E-Mail for Intra-Clinic Communication. In *Proceedings of the 1997 AMIA*

Annual Fall Symposium, pp. 729-33, Oct, 1997.

R. Anderson and M. Kuhn. Tamper resistance-a cautionary note. In *Proceedings of the Second USENIX Workshop on Electronic Commerce.* USENIX Assoc, Berkeley, CA, USA, 1996."

R. Anderson, C. Manifavas, and C. Sutherland. Netcard - A Practical Electronic Cash System. In *Fourth Cambridge Workshop on Security Protocols*, 1996.

R. Armstrong, D. Freitag, T. Joachims, and T. Mitchell. WebWatcher: A Learning Apprentice for the World Wide Web. In *AAAI Spring Symposium on Information Gathering*, 1995.

R. Atkinson, A. Demers, C. Hauser, C. Jacobi, P. Kessler, and M. Weiser. Experiences creating a Portable Cedar. *SIGPLAN Not. (USA), SIGPLAN Notices*, 24(7):322-8, 1989.

R. B. Allen. Interface Issues for Interactive Multimedia Documents. In *Advances in Digital Libraries '95*, 1995.

R. Boisvert, S. Browne, J. Dongarra, and E. Grosse. Digital Software and Data Repositories for Support of Scientific Computing. In *Advances in Digital Libraries '95*, 1995.

R. Chimera, K. Wolman, S. Mark, and B. Shneiderman. An Exploratory Evaluation of Three Interfaces for Browsing Large Hierarchical Tables of Contents. In *ACM Transactions on Information Systems, 12, 4*, pp. 383-406, 1994.

R. Dolin, D. Agrawal, and A. El Abbadi. Scalable Collection Summarization and Selection. In *Proceedings of the Fourth ACM International Conference on Digital Libraries*, 1999.

R. L. Grossman, A. Sundaram, H. Ramamoorthy, M. Wu, S. Hogan, J. Shuler, and O. Wolfson. *Viewing the U.S. Government Budget as a Digital Library.* In *Proceedings of the First Annual Conference on the Theory and Practice of Digital Libraries*, 1994.

R.C. Angell, G.E. Freund, and P. Willett. Automatic Spelling Correction Using a Trigram Similarity Measure. *Information Processing and Management*, 19(4):255-261, 1983.

Ralf G. Herrtwich and Thomas Kaeppner. Network Computers-Ubiquitous Computing or Dumb Multimedia? In *Third International Symposium on Autonomous Decentralized Systems*. IEEE Computer Society Press, 1997.

Raymond J. D'Amore, Daniel J. Helm, Puck-Fai Yan, and Stephen A. Glanowski. MITRE Information Discovery System. In *Proceedings of DL'96*, 1996.

Reka Albert, Albert-Laszlo Barabasi, and Hawoong Jeong. Diameter of the World Wide Web. *Nature*, 401(6749), September, 1999.

Ricardo Baeza-Yates and Berthier Ribeiro-Neto. *Modern Information Retrieval*. Addison-Wesley-Longman, May, 1999.

Richard Fikes, Robert Engelmore, Adam Farquhar, and Wanda Pratt. Network-Based Information Brokers. *In AAAI Spring Symposium on Information Gathering, 1995.*

Richard Furuta, Catherine C. Marshall, Frank M. Shipman III, and John J. Leggett. Physical Objects in the Digital Library. In *Proceedings of DL'96*, 1996.

Richard Furuta. *Defining and Using Structure in Digital Documents*. In *Proceedings of the First Annual Conference on the Theory and Practice of Digital Libraries*, 1994.

Richard Giordano. Digital Libraries and Impacts on Scientific Careers. In *Proceedings of DL'96*, 1996.

Richard P. King, Nagui Halim, Hector Garcia-Molina, and Christos A. Polyzois. Management of a Remote Backup Copy for Disaster Recovery. *TODS*, 16(2):338-68, 1991.

Rob Barrett, Paul P. Maglio, and Daniel C. Kellem. How to Personalize the Web. In *Proceedings of the Conference on Human Factors in Computing Systems CHI'97*, 1997.

Robert Armstrong, Dayne Freitag, Thorsten Joachims, and Tom Mitchell. *WebWatcher: A Learning Apprentice for the World Wide Web*. In *AAAI Spring Symposium on Information Gathering*, 1995.

Robert B. Allen and Jane Acheson. Browsing the Structure of Multimedia Stories. In *Proceedings of the Fifth ACM International Conference on Digital Libraries*, 2000.

Robert B. Allen. A Query Interface for an Event Gazetteer. In *Proceedings of the Fourth ACM/IEEE-CS Joint Conference on Digital Libraries*, 2004.

Robert B. Allen. *Navigating and Searching in Hierarchical Digital Library Catalogs*. In *Proceedings of the First Annual Conference on the Theory and Practice of Digital Libraries*, 1994.

Robert B. Allen. *Two Digital Library Intefaces which Exploit Hierarchical Structure*. In *DAGS '95*, 1995.

Robert B. Kellogg and Madhan Subhas. Text to Hypertext: Can Clustering Solve the Problem in Digital Libraries? In *Proceedings of DL'96*, 1996.

Robert Demolombe and Andrew Jones. *A Common Logical Framework to Retrieve Information and Meta Information*. In *AAAI Spring Symposium on Information Gathering*, 1995.

Robert E. Kahn. *Deposit, Registration and Recordation in an Electronic Copyright Management System*. In *IP Workshop Proceedings*, 1994.

Robert E. Kent and Christian Neuss. Creating a web analysis and visualization environment. In *Proceedings of the Second International World-Wide Web Conference*, 1994.

Robert Engelmore and Tony Morgan. *Blackboard Systems*. Addison-Wesley, 1988.

Robert Gray. Content-Based Image Retrieval: Color and Edges. In *DAGS '95*, 1995.

Robert J. Hall. *Agents Helping Agents: Issues in Sharing How-to*

Knowledge. In *AAAI Spring Symposium on Information Gathering*, 1995.

Robert Johansen. *Teleconferencing and beyond : communications in the office of the future*. McGraw-Hill data communications book series. McGraw-Hill, 1984.

Robert Kahn and Robert Wilensky. *A Framework for Distributed Digital Object Services*. Number tn95-01. CNRI, May, 1995. At http://WWW.CNRI.Reston.VA.US/home/cstr/arch/k-w.html.

Robert P. Futrelle and Xiaolan Zhang. *Large-Scale Persistent Object Systems for Corpus Linguistics and Information Retrieval*. In *Proceedings of the First Annual Conference on the Theory and Practice of Digital Libraries*, 1994.

Robin Burke and Kristian J. Hammond. Combining Databases and Knowledge Bases for Assisted Browsing. *In AAAI Spring Symposium on Information Gathering, 1995.*

Roland Kaye and Stephen Little. Strategies and Standards for Cultural Interoperability in Global Business Systems. In *Proceedings of the 29th Annual Hawaii International Conference on System Sciences*. IEEE Computer Society Press, 1996.

S. Brin and L. Page. The Anatomy of a Large-Scale Hypertextual Web Search Engine. In *Proceedings of 7th World Wide Web Conference*, 1998.

S. Chakrabarti and S. Muthukrishnan. Resource Scheduling for Parallel Database and Scientific Applications. In *8th ACM Symposium on Parallel Algorithms and Architectures*, pp. 329-335, June, 1996.

S. Cheshire and M. Baker. A Wireless Network in MosquitoNet. *IEEE Micro*, Feb, 1996.

S. Cheshire and M. Baker. Internet Mobility 4x4. In *Proceedings of the ACM SIGCOMM'96 Conference*, Aug, 1996.

S. Feiner. Seeing the Forest for the Trees: Hierarchical Display of Hypertext Structure. In *Conference on Office Information Systems, New York:ACM*, pp. 205-212, 1988.

S.B Robertson. Digital Rosetta Stone: a conceptual model for maintaining long-term access to digital documents. Thesis (MSc), Air Force Institute of Technology, Graduate School of Logistics and Acquisition Management, 1996. URL: http://www.au.af.mil/au/database/research/ay1996/afit_la/rober_sb.htm

Sally Jo Cunningham and Nina Reeves. An Ethnographic Study of Music Information Seeking: Implications for the Design of a Music Digital Library. In *Proceedings of the Third ACM/IEEE-CS Joint Conference on Digital Libraries*, 2003.

Sally Jo Cunningham, Chris Knowles, and Nina Reeves. An Ethnographic Study of Technical Support Workers: Why We Didn't Build a Tech Support Digital Library. In *Proceedings of the First ACM/IEEE-CS Joint Conference on Digital Libraries*, 2001.

Sally Jo Cunningham, David Bainbridge, and Masood Masoodian. How People Describe Their Image Information Needs: A Grounded Theory Analysis of Visual Arts Queries. In *Proceedings of the Fourth ACM/IEEE-CS Joint Conference on Digital Libraries*, 2004.

Samuel Gustman, Dagobert Soergel, Douglas Oard, William Byrne, Michael Picheny, Bhuvana Ramabhadran, and Douglas Greenberg. *Supporting Access to Large Digital Oral History Archives*. In *Proceedings of the Second ACM/IEEE-CS Joint Conference on Digital Libraries*, 2002.

Sandra Heiler. Semantic Interoperability. *ACM Computing Surveys*, 27(2):271-273, June, 1995.

Sara Elo. *Augmenting Text: Good News on Disasters*. In *DAGS '95*, 1995.

Sasa Buvac and Richard Fikes. A Declarative Formalization of Knowledge Translation. *In AAAI Spring Symposium on Information Gathering, 1995.*

Saul Greenberg and David Marwood. Real Time Groupware as a Distributed System: Concurrency Control and Its Effect on the Interface. In Richard Furuta and Christine Neuwirth, editors, *CSCW '94*. ACM, New York, 1994.

Scott B. Huffman and David Steier. *Heuristic Joins to Integrate Structured Heterogeneous Data*. In *AAAI Spring Symposium on Information Gathering*, 1995.

Scott Baker and John H. Hartman. The Gecko NFS Web Proxy. In *Proceedings of the Eighth International World-Wide Web Conference*, 1999.

Scott Deerwester, Susan T. Dumais, George W. Furnas, Thomas K. Landauer, and Richard Harshman. Indexing by Latent Semantic Analysis. *Journal of the American Society for Information Science*, 41, June, 1990.

Scott M. Baker and Bongki Moon. Distributed Cooperative Web Servers. In *Proceedings of the Eighth International World-Wide Web Conference*, 1999.

Scott W. Hassan and Andreas Paepcke. *Stanford Digital Library Interoperability Protocol*. Number SIDL-WP-1997-0054; 1997-73. Stanford University, 1997. Accessible at http://dbpubs.stanford.edu/pub/1997-73.

Serge Abiteboul, Sophie Cluet, and Tova Milo. Correspondence and Translation for Heterogeneous Data. In *Proceedings of the 6th International Conference on Database Theory*. Springer, Delphi, Greece, 1997.

Serge Abiteboul, Sophie Cluet, and Tova Milo. Querying and Updating the File. In *Proceedings of the Nineteenth International Conference on Very Large Databases*, pp. 73-84. VLDB Endowment, Dublin, Ireland, 1993.

Sergev Brin, James Davis, and Hector Garcia-Molina. Copy Detection Mechanisms for Digital Documents. *SIGMOD*:398-409, 1995.

Sergey Brin and Lawrence Page. *Dynamic Data Mining: A New Architecture for Data with High Dimensionality*. Stanford University, 1998.

Sergey Brin and Lawrence Page. *The Anatomy of a Large-Scale*

Hypertextual Web Search Engine. In *Proceedings of the Seventh International World-Wide Web Conference*, 1998.

Sergey Brin. *Extracting Patterns and Relations from the World Wide Web*. In *WebDB Workshop at 6th International Conference on Extending Database Technology, EDBT'98*, 1998. Available at http://www-db.stanford.edu/ sergey/ extract.ps

Shirley Browne, Jack Dongarra, Eric Grosse, and Tom Rowan. *The Netlib Mathematical Software Repository. D-Lib Magazine*, Sep, 1995.

Shirley Browne, Jack Dongarra, Ken Kennedy, and Tom Rowan. *Management of the Nationale HPCC Software Exchange- A Virtual Distributed Digital Library*. In *Proceedings of the Second Annual Conference on the Theory and Practice of Digital Libraries*, 1995.

Silvana Castano, Maria Grazia Fugini, Giancarlo Martella, and Pierangela Samarati. *Database Security*. Addison-Wesley, 1994.

Soumen Chakrabarti, Byron Dom, and Piotr Indyk. Enhanced Hypertext Categorization Using Hyperlinks. In *Proceedings of the International Conference on Management of Data*, 1998.

Soumen Chakrabarti, Byron Dom, David Gibson, Ravi Kumar, Prabhakar Raghavan, Sridhar Rajagopalan, and Andrew Tomkins. Spectral Filtering for Resource Discovery. In *ACM SIGIR workshop on Hypertext Information Retrieval on the Web*, 1998.

Soumen Chakrabarti, Byron Dom, Prabhakar Raghavan, Sridhar Rajagopalan, David Gibson, and Jon Kleinberg. Automatic resource compilation by analyzing hyperlink structure and associated text. In *Proceedings of the Seventh International World-Wide Web Conference*, 1998.

Soumen Chakrabarti, David A. Gibson, and Kevin S. McCurley. Surfing the Web Backwards. In *Proceedings of the Eighth International World-Wide Web Conference*, 1999.

Soumen Chakrabarti, Martin van den Berg, and Byron Dom. Focused Crawling: A New Approach to Topic-specific Web Resource Discovery. In *Proceedings of the Eighth International World-Wide Web Conference*, 1999

Stean Gessler and Andreas Kotulla. PDAs as mobile WWW browsers. In *Proceedings of the Second International World-Wide Web Conference*, 1994.

Stefano Ceri and Giuseppe Pelagatti. *Distributed Databases.* McGraw-Hill, Inc. 1984.

Stefano Ceri, Sara Comai, Ernesto Damiani, Piero Fraternali, Stefano Paraboschi, and Letizia Tanca. XML-GL: A Graphical Language for Wuerying and Restructuring XML Documents. In *Proceedings of the Eighth International World-Wide Web Conference*, 1999.

Stephen J. Green. Automated link generation: can we do better than term repetition? In *Proceedings of the Seventh International World-Wide Web Conference*, 1998.

Steve B. Cousins, Andreas Paepcke, Scott W. Hassan, and Terry Winograd. *Towards Wide-Area Distributed Interfaces.* Number SIDL-WP-1996-0037; 1997-67. Stanford University, 1997. At http://dbpubs.stanford.edu/pub/1997-67.

Steve B. Cousins, Andreas Paepcke, Terry Winograd, Eric A. Bier, and Ken Pier. *The Digital Library Integrated Task Environment (DLITE).* In *Proceedings of the Second ACM International Conference on Digital Libraries*, pp. 142-151, 1997. Accessible at http://dbpubs.stanford.edu/pub/1997-69.

Steve B. Cousins, Scott W. Hassan, Andreas Paepcke, and Terry Winograd. *Towards Wide-Area Distributed Interfaces.* Number SIDL-WP-1996-0037; 1997-67. Stanford University, 1996. Available at http://dbpubs.stanford.edu/pub/1997-67.

Steve B. Cousins, Steven P. Ketchpel, Andreas Paepcke, Hector Garcia-Molina, Scott W. Hassan, and Martin Röscheisen.

InterPay: Managing Multiple Payment Mechanisms in Digital Libraries. *Digital Library*, 1995.

Steve B. Cousins, Steven P. Ketchpel, Andreas Paepcke, Héctor García-Molina, Scott W. Hassan, and Martin Roescheisen. *InterPay: Managing Multiple Payment Mechanisms in Digital Libraries.* In *Proceedings of the Second Annual Conference on the Theory and Practice of Digital Libraries*, 1995.

Steve B. Cousins. *A task-oriented interface to a digital library.* In *CHI 96 Conference Companion*, pp. 103-104, 1996.

Steve Cousins. *Reification and Affordances in a User Interface for Interacting with Heterogeneous Distributed Applications.* PhD thesis, Stanford University, 1997.

Steve Hitchcock, Les Carr, Zhuoan Jiao, Donna Bergmark, Wendy Hall, Carl Lagoze, and Stevan Harnad. Developing Services for Open Eprint Archives: Globalisation, Integration and the Impact of Links. In *Proceedings of the Fifth ACM International Conference on Digital Libraries*, 2000.

Steve Jones and Gordon Paynter. Topic-Based Browsing Within a Digital library Using Keyphrases. In *Proceedings of the Fourth ACM International Conference on Digital Libraries*, 1999.

Steve Jones and Gordon W. Paynter. Human Evaluatin of Kea, an Automatic Keyphrasing System. In *Proceedings of the First ACM/IEEE-CS Joint Conference on Digital Libraries*, 2001.

Steven Glassman. A caching relay for the world wide web. In *Proceedings of the First International World-Wide Web Conference*, 1994.

Steven Ketchpel and Hector Garcia-Molina. *A Sound and Complete Algorithm for Distributed Commerce Transactions. Distributed Computing*, 12(1), 1999.

Steven Ketchpel and Hector Garcia-Molina. *Competitive Sourcing for Internet Commerce.* In *Proceedings of*

International Conference on Distributed Computing Systems, 1998.

Steven Ketchpel and Héctor García-Molina. *Making Trust Explicit in Distributed Commerce Transactions.* In *Proceedings of the International Conference on Distributed Computing Systems*, 1996.

Steven Ketchpel, Hector Garcia-Molina, Andreas Paepcke, Scott Hassan, and Steve Cousins. *UPAI: A Universal Payment Application Interface.* In *USENIX 2nd e-commerce workshop*, 1996.

Steven Ketchpel. Distributed Commerce Transactions with Timing Deadlines and Direct Trust. 1997. Poster at International Joint Conference on AI'97.

Steven Ketchpel. *Transaction Protection for Information Buyers and Sellers.* In *DAGS '95*, 1995.

Steven P. Ketchpel, Hector Garcia-Molina, and Andreas Paepcke. *Shopping Models: A Flexible Architecture for Information Commerce.* In *Proceedings of the Second ACM International Conference on Digital Libraries*, 1997. At http://dbpubs.stanford.edu/pub/1997-52.

Stuart K. Card, George G. Robertson, and William York. The WebBook and the Web Forager: An Information Workspace for the World-Wide Web. In *Proceedings of the Conference on Human Factors in Computing Systems CHI'96*, 1996.

Sujata Banerjee and Vibhu O. Mittal. *On the Use of Linguistic Ontologies for Accessing and Indexing Distributed Digital Libraries.* In *Proceedings of the First Annual Conference on the Theory and Practice of Digital Libraries*, 1994.

Sulin Ba, Aimo Hinkkanen, and Andre B. Whinston. *Digital Library as a Foundation for Decision Support Systems.* In *Proceedings of the First Annual Conference on the Theory and Practice of Digital Libraries*, 1994.

Surajit Chaudhuri and Phokion G. Kolaitis. Can Datalog be Approximated? In *Proceedings of the 13rd ACM SIGACT-*

SIGMOD-SIGART Symposium on Principles of Database Systems, pp. 86-96. ACM Press, Minneapolis, Minn. 1994.

Surajit Chaudhuri. Finding Nonrecursive Envelopes for Datalog Predicates. In *Proceedings of the 12th ACM SIGACT-SIGMOD-SIGART Symposium on Principles of Database Systems*, pp. 135-146. ACM Press, Washingtion, D.C., 1993.

Susan Gauch, Ron Aust, Joe Evans, John Gauch, Gary Minden, Doug Niehaus, and James Roberts. *The Digital Video Library System: Vision and Design*. In *Proceedings of the First Annual Conference on the Theory and Practice of Digital Libraries*, 1994.

Susan T. Dumais, George W. Furnas, Thomas K. Landauer, Scott Deerwester, and Richard Harshman. Using Latent Semantic Analysis to Improve Access to Textual Information. In *Proceedings of the Conference on Human Factors in Computing Systems CHI'88*, 1988.

Susumu Harada, Mor Naaman, Yee Jiun Song, QianYing Wang, and Andreas Paepcke. Lost in Memories: Interacting With Photo Collections on PDAs. In *Proceedings of the Fourth ACM/IEEE-CS Joint Conference on Digital Libraries*, 2004.

T. Alanko, M. Kojo, M. Liljeberg, and K. Raatikainen. Mowgli: improvements for Internet applications using slow wireless links. In *Waves of the Year 2000+ PIMRC '97. The 8th IEEE International Symposium on Personal, Indoor and Mobile Radio Communications. Technical Program, Proceedings (Cat. No.97TH8271)*, pp. 1038-42. Vol. 3. 1997.

T. Goldstein. The Gateway security model in the Java electronic commerce framework. In R. Hirschfeld, editor, *Financial Cryptography First International Conference, FC'97. Proceedings*. Springer-Verlag, Berlin, Germany, 1997.

T. Joachims, D. Freitag, and T. Mitchell. WebWatcher: A Tour Guide for the World Wide Web. In *Proceedings of IJCAI97*, 1997.

T. Kirste and U. Rauschenbach. A presentation model for mobile information visualization. *Computers & Graphics*, 20(5):669-81, 1996

T. Todd Elvins, David R. Nadeau, Rina Schul, and David Kirsh. Worldlets: 3D Thumbnails for 3D Browsing. In *Proceedings of the Conference on Human Factors in Computing Systems CHI'98*, 1998.

Taher Haveliwala. *Efficient Computation of PageRank*. Number 1999-31. Database Group, Computer Science Department, Stanford University, February, 1999. Available at http://dbpubs.stanford.edu/pub/1999-31.

Tammara T.A. Combs and Benjamin B. Bederson. Does Zooming Improve Image Browsing? In *Proceedings of the Fourth ACM International Conference on Digital Libraries*, 1999.

Tao Guan and Kam-Fai Wong. KPS: a Web Information Mining Algorithm. In *Proceedings of the Eighth International World-Wide Web Conference*, 1999.

Tarek F. Abdelzaher and Nina Bhatti. Web Content Adaptation to Improve Server Overload Behavior. In *Proceedings of the Eighth International World-Wide Web Conference*, 1999.

Task Force on Archiving Digital Information. Preserving Digital Information: Final Report and Recommendations. May 20, 1996. URL: http://www.rlg.org/ArchTF/index.html PDF: http://www.ifla.org//documents/libraries/net/tfadi-fr.pdf

Terry Kuny and Gray Cleveland. Digital Libraries: Myths and Challenges. Paper delivered at the 62nd IFLA General Conference - August 25-31, 1996. PDF: http://www.ifla.org/IV/ifla62/62-kuny.pdf

Terry L. Harrison, Michael L. Nelson, and Mohammad Zubair. The Dienst-OAI Gateway [short paper]. In *Proceedings of the Third ACM/IEEE-CS Joint Conference on Digital Libraries*, 2003.

The Library and Information Commission. (UK) Virtually New - Creating the Digital Collection: A Review of Digitisation Projects in Local Authorities, Libraries and Archives. URL: http://www.ukoln.ac.uk/services/lic/digitisation/

The URN Implementors. *Uniform Resource Names: A Progress Report. D-Lib Magazine*, Feb, 1996.

Thomas Ellman. *Approximation and Abstraction Techniques for Generating Concise Answers to Database Queries.* In *AAAI Spring Symposium on Information Gathering*, 1995.

Thomas Kirk, Alon Y. Levy, Yehoshua Sagiv, and Divesh Srivastava. The Information Manifold. *In AAAI Spring Symposium on Information Gathering, 1995.*

Time and Bits. An integrated technical and philosophical discussion of digital archives and their future that includes the socio-cultural and economic implications of both the problems and the solutions that could provide a framework for long-term digital cultural preservation. URL: http://www.getty.edu/bookstore/titles/time.html

Timothy C. Bell, Alistair Moffat, and Ian H. Witten. *Compressing the Digital Library*. In *Proceedings of the First Annual Conference on the Theory and Practice of Digital Libraries*, 1994.

Timothy W. Bickmore and Bill N. Schilit. Digestor: Device-independent Access to the World Wide Web. In *Proceedings of the Sixth International World-Wide Web Conference*, 1997.

U. Andersson. Short version of the Sesam report: philosophy and rules concerning electronic archives and authenticity. In: Proceedings of the DLM-Forum on Electronic Records, Brussels, 18-20 December 1996. INSAR: European Archives News, Supplement II. Luxembourg: Office for Official Publications of the European Communities, pp. 175-189, 1997.

Ullas Gargi. *Consumer Media Capture: Time-Based Analysis*

and Event Clustering. Number HPL-2003-165. HP Laboratories, August, 2003.

V. Christophides, S. Abiteboul, S. Cluet, and M. Scholl. From Structured Documents to Novel Query Facilities. In *Proceedings of the International Conference on Management of Data*, pp. 313-324. ACM Press, 1994.

Vannevar Bush. *As We May Think. The Atlantic Monthly*, July, 1945. Available at http://www.theatlantic.com/unbound/flashbks/computer/bushf.htm.

Various. Some Considerations on the Archiving of Digital Information. January, 1995. URL: http://www.ifla.org/documents/libraries/net/waters1.htm

Vinod Anupam, Alain Mayer, Kobbi Nissim, Benny Pinkas, and Michael K. Reiter. On the Security of Pay-per-click and Other Web Advertising Schemes. In *Proceedings of the Eighth International World-Wide Web Conference*, 1999.

Virgilio A.F. Almeida, Wagner Meira, Jr., Vicotr F. Ribeiro, and Nivio Ziviani. Efficiency Analysis of Brokers in the Electronic Marketplace . In *Proceedings of the Eighth International World-Wide Web Conference*, 1999.

Virgilio Almeida, Azer Bestavros, Mark Crovella, and Adriana de Oliveira. Characterizing Reference Locality in the WWW. In *Proceedings of PDIS'96: The IEEE Conference on Parallel and Distributed Information Systems*, 1996.

W. B. Frakes and R. Baeza-Yates. *Information Retrieval Data Structures & Algorithms.* Prentice Hall, Englewood Cliffs, N.J., 1992.

W. Bruce Croft, Robert Cook, and Dean Wilder. *Providing Government Information on the Internet: Experiences with THOMAS.* In *Proceedings of the Second Annual Conference on the Theory and Practice of Digital Libraries*, 1995.

W. Bruce Croft. *What Do People Want from Information Retrieval? (The Top 10 Research Issues for Companies that Use and Sell IR Systems). D-Lib Magazine*, Nov, 1995.

W. Hill and J. Hollan. History-Enriched Digital Objects: Prototypes and Policy Issues. *The Information Society,* 10(2), April-June, 1994.

W. Hill, L. Stead, M. Rosenstein, and G. Furnas. Recommending and evaluating choices in a virtual community of use. In *Proceedings of the Conference on Human Factors in Computing Systems CHI'95.* ACM, New York, 1995.

W. V. Citrin and M. D. Gross. PDA-based graphical interchange for field service and repair workers. *Computers & Graphics, vol.20, no.5, p. 641-9,* 20(5):641-9, 1996.

W.J. Hutchins and H.L. Somers. *An Introduction to Machine Translation.* Academic Press, 1992.

Walter B. Hewlett and eds. Eleanor Selfridge-Field. *Melodic Similarity. Concepts, Procedures, and Applications.* MIT Press and Center for Computing in the Humanities (CCARH), Stanford University, 1998.

Wei Chai and Barry Vercoe. Structural Analysis of Musical Signals for Indexing and Thumbnailing. In *Proceedings of the Third ACM/IEEE-CS Joint Conference on Digital Libraries,* 2003.

Wei Ding, Gary Marchionini, and Dagobert Soergel. Multimodal Surrogates for Video Browsing. In *Proceedings of the Fourth ACM International Conference on Digital Libraries,* 1999.

Wesley W. Chu, M. A. Merzbacher, and L. Berkovich. The Design and Implementation of CoBase. In *Proceedings of the International Conference on Management of Data,* pp. 517-522. ACM Press, Washington, D.C., 1993.

William B. Cavnar and Andrew M. Gillies. *Data Retrieval and the Realities of Document Conversion.* In *Proceedings of the First Annual Conference on the Theory and Practice of Digital Libraries,* 1994.

William C. Janssen. Collaborative Extensions for the UpLib System. In *Proceedings of the Fourth ACM/IEEE-CS Joint Conference on Digital Libraries,* 2004.

William P. Birmingham, Edmund H. Durfee, Tracy Mullen, and Michael P. Wellman. The Distributed Agent Architecture of the University of Michigan Digital Library (Extended Abstract). *In AAAI Spring Symposium on Information Gathering, 1995.*.

William P. Birmingham, Karen M. Drabenstott, Carolyn O. Frost, Amy J. Warner, and Katherine Willis. *The University of Michigan Digital Library: This is Not Your Father's Library.* In *Proceedings of the First Annual Conference on the Theory and Practice of Digital Libraries,* 1994.

William P. Birmingham. *An agent-based architecture for digital libraries. D-Lib Magazine,* July, 1995.

William T. Crocca and William L. Anderson. *Delivering Technology for Digital Libraries: Experiences as Vendors.* In *DL '95*, 1995.

William W. Cohen and Wei Fan. Learning Page-independent Heuristics for Extracting Data from Web Pages. In *Proceedings of the Eighth International World-Wide Web Conference,* 1999.

William Y. Arms. *Key concepts in the architecture of the digital library. D-Lib Magazine,* Jul, 1995.

Y. J. Gao, J.J. Lim, and A.D. Narasimhalu. Fuzzy Multilinkage Thesaurus Builder in Multimedia Information Systems. In *Advances in Digital Libraries '95*, 1995.

Yee-Hsiang Chang and Ellis Chi. *HTGraph: A New Method for Information Access Over the World Wide Web.* In *DAGS '95*, 1995.

Yi-Chun Chu, David Bainbridge, Matt Jones, and Ian H. Witten. Realistic books: A bizarre homage to an obsolete medium? In *Proceedings of the Fourth ACM/IEEE-CS Joint Conference on Digital Libraries,* 2004.

Yi-Chun Chu, Ian H. Witten, Richard Lobb, and David Bainbridge. How to turn the page [short paper]. In *Proceedings of the Third ACM/IEEE-CS Joint Conference on Digital Libraries,* 2003.

Y-Ming Chung, Qin He, Kevin Powell, and Bruce Schatz. Semantic Indexing for a Complete Subject Discipline. In *Proceedings of the Fourth ACM International Conference on Digital Libraries*, 1999.

Yuan Chen, Jan Edler, Andrew Goldberg, Allan Gottlieb, Sumeet Sobti, and Peter Yianilos. A Prototype Implementation of Archival Intermemory. In *Proceedings of the Fourth ACM International Conference on Digital Libraries*, 1999.

Yueyu Fu and Javed Mostafa. Integration of Biomedical Text and Sequence OAI Repositories. In *Proceedings of the Fourth ACM/IEEE-CS Joint Conference on Digital Libraries*, 2004.

Yueyu Fu and Javed Mostafa. Toward Information Retrieval Web Services for Digital Libraries. In *Proceedings of the Fourth ACM/IEEE-CS Joint Conference on Digital Libraries*, 2004.

Zan Huang, Wingyan Chung, Thian-Huat Ong, and Hsinchun Chen. *A Graph-based Recommender System for Digital Library*. In *Proceedings of the Second ACM/IEEE-CS Joint Conference on Digital Libraries*, 2002.

Zubin Dalal, Suvendu Dash, Pratik Dave, Luis Francisco-Revilla, Richard Furuta, Unmil Karadkar, and Frank Shipman. Managing Distributed Collections: Evaluating Web Page Changes, Movement, and Replacement. In *Proceedings of the Fourth ACM/IEEE-CS Joint Conference on Digital Libraries*, 2004.

Index